ARCHITECTURE

Nottingham

D1091706

PEVSNER ARCHITECTURAL GUIDES

Founding Editor: Nikolaus Pevsner

PEVSNER ARCHITECTURAL GUIDES

The *Buildings of England* series was created and largely written by Sir Nikolaus Pevsner (1902–83). First editions of the county volumes were published by Penguin Books between 1951 and 1974. The continuing programme of revisions and new volumes has been supported by research financed through the Buildings Books Trust since 1994.

The Buildings Books Trust gratefully acknowledges
Grants towards the cost of research, writing and illustrations
for this volume from

ENGLISH HERITAGE

Nottingham

ELAIN HARWOOD

PEVSNER ARCHITECTURAL GUIDES

YALE UNIVERSITY PRESS

NEW HAVEN & LONDON

ARCHITECTURE

For my parents, the best B'n'B in town

The publishers gratefully acknowledge help in
bringing the books to a wider readership from
ENGLISH HERITAGE

YALE UNIVERSITY PRESS
NEW HAVEN AND LONDON
302 Temple Street, New Haven CT06511
47 Bedford Square, London WC1B 3DP

www.pevsner.co.uk
www.yalebooks.co.uk
www.yalebooks.com

Published 2008
10 9 8 7 6 5 4 3 2 1

Designed by Sophie Kullmann
Set in Adobe Minion by SNP Best-set Typesetter Ltd., Hong Kong
Printed in China through World Print

Library of Congress Cataloging-in-Publication Data

Harwood, Elain.
Nottingham / Elain Harwood.
    p. cm. -- (Pevsner architectural guides)
  Includes bibliographical references and index.
  ISBN 978-0-300-12666-2 (alk. paper)
  1. Architecture--England--Nottingham--Guidebooks. 2. Historic buildings--
England--Nottingham--Guidebooks. 3. Nottingham (England)--Buildings,
structures, etc.--Guidebooks. 4. Nottingham (England)--Guidebooks. I. Title.
  NA971.N85H37 2008
  720.9425´27--dc22
                          2008015846

Contents

1. Nottingham, showing areas covered by Walks and Excursions

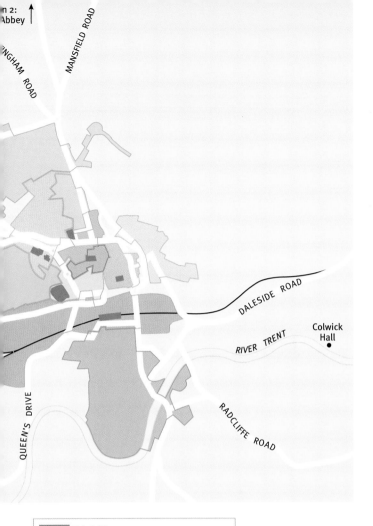

n 2:
Abbey ↑

NGHAM ROAD

MANSFIELD ROAD

DALESIDE ROAD

RIVER TRENT

Colwick
Hall
●

QUEEN'S DRIVE

RADCLIFFE ROAD

Acknowledgements

Nottinghamshire was, with *Cornwall*, the first of Nikolaus Pevsner's guides, published in 1951. His succinct text still evokes the city centre's spirit, though many of the structures he describes have gone. Elizabeth Williamson's revision in 1979 provided the mainstay of this book. She also introduced me to John Beckett, Director of the Victoria County Histories, and thence to Ken Brand of the Nottingham Civic Society, whose generosity of time and knowledge has been exceptional. Stephen Best has been similarly generous in answering queries on Sneinton and reading its text. David Durant, Geoffrey Oldfield, Hilary Silvester and Ian Wells (also of the Civic Society) have volunteered help and much encouragement. Ken Powell provided much information and useful contacts for current schemes.

Particular thanks are due to Trevor Foulds, whose comments on the draft texts for Nottingham Castle were invaluable. I would especially like to record my thanks to Dr Rosalys Coope and Haidee Jackson at Newstead, for giving up so much time, despite the floods of May 2007. Ivan Hall imparted freely of his expertise on John Carr and Colwick Hall. Tim Brittain-Catlin generously advised on Pugin's clergy houses and convents, and Pauline and Brian Miller shared their research on St Mary's. Richard Garnier has advised on Bromley House. At English Heritage, a Nottingham guide was encouraged by Sir Neil Cossons, then Chairman, and its grant-giving team. Linda Monckton brought St Mary's to life, and she drafted the medieval section of the Introduction; any mistakes there are mine. Pete Smith and Bernard Baptist provided local support, while Steve Cole took many splendid interior photographs. Ian Leith advised on sculpture, while Susie Barson and John Cattell generously acceded to my secondment.

It is a pleasure to acknowledge the marvellous people who kindly allowed access to their buildings. It is impossible, sadly, to name them all. At Boots, Rob Robinson showed exceptional patience, aided by Katey Logan, David Hunt, Clare Farrelly, Sophie Clapp, Judith Wright and their archives team. Ken Marshall at the Theatre Royal was similarly tolerant, as was Rebecca Dollman at Nottingham Playhouse, and Emma Ward at Shire Hall. Carol Allison and staff, Simon Boardman, Richard Clark, Professor Ted Cocking, Michael Collins, Fr Malcolm Crook, Rob Dunmore, Jeremy Dunn, John Ellison, Jeremy Farrell, Chris Gempton, Nicholas Forman Hardy, Ann Insher, Alan

Johnson, Martin Kirkbride, Ian Littlehayes, Fr Macgillivray, John Michalak, Josie O'Dowd, Major Radford, Clarence Rickards, Anne Scotney, Chris Scott, Ashley Smart, Greg Smith, Amy Sutton, Dean Throop, Fr Andrew Waude, John Webb, Clifford Wilton, and Fr Michael and Mr Potik at St Alban's Ukrainian Church, made visits to their buildings particularly memorable.

The architects Graham Brown, Adam Caruso, Stefanie Fischer, Julian Marsh, Mark Hobson (Maber Associates) and Bill Stonor (Faulkner Browns) patiently answered questions about their buildings and suggested others for inclusion. Jackie Wilkinson and David Ward in Nottingham Planning Department permitted me to consult their indexes and microfiches, and Dorothy Ritchie and Ann Crooks of the Nottingham Local Studies Library patiently produced cuttings, books and maps. Nottingham Archives became a second home. I would like to thank the Principal Archivist Mark Dorrington, Chris Weir, and their team: Dona Bickerdyke, Nicholas Clark, Matthew Hallworth, Jaime Harris-Hughes, Peter Lester, Beverley Lockyer, Alexa Rees, Jo Peet, Nicholas Smith and Gabriella Stenson.

Special thanks go to the editorial team at Yale University Press. Simon Bradley's painstaking editing greatly broadened and enriched this survey. The Commissioning Editor, Sally Salvesen, oversaw the design and production, with Sophie Kullmann providing the thankless graft. Bernard Dod copy-edited the volume and Judith Wardman compiled the indexes. Ruth Harman advised on how to survive writing a city guide, David and Felicia Trevor-Jones chauffeured, Tom Muirhead enlivened railway journeys, while Peter Stawowsky and John Carlyle's Spin classes proved the best respite.

Finally, in the long tradition of the Pevsner volumes, an appeal to readers for any corrections or significant omissions.

How to use this book

This book is designed principally as a guide for exploring the buildings of Nottingham's city centre and immediate suburbs. The divisions between the sections are shown on the map on pp. vi–vii. Following a chronological introduction, the gazetteer begins on p. 29 with seven Major Buildings, all in the central area. This area, between the Castle, Broadmarsh Centre and Upper and Lower Parliament streets, is divided into four walks. Each has its own street map, with the main buildings and landmarks marked and arrows indicating the suggested route. Walks around the surrounding area begin on p. 57 and are arranged in a clockwise sequence, beginning by the Castle, w. There are then eight outlying walks, again beginning at the w, and three excursions further afield. Readers should note that the description of the interior of a building does not indicate that it is open to the public.

In addition certain buildings, topics and themes have been singled out for special attention and presented in separate boxes:

Architects: The Stretton Family, p. 10; Watson Fothergill, p. 20

Building Types: Nottingham Caves, p. 6; Nottingham School Board, p. 17

City-centre Buildings: Bromley House, p. 60; Old Market Square and the Exchange, p. 76; The Lace Warehouses, p. 108

Inner-city Themes: Tractarianism in Sneinton, p. 150; The Nottingham and Beeston Canal, p. 172

Major Buildings and Objects: St Mary's Church, Restorations, p. 36; Nottingham Castle, The Duke of Newcastle, p. 42, Council House: Classicism, a Valid Style for the 1920s?, p. 49; St Barnabas's Cathedral: Pugin and his Patrons, p. 52; Holy Trinity, Lenton: The Lenton Font, p. 181

Introduction

Introduction

In 1675 Thomas Baskerville described Nottingham as 'paradise restored, for here you find large streets, fair built houses, fine women and many coaches rattling about, and their shops full of merchantable goods'. Today there are many fair buildings, if few Baskerville would recognize.

Nottingham owes its existence to its position on the River Trent, at the head of regular navigation, a crossing point protected by sandstone bluffs to the N. Although prehistoric hunter-gatherers worked on the Trent flood plains, settlement on the escarpment was recorded only with the arrival of Danish invaders in A.D 868.* It occupied the broad hill nearest the river and its tributary, the Leen, while, on the next hill E was the village of Sneinton. In the Middle Ages Nottingham marked the gateway to the North, and even today it enjoys an indeterminate character, not quite northern, yet distinct from the rest of the Midlands. Nottingham has see-sawed in popular estimation: a town admired for its elegance in the C18, a notorious slum in early C19; noted for its garden suburbs by 1940, in the early C21 culturally diverse but over-shadowed by a reputation for heavy drinking and crime.

What characterizes Nottingham through the centuries is its small centre. There is little medieval work above ground, yet the street pattern largely survives, and with it the tightness and complexity of an old town. While northern cities like Hull and Newcastle have old enclaves and a later commercial hub, in Nottingham the historic and modern centres share a common footprint. Beyond this ring, roughly bounded by Upper and Lower Parliament streets, Canal Street and the Castle, the intensity of building loosens. There were three common fields here: the Sand and Clay fields, N, and the Meadows towards the river; to the w was the Duke of Newcastle's Park Estate and to the E Earl Manvers's land. Together they strangled the town's growth until 1845. Then the fields were divided into small building lots, and each was developed to a separate pattern. Only the public parks and the roads radiating s followed a more comprehensive plan. One feature of Nottingham's working-class neighbourhoods is the red textile-mill building rising amidst late C19 bylaw housing. Surrounding them are C20 estates, their crescent patterns reflecting the dumb-bell plan chosen for the Park Estate, Nottingham's premier Victorian middle-class enclave.

*Nottingham's early history is based on a draft text by Linda Monckton.

Building Materials

Nottingham's buildings were largely timber-framed until the C17, when coppices on The Forest and at Mapperley were exhausted. Hard gypsum plaster from Cotgrave and Gotham, along the Trent, lined upper floors into the C19. Associated geologically is alabaster, worked at Chellaston just inside Derbyshire, the basis of Nottingham's medieval sculpture industry. Thatched roofs gave way to tile, and thence emerged a brick industry. **Brick** was used at Wollaton Hall for internal walls in the 1580s; the C18 antiquary Charles Deering noted that Nottingham's earliest dated brick building was the Green Dragon inn of 1615.

Nottingham itself has no useful **building stone.** Its founding hills are formed of Bunter sandstone (now called Sherwood sandstone by geologists). Too friable for building, though used at the Castle [3], it is easily excavated for caves (*see* topic box, p. 6). Basford, Wollaton, Trowell and Stanton supplied well-cemented Coal Measures sandstones. Bulwell marked the s extremity of magnesian limestone, grey or honey-coloured, the best quarries being N of Mansfield. Two related and popular building stones are Mansfield 'white' (actually yellow or grey) and red, judged sandstones for their high silica content. Gedling provided a greenish waterstone, used over a long period but in small quantities. Its softer texture typifies the Keuper marls that form the hills of Carlton and Mapperley, including Nottingham's pre-enclosure Clay Field, roughly E of Mansfield Road and contrasting with the Sand Field on the sandstone to the w. Ancaster oolite was transported from near Grantham for Wollaton Hall, and became popular in the C19, along with Derbyshire limestones, as used at the Guildhall (1884–8). Swithland slate from Leicestershire was used for gravestones, crisply carved with flowing script, many signed by their makers.

More varied bricks were manufactured in the C19, including the hard reds favoured by Fothergill Watson [3] and Alfred Waterhouse [52].

3. Castle Gatehouse, showing medieval and Edwardian sandstone with brick patching (left); detail of Watson Fothergill's terracotta facade No. 15 George Street (right)

4. Nottingham Castle, set on the Castle rock. The River Leen originally ran at its foot, serving Brewhouse Yard, right

Terracotta was used for details and sometimes for whole façades – including A.E. Lambert's Midland Station [110] and Albert Hall, and the Co-operative [58] and Boots stores [60]. In the C20 this richness of colour and texture gave way to faience tiles and Portland stone, favoured by Wren and popularized by John Belcher and fellow classicists in the late C19, which exemplified civic dignity in the C20. In Nottingham it appears at Highfields in 1922–8, having been used by the national clearing banks from the 1900s.

Medieval Nottingham

There was no apparent Roman occupation, for the Fosse Way by-passed Nottingham ten miles E. Some pre-C9 history is indicated by its **Saxon** name – Snotingeham, homestead of the Snots – and that of Sneinton, but physical evidence is limited to ditch features on its central hill. Nottingham was one of the five boroughs of the Danelaw, the origin of its county status, but in 921 it was recovered by the Saxons. Edward the Elder then built a ditch and timber wall around the hill, their line denoted by the parallel streets that developed to either side: Bridlesmith Gate and Fletcher Gate, w, and Warser Gate and Carlton Street/Goose Gate to the N. A market may have stood N of St Mary's, where the E–W line of Barker and Pilcher gates is interrupted. Edward also built the first bridge over the Trent; two arches of its C12 successor survive.

Nottingham's **castle** was constructed c. 1068 by William Peveril at the order of William the Conqueror, on a still steeper sandstone

The earliest reference to Nottingham, in 868, uses an old British name, Tigguacobauc, 'dwelling of caves'. Caves cannot occur naturally in Nottingham's sandstone, but its softness, cross-bedding and lack of fractures mean they can be easily excavated. Larger caves were created after 1600, and more as Nottingham expanded N after 1845. Houses were recorded in the rock in 1518; the last were condemned *c.* 1900.

Twenty-eight malt-kiln caves have been found, including medieval examples, distinguished by a circular malt kiln, a larger germination room and a nearby well. Caves were also used for brewing and storing ale, and for drinking. Celia Fiennes (1697) describes caves 'all dugg out of the rocks and . . . very coole; at the Crown Inn is a Cellar of 60 stepps down all in the Rock like arch worke over your head, in the Cellar I dranke good ale.' More extensive cellars were excavated under the Nottingham and Star (Shipstone's) breweries in the late C19, and for large sand mines under Mansfield Road from *c.* 1785. Further excavations were made at the Rock Cemetery as catacombs, 1859–63. Ornamental caves were also created, the most famous by Alderman Herbert, who from 1839 linked No. 32 The Ropewalk to its garden below Park Terrace by a staircase inspired by Haddon Hall. It survives with a tableau, Daniel's Den, including lions [5].

5. Daniel's Den, under Park Terrace, for Alderman Herbert, 1856–72

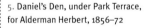

escarpment, W [4]. Between the hills a second settlement emerged, known as the French Borough, with roads fanning out from the castle. The boroughs remained administratively distinct until at least the C13, when a common town wall was built. The pattern of appointing separate bailiffs, introduced with a charter of 1284, was continued by the appointment of two Sheriffs until 1835. Both boroughs probably had small **markets**, that of the pre-Conquest Saxon borough held at Weekday Cross. In the intervening shallow valley evolved a shared marketplace (the Saturday Market), described *c.* 1540 by Leland as 'the most Fairest without exception in all England', and quickly surrounded by long, narrow burgage plots.

The centre of the Saxon borough was St Mary's, through Nottingham's history its largest and most important **church** (*see* p. 31).

Two more churches were established in the French Borough after 1068. Of far greater importance in the early Middle Ages was Lenton Priory, founded by William Peveril, to which in 1109 the three church livings were granted. Lenton perhaps prevented more parish churches from being created, while chapels at the castle consumed court patronage. Grey Friars settled in Broad Marsh in 1230, and the White Friars secured a prime site near the Saturday Market before 1271. The town churches and castle were remodelled in the later Middle Ages. But while St Peter's [46], with its modest retained E.E. arcades, typifies church building in the county, the rebuilding of St Mary's in c14–c15 places it in a national group of Perp town churches promoted by guild interests.

The River Leen was important for **industries** such as tanning, and carried coal from Wollaton by the c15. This was the source of Sir Francis Willoughby's prosperity that led him to build Wollaton Hall in 1580–8, the earliest and most southerly of the sequence of houses by the Smythson family along the Notts and Derbyshire border (*see* p. 196). A cloth industry appeared by the late c12, and textiles dominated Nottingham's economy into the c20. Its importance as a county town is reflected in charters and privileges, culminating in a charter of 1449 making it a county borough. The Shire Hall survives, as rebuilt in the c18 and remodelled in the c19 [67], although the nearby Guildhall, built in the c14–c15, was demolished in 1894. Plumptre Hospital and the High School survive as c19 re-foundations.

Leland described the town wall as partly 'now down'. The remains of the Castle were swept away in the late c17, leaving only the gatehouse and fragments of the bailey walls. Earlier structures, including an aisled c12 hall, have been excavated on Drury Hill, whence the c14 house Severns was moved to Castle Road in 1969. Otherwise there are few **pre-1600 buildings**: the Bell Inn [41], like Severns with a simple crown-post roof [6], the Salutation, and one shop on Bridlesmith Gate.

6. Severns, Castle Road. c14 crown-post roof

Nottingham from *c.* 1600

The Interregnum was a busy building period, especially for new-made men. Col. Francis Pierrepont built a mansion *c.* 1650 close to St Mary's Church, and nearby the physician Huntingdon Plumptre refronted Plumptre House before 1654. Most brick **houses** were three storeys high with many gables, shown on Leonard Knyff's drawing of Nottingham, commissioned in 1699, and demonstrated at Brewhouse Yard [44]. Brick also served for the modest rebuilding in 1671–8 of St Nicholas's church, destroyed in the Civil War.

More **classical façades** were, however, beginning to be built. William Toplady, who married an heiress in 1657, claimed to have set a fashion for parapet roofs. Newdigate House [7], of the 1670s, has a façade alternating triangular and segmental pediments over bolection-moulded window surrounds, motifs repeated in the demolished Howitt House on South Parade and the 'Oriental Café' in Wheeler Gate. Such artisan endeavours

7. Newdigate House, Castle Gate, 1670s

8. Bromley House, Angel Row, stair, begun 1752

paled before the rebuilding of Nottingham Castle in 1674–9 by *William Cavendish, 1st Duke of Newcastle*. Enough survives of its monumental E front to indicate a design of impeccable Continental provenance, though with the solecisms of an architectural amateur [31]. Alternating pediments and Gibbs surrounds featured in the surprisingly decorative E front rebuilt at Plumptre House by *John Plumptre* M.P., another amateur architect, working in 1724 with *Colen Campbell* (demolished). Celia Fiennes in 1697 admired 'severall good houses' and also noted that a 'pyazza' (as Inigo Jones had described his Covent Garden) provided a covered walk alongside the Market Square, with 'long Streetes much like London'.

More **town houses** survive, with their interiors, from the 1730s onwards. A feature of Nottingham houses is their symmetry, with main and service stairs against the cross-walls facing each other. The most geometrically complex town house is Bromley House, begun in 1752 and with a top-lit stair hall [8]; some details are typical of Nottingham, others of London fashion. Stairs placed at the sides permitted large rear rooms, and on Low Pavement and Castle Gate gave unobstructed views across the Trent valley. Where the stairs are behind the entrance on the rear elevation, there was generally no back garden, but a 'vista' over open land in front instead. Examples include County House and Morley House (1750), in the Saxon town, and No. 64 St James's Street (Sheriff House, 1767) [42]. Willoughby and Morley houses have severe

John Carr's builder in Nottingham was *Samuel Stretton* (*c.* 1732–1811). He also practised as an architect, from 1782 with his son *William* (1755–1828), an enthusiastic antiquary. Their work included Richard Arkwright's cotton mill, Green's mill in Broad Marsh, lace factories and many public works. But their private houses are the principal survivors. From known buildings, such as Wilford House, built by Samuel in 1781 for the Loughborough architect William Henderson, and William's alterations to No. 26 Low Pavement (1792–4) [9], a distinctive style emerges, from which it is possible to attribute other houses. Wilford House features a circular 'piecrust' motif, repeated as a lintel in Low Pavement, while bucrania and swag friezes are shared internal features. Fluted dadoes and anthemion mouldings are also distinctive. Houses that exhibit similar features include Stanford House, No. 72 St James's Street and No. 27 St Mary's Gate. William Stretton in 1802 built himself a house with machicolations and Gothick mouldings to the s of the priory at Lenton, where he excavated several piers and the Romanesque font, now at Holy Trinity, Lenton (*see* topic box, p. 181).

façades, but at Sheriff House the dining room hints at a more refined Neoclassicism seen more fully at Stanford House, Castle Gate (*c.* 1775).

A distinctive feature of smaller Nottingham houses is the stone lintel, preferred to gauged brick heads, usually cut as a wedge shape and sometimes with an elaborate central 'keystone'. Patterns change little between 1750 and 1850, making terraced houses difficult to date.

Public buildings also became more sophisticated. The Exchange, built at the E end of the Market Square in 1724–6, was still artisanal in its design. By 1770 architects from outside Nottingham were introducing a more considered style, which local builders personalized in turn. *James Gandon*, a Londoner, won a competition in 1768 for a new Shire Hall, its details inspired by William Chambers. Of greater influence was *John Carr* of York, who worked for Whig patrons around Nottingham at Colwick Hall in 1774–6 and Clifton Hall in 1778–9. He designed new assembly rooms and a grandstand for Nottingham Racecourse (dem.) in 1776–8 at the behest of Lord Edward Bentinck, brother of the Duke of Portland.

The diarist Abigail Gawthern (1757–1822), owner of No. 26 Low Pavement [9], recorded a social round of race meetings, card parties and assemblies. But Nottingham was changing: Gawthern also noted riots prompted by parliamentary elections and economic discontent. Many 'urban gentry' moved out, notably to Lenton where from 1797 the

9. No. 26 Low Pavement, remodelled by William Stretton, 1792–4

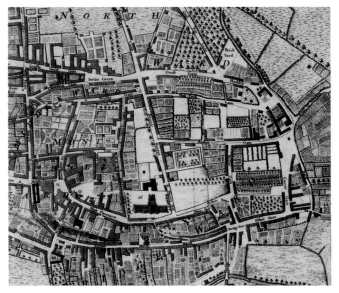

10. Badder & Peat's map, 1744, detail of the Lace Market area showing it still occupied by orchards and gardens. Plumptre House is just north of St Mary's church

Milward Estate was auctioned in commodious lots. In 1807–10 *William Stretton* laid out Standard Hill as a middle-class suburb. The 4th Duke of Newcastle commissioned architects to lay out Park Terrace and the Ropewalk from the 1820s, mainly with stuccoed semis.

Industrialization, *c.* 1750–1830

Nottingham's population grew exponentially from the C18. In 1700 it was 6,000, in 1751 11,000. By 1801 it was 28,861, by 1831 50,220. The first incomers were attracted by the **hosiery industry**. The stocking frame was invented in 1589 by William Lee, curate of nearby Calverton, and Celia Fiennes noted framework knitting as Nottingham's leading industry. Deering estimated in 1739 that there were 1,200 stocking frames in the town, and in 1754 that a third of its burgesses were hosiers. Richard Arkwright opened a cotton mill in Hockley, in 1769. Cotton did not become established, but enterprising hosiers began to adapt frames for the machine-lace industry from the 1780s. In 1809 John Heathcoat invented the bobbin-net machine for more intricate patterns, and John Leavers's action of bobbins and warps, invented in 1813, was adopted for steam-driven machinery by Hooton Deverill in 1841. By 1831 there were nearly 1,400 individual net manufacturers.

For good light, stocking frames and some lace machines were set in attics with long, horizontal windows, e.g. at the side of Brewhouse Yard [44]. Workshops survive in ribbon developments along Alfreton and Mansfield roads, built into the 1840s, and at Sneinton. Bobbin-net machines were so large, and secrecy so intense, that many manufacturers rented space or 'standings' in shared factories. Nottingham remained the hub for design, finishing and selling, but manufacture of all save the most experimental and delicate lace moved from *c.* 1870 to Long Eaton, 7 m. w, where cheap land permitted single-storey factories for larger machines. The Saxon town became the centre of lace trading from the mid 1840s, and is still known as the Lace Market [11]. The River Leen was superseded for haulage by the Nottingham Canal, opened in 1793 from Trent Bridge to the town, and in 1795 to join the Erewash Canal at Langley Mill.

Nottingham's Corporation was Whiggish, oligarchic and by the c19 overwhelmingly Nonconformist. The burgesses who elected the aldermen had the rights to the common fields around Nottingham, and in 1787 rejected proposals for their enclosure. James Granger in 1902 described how 'in living memory it was possible . . . to be in a field but little more than two hundred yards from the Market Place where hay was being made.' With more space, Carrington, New Lenton, New Radford and Sneinton grew rapidly. But most incomers squeezed into the old town. Piecemeal development encouraged a pattern of courtyards lined with back-to-back houses, entered under an archway, often sharing a single pump and closet. Conditions were aggravated from 1810 by the downturn of the hosiery industry, blamed on Napoleon's import embargo and the fashion for trousers, and Nottingham gained a reputation for political radicalism. In October 1831 attacks on Tory opponents of the Reform Bill included the looting of Colwick Hall and Lenton House, while Wollaton was threatened, and the Castle was gutted by arsonists.

11. The Saxon Town and Lace Market, with High Pavement Chapel and St Mary

The worst **housing** was by the River Leen, an area of long, narrow burgage plots already insalubrious before being crammed with court-yards, where cholera struck in 1832. A Royal Commission in 1844 recorded that Nottingham 'had been forced to receive at least three times the amount of population which could have been prudently and healthfully located within so narrow a limit'. Most courts were cleared for lace warehouses around 1900. The last, around Narrow Marsh, were replaced by council housing in the 1930s. Back-to-back terraces towards Sneinton lingered into the 1950s. Small terraced houses, e.g. on Plumptre Street from *c.* 1800, survived in the Lace Market as factories. A late courtyard is Brewitt's Place, *c.* 1845, entered through a doorway off George Street and still with workshop windows on the top floor.

Enclosure

The 1835 Municipal Reform Act broke the old oligarchy by enlarging the franchise, and with the promise of compensation for their rights the burgesses accepted **enclosure**. An early beneficiary was the Midland Counties Railway, though not before Derby had established itself as the East Midlands' railway hub. In 1837 the Corporation agreed to enclose the Westcroft Field, and an Act allowed the company to open a line from Derby and a Neoclassical station in 1839. It lay s of the canal, opposite the present Baroque station of 1902–4. Railway workings thus disturbed Nottingham relatively little, until in 1894–9 the Great Central Railway cut a swathe through central slums for its Victoria Station (dem. 1968). An Act in 1839 also enclosed the Lammas lands between Derby Road and Park Row as a smart residential area, and Burton Leys, given over to churches and the Mechanics' Institute (dem.). Similarly Neoclassical designs survive among the cluster of charitable buildings around George Street, cut *c.* 1800.

The largest Nottingham fields were finally enclosed in 1845. It was hoped that land values would fall and enable decent housing to be built,

12. Arboretum, opened in 1852; postcard of *c.* 1900

THE ARBORETUM, NOTTINGHAM.

13. Papplewick Pumping Station, engine room, by M.O. Tarbotton, 1882–6

but enclosure had little benefit for the very poor, for even on the artisanal Clay Field rents could not be kept below 3s. a week. The former
Sand Field, around the Arboretum, was laid out with middle-class
housing. By the 1840s Enclosure Acts were required to set aside public
space, so the 77-acre common of The Forest was left open, with two
cemeteries, two cricket grounds and the Arboretum [12] (opened in
1852). Land was also given for public baths (1851). Elm Avenue,
Corporation Oaks and Robin Hood Gardens led from the Arboretum
to the beauty spot of St Ann's Well, with Waterloo Promenade to the w
and Queen's Walk in the Meadows; Leicester's New Walk (1785)
provided a model. The result was a green band threaded through the N
of the town. To the NE, common land in Mapperley at Hunger Hills was
partly occupied by allotments.

Thomas Hawksley established a high-pressure constant **water system**,
drawn after 1850 mainly from aquifers in the sandstone, and this did
most to limit further cholera outbreaks. Only in 1859 was a Borough

Engineer appointed, *Marriott Ogle Tarbotton* (1834–87), a man of exceptional vision and energy. He was responsible for culverting the noxious River Leen; for initiating the first subway system of sewers outside London, set below Victoria Street, cut in 1861–3; for a new Trent Bridge (1868–71); and for Papplewick Pumping Station (1882–6) [13], N of the area covered by this book. He also prepared competition briefs for Nottingham's public buildings, including model dwellings erected in 1875–7 – among the earliest in the country.

Nottingham becomes a Victorian City, *c*. 1860–1914

In 1871 a brochure proclaimed Nottingham as the 'Queen of the Midlands', a reflection of its growth and increasing respectability. Sneinton, Lenton, Radford, Basford, and Bulwell parishes were absorbed in 1877, with Wilford lands N of the river. City status followed in 1897.

Nottingham had been a centre of religious **Nonconformity** since the Civil War. High Pavement (Unitarian) and Castle Gate Congregational Chapel, with the Society of Friends, built larger and more fashionable premises after 1860, High Pavement following a national competition. Its stained glass is the best in the city. Chapels proliferated in the new suburbs, as did **Anglican churches**. The latter survive in the Meadows and Sand Field. *W.B. Moffatt* and *Sir George Gilbert Scott* worked in turn on the restoration of St Mary's. Subsequent works reflected its growing social role under Canon Morse, vicar 1864–84, with frustrated aspirations to cathedral status, and an attempted aggrandizement after 1918 as the centre for the county's war memorials. St Peter's lost its C17 chancel to a more 'correct' Gothic design, by *Evans & Jolley*, 1875–7. Most of the Anglican churches built in 1840–80 were by local architects. *T.C. Hine* proved remarkably conventional at All Saints, in the manner of Sir Gilbert Scott [92], while *William Knight* was bombastic at

14. St Andrew's, interior looking east, by William Knight, 1869–71

Nottingham School Board

15. Ilkeston Road Board School, by A.H. Goodall, 1882–3

Education in Nottingham faced a particular challenge, for many children were employed in the textile industries. The School Board, elected in 1870, established a programme of elementary education and by 1903 had also achieved great advances in secondary education.

The Nottingham Board was spared the hostility between Anglicans and Dissenters found elsewhere, probably because Canon Morse and the Congregational teacher Dr Paton shared friendship and a commitment to education. More usual was the situation in Sneinton, where the Board imposed in 1875 was stoutly contested by the Tractarians (*see* p. 150). Sneinton, with the Basford, Lenton and Radford boards, was subsumed when Nottingham expanded its boundaries in 1877.

Nottingham was not short of schools in 1870, but those E and S of the centre were poor and overcrowded. *M.O. Tarbotton*, consultant surveyor, recommended a competition to rebuild St Mary's schools in Bath Street. New buildings by *Evans & Jolley* duly opened in 1874. A second competition that year was won by *A.N. Bromley*. Having been awarded a school, his practice and its successors took responsibility for all subsequent maintenance and extensions. Thus Nottingham's first Board Schools follow no one style.

More urgent building followed the boundary extensions. Bromley became the Board's consultant in 1891, and, although other architects were commissioned, his severe Renaissance style became dominant. Workshops, cookery blocks and swimming baths were added to earlier schools. *A. Henry Whipple*, Director of Education 1924–40, instituted a programme of single-storey buildings designed to maximize natural light.

Evangelical St Andrew's [14]. Outside architects arrived only in the 1880s when new churches were built by the Tractarians: St Alban in Sneinton [97] and St George [102] in the Meadows. Their preferred architect was *G.F. Bodley*, with his successor *C.G. Hare*, working in an airy, sophisticated late Perp style. Roman Catholicism in the city centre means *A.W.N. Pugin*'s St Barnabas's Cathedral (*see* p. 50), built in 1841–4 and based firmly in Midland Decorated traditions.

Charity **schools** moved from the Lace Market to the more whole-some Sand Field. The Bluecoat School [90], founded in 1709, moved in 1853 to new buildings on Mansfield Road by *T.C. Hine*. Nottingham High School moved in 1868, its tall Gothic building accentuating the commanding site between the Arboretum and The Forest. High Pavement School, founded in 1788 for Nonconformists, was taken over by the School Board (*see* topic box, p. 17) as a senior school and moved to Forest Fields in 1893.

Thanks to Tarbotton and *Sir Samuel George Johnson*, the Corporation embarked on an adventurous **road programme** in the 1880s. New arterial roads began in 1883 with Gregory Boulevard, built in conjunction with the Gregory Estate, and Lenton/Castle Boulevard in 1884; more unusually, they were linked in 1887 by Radford Boulevard, to make a very early ring road w of the town. More prestigious schemes were for a University College, Public Library and Museum in 1876–81; and a Guildhall containing law courts and accommodation for its police and fire services, in 1884–6: competitions won by architects from outside Nottingham, respectively *Lockwood & Mawson* (Gothic) and *Verity & Hunt* (French classical).

Victorian Nottingham, especially the commercial core rebuilt *c.*1870–1914, is otherwise distinctively the work of **Nottingham architects**, trained by apprenticeships within the profession, enhanced from 1865 by courses at the Government School of Design (founded in 1843 at Morley House to improve design in the textile industries). In 1928 this became a School of Architecture, and in 1964 was transferred to the University of Nottingham.

T.C. Hine (1813–99) enjoyed pre-eminence as 'the father of Nottingham architects'. His commercial and domestic work spanned Italian and Elizabethan styles, most with an underlying classical structure. Hine's first major building was the Corn Exchange, Thurland Street, 1849, in a style he termed Anglo-Italian, which combined c17 classical details with strapwork. Factories and warehouses followed, the first (1851) for the family hosiery firm, Hine and Mundella, in Station Street, with a Jacobean corner gable. Warehouses from 1853–5 in Broadway and Stoney Street [68, 69] made Hine's reputation. Through the client Richard Birkin, they led to commissions for the General Hospital [78] and the Great Northern Railway station [112] on London Road. In 1854 Hine was appointed surveyor for The Park. He produced a concentric plan of crescents [77] around two circuses, which he and others (under his surveillance) lined with middle-class housing over

16. Nottingham Castle, Long Gallery, by T.C. Hine, 1875–8

the next fifty years, forming a distinctive red brick and leafy enclave. A similar development with his brother John at Alexandra Park (1854–7), failed. Hine also considered himself an antiquary, and his greatest work to be the sensitive restoration of Nottingham Castle as the City Museum and Art Gallery [16]: a contrast to his aggressive French Renaissance rebuilding of the Shire Hall after fire damage in 1876.

Other manufacturers' sons followed Hine into architecture. The work of his erstwhile partner *Robert Evans* and assistant *William Jolley*, who formed a practice in 1871, typifies the Northern Renaissance style in which central Nottingham was rebuilt in the late C19. The style, updating mercantile Bruges or Antwerp for a modern textile centre, was used indiscriminately for warehouses, offices and Board Schools. *S. Dutton Walker* added distinctive tile patterning to gables of red brick and terracotta, materials adopted enthusiastically by *John Howitt* and *G.S. Doughty*, architects of the most vibrant-hued showrooms and offices along Derby Road and on Bridlesmith Gate. Terracotta was also embraced by *Albert Nelson Bromley*, who dominated public building in the 1890s as architect to the tramways company and School Board, and who worked across Britain for Boots and the National Telephone Co. Bromley came to architecture through his uncle, *Frederick Bakewell*; other architectural dynasties included the *Evans, Sutton* and *Heazell* families.

The most interesting **houses** in the Gothic style were by *R.C. Sutton* and *Henry Sulley*. Undistinguished individually, *Arthur W. Brewill* and *Basil Baily* together moved from Jacobean shaped gables to a refined Arts and Crafts style, seen in Mansfield Road's Christian Science church

(1898). There are few truly Queen Anne houses, the best perhaps in Forest Road West, by *Sidney R. Stevenson*, 1884, for a Dr Chicken. Doctors elsewhere made progressive architectural clients, seen in Arts and Crafts houses by *William R. Gleave* in Arkwright Street, 1902, and by *H.E. Woodsend* in Sneinton, 1907. The most interesting Arts and Crafts architect was *Arthur Marshall* (1858–1915), designer of the Bagthorpe workhouse (1903, now City Hospital), and two houses of 1896 for the Player family with panelled living-room halls, Fernleigh, Woodborough Road (a substantial remodelling), and Lenton Hurst, at the University. For Nottingham's most eccentric architect, Watson Fothergill, *see* below.

Watson Fothergill

The idiosyncrasies of Nottingham's most charismatic architect begin with his name. *Fothergill Watson* (1841–1928) was born in Mansfield, eldest son of lace manufacturer Robert Watson and Mary Ann Fothergill. A fascination for genealogy led him to explore the Fothergills' putative links to William I and in 1892 to swap his forename and surname. 'Fothergill' is used as a common abbreviation.

Fothergill was articled (1856–60) to the surveyor Frederick Jackson, and his extensive speculative housing, as in Foxhall Road, 1901, may derive from this background. He worked for Arthur Blomfield in London and with John Middleton in Cheltenham before beginning practice in Nottingham in 1864. In 1873 Fothergill won a competition for the Temperance Albert Hall, polychromatic with a Rhenish tower, followed by offices for the Nottingham Daily Express [54] in 1876 – a cacophony of gables, oriels and a corner tourelle. The building features Fothergill's signature, first 'FW', and in 1899 'Watson Fothergill', when he added further storeys.

Other clients included the Nottingham and Notts Bank, and Brunt's Charity, for whom he built housing in the Meadows and the Black Boy Hotel from 1887 (dem. 1970). This, like the bank's headquarters in Thurland Street, had a rollicking central tower. Imaginative animal carvings and figurative friezes (the later ones by *Benjamin Creswick*), have made Fothergill's work popular with the Nottingham public. Later buildings combine hard red brick and granite with squat timber-fronted attics, some with box-like dormers under pyramidal hats.

Fothergill is best known for his commercial work, but he designed many houses, almshouses and churches here and in Mansfield. The ultimate conceit was his own offices [17] in George Street (1894–5), where he commemorated his architectural heroes in stone, above a sculpture of an architect pointing to plans for a cathedral – an aspiration Fothergill never realized.

17. Watson Fothergill's office, No. 15 George Street, 1894–5

18. Boots, interior of D10, 'Wets Building', by Sir Owen Williams, 1930–2

The Twentieth-century City

Nottingham's growth since 1900 has been in physical size rather than population. A proposed **borough extension** was rejected in 1920, but in 1933 Bilborough and Wollaton were incorporated to the w, Bestwood to the n, and parts of Arnold, Gedling and Colwick in the e. In 1952 the parishes of Clifton and Wilford s of the river were added. West Bridgford resisted incorporation, giving Nottingham its ungainly s boundary. The population of 260,000 in 1911 rose to 311,000 over this larger area in 1961, declining to 277,000 in 1981 (278,700 in 2005).

The Housing and Town Planning Act of 1919 forced the Corporation to review its languishing building programme. There were forty **slum-**

clearance schemes, and in 1937 St Mary's reported that 'scarcely any residents are left in the parish'. Back-to-back terraces were demolished for Sneinton's wholesale market (opened 1938). **Streets** were widened in 1932 to make an inner ring road, N and E of the city core, and a new northern artery, Huntingdon Street, with a retail market and bus station (demolished 1985). Twenty new **housing estates** were built, mainly to the N and W, to low densities. Wollaton Hall was bought in 1924, becoming a public park and museum, and an outer ring road was opened between 1928 and 1938.

The centrepiece of this civic aggrandizement was the Council House (*see* p. 46), by the Housing Architect *Thomas Cecil Howitt* (1889–1968). He was among the first architects anywhere to move from a local authority into independent practice. Lesser architects turned to Art Deco, notably *Cyril F. W. Haseldine*, who designed Moderne houses into the 1950s. *Alfred J. Thraves* moved from chapel work into cinema design, a specialism refined by his one-time assistant, *Reginald Cooper*. J.B. Priestley's *English Journey* (1934) considered Nottingham the 'most frivolous' of provincial towns for its commercial entertainment, criticizing Goose Fair (first recorded in 1284) and its sporting institutions.

The lace industry stagnated in the 1920s, and Nottingham was slow in adapting to the market for ready-made clothes. High female employment secured Nottingham's tradition for pretty girls but kept general wage rates low. However, the suburbs and satellite towns developed a skilled workforce in **light engineering**, developed around Raleigh bicycles (founded 1886) and Humber cars, based at Beeston 1898–1908, and supported by 'night schools' such as the People's College. Raleigh and Player's, the cigarette manufacturers, built imposing Neoclassical offices. Hollins & Co., manufacturers of 'Viyella' fabrics, were Nottingham's one leader in ready-made clothing. Their second factory, by *Frank Broadhead*, 1931–3, adopted the progressive flat-slab system with mushroom columns first used in Britain at Garston, Liverpool, in 1919. But the most important industrial architecture was at Boots' new site, where *Sir Owen Williams* produced Nottingham's one building of international stature, D10 [18, 148] or the 'Wets' building, in 1930–2. He pushed flat-slab construction to incorporate a cantilever, with only the thinnest of floor slabs interrupting the curtain walling, and turned storing and packing toiletries into high drama. Williams followed this with D6 [149] for dry goods, in 1935–8, more inventive in its cantilevers, but a tighter budget meant there was no place for spatial effects.

The **University College** was gifted a suburban campus in 1921 by Jesse Boot at Lenton, based on three Late Georgian villas and their grounds. Boot's favoured architect *Percy Morley Horder* designed the first new buildings. They epitomise inter-war civic architecture, the classical clock tower of the central Trent Building [126] (1922–8) a striking landmark set on axis from the park entrance across a lake. Full university status was granted only in 1948, but expansion rapidly followed.

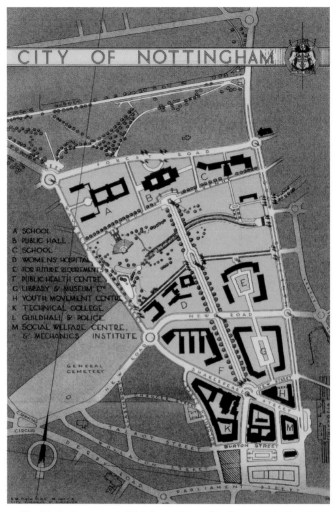

A SCHOOL
B PUBLIC HALL
C SCHOOL
D WOMENS' HOSPITAL
E FOR FUTURE REQUIREMENTS
F PUBLIC HEALTH CENTRE
G LIBRARY & MUSEUM ℃°
H YOUTH MOVEMENT CENTRE
K TECHNICAL COLLEGE.
L GUILDHALL & POLICE.
M SOCIAL WELFARE CENTRE.
  & MECHANICS INSTITUTE

GENERAL
CEMETERY

19. City of Nottingham, proposed Civic Centre, Report of the Reconstruction Committee, CA/PL/16/1, 1943

Post-war Nottingham

Nottingham suffered little war damage,* but in 1942 a Reconstruction Committee was appointed to plan post-war development. Its **report**, 1943, had three major proposals. The most ambitious – and never realized – was for a new civic centre [19], stretching N from the Guildhall to the High Schools. The other proposals, for new housing and roads, had greater impact.

*There was damage to the University College; St John, Canal Street; St Christopher, Sneinton; buildings at the SE corner of Friar Lane and in the Lace Market.

In 1952 a large estate was bought to the s at Clifton, developed with mainly low-rise **housing** in 1957–73. Tall point blocks formed part of Nottingham's slum-clearance programmes at Sneinton, Lenton and elsewhere in the 1960s. System building was taken further following the appointment of *David Jenkin* in 1964 as the first City Architect to head his own department. Two major slum clearance programmes included St Ann's, where 10,000 houses were replaced in 1967–76 by 3,500 new homes, mostly following a regular courtyard grid. A higher density and irregular plan were adopted at the Meadows, 1972–80, but the area's former vibrancy was lost.

Of greatest damage to historic Nottingham was the third initiative from 1943, of completing the **inner ring road** with a w section from Chapel Bar to Castle Boulevard [20]. The area lay strategically between the Castle and Market Square. The demolition of Collin's Almshouses of 1709, described by Pevsner as 'one of the best almshouses of its date in England', and the break-up of the radial street pattern were approved with little opposition. Work began in 1957. Arthur Ling, Professor of Town Planning at Nottingham University, decried the road in 1966 as 'an insult to Maid Marion [sic], for the street must qualify as being one of the ugliest in Europe', a reflection of the quality of the new buildings

20. Maid Marian Way under construction, photo of 1965. Building at the junction with Friar Lane

lining it. Reacting to rival Leicester's economic acceleration, Nottingham allowed developers a free hand to build offices of poor design and unsympathetic scale in a bid to be 'go-ahead'.

Two vast **shopping centres** followed. The Victoria Centre, by *Arthur Swift & Partners* and opened in 1972, filled the railway cutting formerly occupied by Victoria Station. More controversial was the Broadmarsh Centre, built in 1970–3 despite objections to the loss of Drury Hill, one of Nottingham's oldest streets. That central Nottingham survived into the 1960s relatively unscathed only highlighted its subsequent denudation.

It could have been worse. That nothing was built of Robin Hood Way and Park Way, and little of Sheriff's Way, reflects the move towards **preservation**. Most importantly, a planned road E–W through the Lace Market was abandoned when in 1969 a Conservation Area was created. This was expanded N of Goose Gate in 1974. A mix of smart restaurants, new flats and residential warehouse conversions now rubs shoulders with down-at-heel workshops and derelict sites, but the area's tight-knit character has been retained. A greater change has been the redevelopment of the canalside as an area of offices, flats and bars since the early 1990s.

Nottingham has more good **post-1945 buildings** than most provincial cities. The continuing classicism at the University of Nottingham, derided by Modernists, became fashionable in the 1980s. At halls of residence along Beeston Lane, *Donald McMorran* and *Brian O'Rorke* speculated on what might have happened had the Gothic Revival not intervened, while drawing on details from 1920s Swedish classicism. T.C. Howitt also built in the classical tradition at the University and the College of Technology (Nottingham Trent University since 1992).

Modernism followed slowly. Gentle 1950s functionalism is represented by locals *Bartlett & Gray*, designers of the Friends' Meeting House (1960–1). *Basil Spence* passed his commission for the University's Science Area to his partner *Andrew Renton*, and the Pope and Chemistry [131] buildings, both opened in 1961, combine elegance with fine materials. More dramatic are *Peter Moro*'s Nottingham Playhouse [21, 38], and *Skidmore, Owings & Merrill*'s offices at Boots [150], updating ideas by Gropius and Mies van der Rohe for the 1960s. The John Player Horizon Factory [151], 1968–71, represents the best of British factory design, the culmination of *Arup Associates*' ideas on the integration of architecture and services. Postmodern classicism was favoured for 1980s offices by local practices, led by *Crampin Pring* with the Atrium (1989–91) and by *James McArtney*, more significant as conservation planners than as designers. The two practices have now merged. *Graham Brown* used welded steel in the manner of the

21. Nottingham Playhouse, by Peter Moro, 1961–3, interior, view of main staircase through entrance foyer

22. Centre for Contemporary Art, Weekday Cross, by Caruso St John, 2006–9, model perspective

Californian architect Craig Ellwood for his own house (1986), at the same time as designing Postmodern offices and the Djanogly Arts Centre (1989–92).

The **Modernist revival** of the 1990s came early to Nottingham, when in 1992 *Michael Hopkins* won a competition for Inland Revenue offices [117] on a sensitive site below the Castle, with vistas between the blocks and contextual materials. It was an early user of green technology. Hopkins refined the formula with his Jubilee Campus at Nottingham University [133] (first phase 1996–9), a necklace of glazed teaching units strung along a canal – maybe too sophisticated for student life, but still impressive a decade later. *Ken Shuttleworth*'s *Make Architects* promise a more dynamic image with their campus extensions. Most new building in Nottingham is now in the conservative Modernism established since the late 1990s, mixing materials and geometries. *Hawkins\Brown*, a London firm with Nottingham roots, has three large projects in the city, including the New Art Exchange, completed 2008. *Maber Associates*, founded in 1983, specialize in large commercial projects, while *Marsh Grochowski* have since 1985 undertaken bijou housing, offices and arts projects, their elegance combined with an increasing emphasis on green issues.

It is difficult to be as upbeat about Nottingham as the editors of its Centenary History were a decade ago. This guide is written amid economic uncertainty, while the loosening of planning controls threatens conservation principles. Yet has there been a better time for new architecture here? Prominent national firms working in the city include, additionally, *Caruso St John*, whose Centre for Contemporary Art is under construction [22], and a shopping centre and hotel by *Benson & Forsyth* opened in 2007–8 [63], both deliberately eye-catching works that nevertheless fit the traditional street pattern.

Major Buildings

23. St Mary, High Pavement, exterior

St Mary's Church

Next to Newark, St Mary's is the largest parish church in the county, dominating the skyline of the Saxon town despite the increased scale of c18 and c19 rebuilding around it.* It was probably a Saxon minster much rebuilt in the c12 and early c13 – perhaps following town fires in 1140 and 1171. Two c12 arches survive *ex situ* in the side of Birkin's warehouse in Broadway (p. 105), with no capitals between jambs and voussoirs; fragments of early c13 piers, with fat roll mouldings, can be seen under the third of the nave N piers (floorboarding can be lifted). More remains were noted in the 1840s rebuilding. Today the church is almost entirely mature Perp, described glowingly by Leland in 1532 as 'excellente, newe, and unyforme yn worke, and so manie faire windows yn itt yt no artificer can imagine to set more'. It has been much restored (*see* topic box, p.36), especially in 1846–50 by *W.B. Moffatt*, who rebuilt the W front. The S chancel chapel was added by *Temple Moore*, 1912–15, the chapter house by *Bodley & Garner*, 1887–8, and the nave vestry by *Ernest A. Heazell & Son*, 1939–40. St Mary's hoped to be raised as the cathedral of the Diocese of Notts and Derbyshire, created in 1884, but Southwell Minster was preferred. The plan is cruciform, with a 108-ft (33-metre) nave of six bays and aisles, an originally aisleless four-bay chancel (72 ft, 22 metres, long), and transepts (100 ft, 31 metres, N–S). The tower (126 ft, 39 metres, to parapets) is over the crossing.

The C15 Church

The **rebuilding** from *c.* 1400 of the nave and transepts, i.e. those parts for which the town and its guilds were responsible, has an invention and logic that inform every element of its design. The work began in the S transept and S aisle, heading westwards and then back to the N transept, replacing the old church section by section. The earliest parts suggest a little Lincolnshire influence, but the most important model is Gloucester Cathedral and particularly its S transept rebuilding from the 1330s into the c15, perhaps introduced to Nottingham via the West Midlands; the great guild churches of Coventry – Holy Trinity and St Michael – and Kenilworth Castle have similar details. Nottingham's guilds were small compared to Coventry's, with 167 members in 1370,

*This account owes much to unpublished research by Richard Morris and Linda Monckton.

24. St Mary, interior, mostly c15, looking east

but St Mary's stands as one of a wave of big town church rebuildings of the early c15. It is based on a meticulous grid of thick roll mouldings with a canted fillet behind, particularly inside, giving a subtle pattern of light and shade. With its sense of frame and infill, no wonder Perp was popular with mid-c20 Modernists! The uprights and horizontals of this scaffolding give the church a solid, four-square appearance. This is very different, for example, from Newark and also from Melton Mowbray in Leicestershire, with which, however, the clerestory fenestration and detail of the crossing tower – and the emphasis given the latter – are evidently connected.

Exterior

The s porch is both the normal entrance and one of the two set-pieces of the earliest rebuilding phase – the other is the recessed tomb canopy [26] on the s wall inside the s transept – and as both are bonded into the wall, with which they share masons' marks,* they and the wall must be contemporary. The **porch** [25] has solid double cusps, heavily articulated, hanging from an ogee moulding, as at St Botolph, Boston, but closer in style is the w cloister door at Gloucester Cathedral, *c.* 1330. The walls have a grid of roll mouldings that continue as transverse arches into the vault, with trefoil decoration between. The inner doorway is enriched by niches placed diagonally in the typical c14 way. Above

*I am grateful to Jenny Alexander and Pauline Miller for this information.

them, the voussoirs of the arch are decorated by large square fleurons. The tracery of the s transept **window** owes much to Gloucester. The paired aisle windows, unusual for a Perp church, may hark back to the C13 church it replaced – particularly in the s aisle with its tripartite pattern of lights; the clerestory windows are also doubled, a more common feature.

The exterior stonework was renewed in campaigns by *William Stretton* and especially *W.B. Moffatt*. The **tower** has three stages, the first with a blank arcade, the second with one large window (like those in the chancel N and s) on each side, the third with four arcades of which the two middle ones are pierced. It is crowned by battlements and pinnacles. The body of the church is also castellated, the chancel plainly, the nave and aisles with panelled battlements; panelling extends to the buttresses. The richest decoration is lavished on the show fronts of the transepts, with ogee gables and pinnacles. The s and N transept windows are huge – twelve lights, three transoms, depressed four-centred tops. The w and N aisle windows have Y-tracery, and those on the w front and first two N bays have roll mouldings and canted fillets. Their absence from the N aisle E of the first two bays indicates that rebuilding progressed from the s transept through the w end and then eastwards to the N transept. The w porch follows the detailing of the s porch, but there are two windows at the w end of each aisle instead of the one shown in Thoroton's view (*see* topic box, p. 36). Moffatt also renewed the nave roof and clerestory. On the N side are additions, the low 1940 nave vestry allowing *Bodley & Garner*'s four-bay vestry of 1887–8, denoted by its prominent piers, to be used as a **chapter house**, linked by a door to the N aisle in 1939. To the E, the high gable and large N Perp window of the vestry shows that it is part of the C15 rebuilding.*

25. St Mary, south porch, late C14 detailing, with door by Henry Wilson, 1904–5

*Plans of 1890 by *Bodley & Garner* for a lavatory and coal store on the site of the nave vestry were unrealized. In 1919 proposals were made for a war memorial Lady Chapel on the site of the chapter house, by *C.G. Hare*, but funds could not be raised.

The **chancel** is significantly simpler. The living was granted to Lenton Priory, 1109, and perhaps the Priory was shamed into rebuilding *c.* 1470 by the richness of the town's work. Four-light windows, tall with two transoms and two-centred arches, save for the E window which goes to nine lights and three transoms. Though there are similarities to the external face of the later N aisle, without mouldings they are difficult to date. Archdeaconry records (1590–1635) dismiss the tradition that the chancel was rebuilt in Elizabeth's reign, but report its poor condition; it was finally repaired in 1635. *Temple Moore* built the S chancel aisle for the organ, 1912–15, re-setting the windows and buttresses and including a new turret stair and furnishings.

Interior

The sense of a glasshouse is countered by the darkness of the stonework within [24]. In the S transept the recessed **tomb canopy** to John Samon [26], d.1416, has the solid cusping and panels found in the S porch. Samon's father (also John, d.1371) first mooted the rebuilding, and bequests continued until the mid C15. A distinctive feature of the early C15 rebuilding, well seen on the former chantry (now vestry) doorway, nave N, is a big roll moulding springing vertically from the doorhead as part of the overall grid. A hierarchy of similar roll mouldings and canted fillets defines the nave piers, which have hexagonal bases – again already found at Gloucester. These piers are of graceful lozenge shape, maximizing transverse light, and have only meagre capitals – most ribs run through from shaft to arch without a break. The clerestory stands immediately on the apex of the arcade. The end of the rebuilding is marked in the N transept by the tomb to Thomas Thurland, d.1473, though not integrated into the wall. Its canopy has pretty little fan vaults, yet echoes across some sixty years the double cusping of Samon's tomb facing it.

Moffatt rebuilt the four composite tower piers. *William Stretton* replicated the fan vault under the tower (likened by Pevsner to the Tudor vault at Rotherham) in wood and plaster, 1811–12. It was suggested that Heazell replace it in stone, 1934–5, but there is no evidence this was done. The vestry, described as in poor condition by 1625, has an C18 plaster ceiling. The chancel roof is thought to have been renewed by *Sir Gilbert Scott*, 1872, and was decorated by *Lawrence Bond* in 1965.

Furnishings

Chancel stalls and **sedilia** by *Sir Gilbert Scott*, 1872; spiky **bishop's throne at** its end. – **Screen** and **reredos**, 1884–5 by *Bodley & Garner*; the screen made by *Kett* of Cambridge, the reredos panels painted by *Burlison & Grylls*. E end panelling, 1931. – **Altar table**, N transept, Jacobean. – Other fittings late C19–C20. – **Organ**, E wall of S transept. One of the first in Britain by *Marcussen* of Denmark, installed 1973. – Octagonal **font**, w end of S aisle. C15, with Perp panelling under ogee arches. Lowered in 1948, and with a cover of 1957. – **Royal arms**. Lion and Unicorn, free-standing figures of *c.* 1710, nave w end.

Sculpture. In the s chancel chapel wall, a small C15 **alabaster** possibly from a reredos, local in style, found under the sanctuary floor. It depicts St Thomas; faces of great calm. Also in the s chancel chapel a terracotta **maquette** by *George Tinworth* of Doulton's, exhibited 1875. – Sumptuous s bronze **doors**, 1904–5 by *Henry Wilson* commemorating Canon Morse, vicar 1864–86; scenes of Christ with Our Lady. Tautly drawn low-relief figures with great expression, comparable with Wilson's work at Welbeck Abbey, N of Nottingham.

Stained Glass

Unimportant C15 fragments in lower windows of the s chapel, and in the upper lights of the fourth window from the E; Throsby in 1795 recorded only a figure of St Andrew surviving (and a faint wall painting over the vestry door, perhaps of St Christopher). A thorough programme of stained glass began in 1867 with the gift of the s transept window by the Smith banking family. The programme soon left its planned themes. Some glass swapped sides with the installation of the organ, 1973. The following runs from the E end, s to the w end, and then back along the N side.

26. St Mary, south transept, recessed tomb canopy to John Samon, d.1416

St Mary's Late Georgian appearance was very different [27]. In 1762, as it threatened to fissure, the w front was replaced by a classical design by *William Hiorn* of Warwick, with a heavy pediment surmounted by an urn, and a Doric doorcase. A new roof was placed over the nave, destroying the clerestory tracery. The s transept and aisle were refaced by *William Stretton* in 1818–20. In 1842 the church was closed as the tower was declared unsafe, and a proposal to demolish the whole was narrowly defeated. *L.N. Cottingham* organized scaffolding while he investigated the problem, attributed to gravediggers undermining the foundations. He was replaced by *Scott & Moffatt* after an argument about money, and when that partnership was severed in 1845 *W.B. Moffatt* took the job. In 1846 the public finally raised a subscription and the work began. The w front was rebuilt in accordance with Thoroton's view of 1677 and surviving evidence behind Hiorn's work. The chancel was re-roofed and repaired at the charge of the patron, Earl Manvers, and the c15 oak stalls were salvaged for St Stephen, Sneinton (*see* p. 152). In 1867 the galleries and high pews were removed, and the side aisles and transepts re-roofed.

27. St Mary, c18 frontage, engraving, 1840

Chancel. E, 1863, to the Prince Consort (pre-dating the formal programme), by *Hardman*. The earliest and most garish c19 piece in the church, partly concealed by the reredos. s **chapel**. E window to Katherine Mary Monica Wade-Dalton, d.1918 of influenza a week after her marriage, depicted in the lace wedding dress made by her father's company. 1920 by *Burlison & Grylls*. s side, 1st, 1878 by *Hardman*; 2nd and 3rd, 1868 by *Ward & Hughes,* moved after 1912. s **transept**. E, 1882 and 1903, by *Burlison & Grylls*. s, 1867 by *Heaton, Butler & Bayne*, a major mid-Victorian design, with a wide and glowing colour range. w side, 1876 by *Ward & Hughes*.

s **aisle.** From the E: 1st, to Crimean and Indian Mutiny veterans, designed 1933 by *Denholm Davis*; installed 1936, by *Hinchcliffe, Hincks & Burnell* of Nottingham. 2nd, 1922 by *Burlison & Grylls*. 3rd, to the Scout movement, by *Ernest C. Carter* of *Hincks & Burnell*, 1928. 4th–7th, 1899–1902, and 8th, 1895, all by *C.E. Kempe*. 9th and 10th, by *Burlison & Grylls*, 1920 and 1882. Their work seems pasty in comparison to that of *Clayton & Bell* alongside, 11th (1888), and 12th (1900, to T.C. Hine the architect). **w end.** 1887 and 1884, also by *Clayton & Bell*; all designed as a group around the font. w centre window by *Hardman*, to Thomas Adams, lace manufacturer, 1876. Much finer than the E window, showing the Life of Christ with rows of pharaohs, prophets and kings.

N **transept.** Mostly *Clayton & Bell*: N 1874; E side, 1876, 1880 (by *Hardman*), 1883, 1876. **Chancel.** N side, 1st and 2nd, 1880 and 1891, by *Clayton & Bell*; 3rd, 1890 by *E.R. Frampton*.

Monuments

Battered alabaster effigy in the N aisle, later C14. – John Samon, d.1416, alabaster, in the s transept recess already mentioned. – N transept, the tomb of Thomas Thurland, d.1473, contains an alabaster chest made probably for John Tannesly, d.1414, and his wife. Small figures of the Annunciation. On this rests a Purbeck slab probably from the tomb of William Amyas *c.* 1348–69. Additionally an early C15 alabaster of a bishop, possibly from the tomb-chest of Robert English, d.1475. – Also in the N transept Robert Plumptre, d.1693. Acanthus scrolls. – Many minor tablets in the N aisle. – s aisle, Thomas Smith, d.1727, a Baroque plaque with putti and a skull. Chancel, war memorials: South Notts Hussars, unveiled 1922, topped by pith helmets; the three Robin Hood battalions of the Sherwood Foresters, a large rectangular bronze relief by *Henry Poole* with *Brewill & Baily*, 1921.

Churchyard

This assumed its present dimensions in 1806. Typical Notts slate **headstones**, mainly laid flat in 1948, by local sculptors including *Valentine Johnson*, *William Charles*, *J.E. Hall* and *Job Turton* of Nottingham, and *Surplice* of Beeston. Near the N wall, **monument** (and modern plaque) to George Africanus (1763–1834), brought from Sierra Leone as a child and trained as a brass founder. By the NW gate, nearly illegible, a terracotta headstone to young sisters, d.1704, made by their father *William Sefton*, maker of earthen pipes. City and County **war memorial** at the sw entrance to the churchyard, 1921–2 by *C.G. Hare*, a central stone cross flanked on either side by tapering flights of steps, with gates; inset tablets inscribed with the names of Notts parishes and their 1,200 dead.

Nottingham Castle

Nottingham Castle today is not a medieval fortification but a mansion begun in 1674 by William Cavendish, 1st Duke of Newcastle, and completed by his son Henry, the 2nd Duke, in 1679 [4, 28]. It was recast as the city's museum and art gallery in 1875–8. Novel in English architecture, it looks at first, in its general shape with the top balustrade, as if it stood in northern Italy or Prague. Its direct origins are, however, Flemish.

The first castle on the 133-ft-high sandstone crag w of the city was built by William I in 1067–8. So prominent a hill may have had earlier defences, although only scanty Saxon pottery shards have been found. It became one of the most important royal castles, overseeing the Trent crossing linking northern and southern England. The castle had a hand in the county's justice system. Henry II, Henry III, Edward III and Edward IV built extensively, and it was a favourite of Richard III, who spent his last nights before the Battle of Bosworth here.

By 1525 all was 'in great ruin and dekay'. The outer defences were repaired in 1536 (the crisis of the Pilgrimage of Grace), and twice during Elizabeth I's reign. But in 1622 James I leased Nottingham Castle to Francis Manners, 7th Earl of Rutland, and his heirs, who stripped it of materials. By 1641 it was uninhabitable. Charles I raised his standard here in August 1642, but the castle was taken for Parliament, and Colonel John Hutchinson installed defences. Following Parliament's victory the Council of State agreed that it should be demolished. The *Duke of Newcastle* bought the site in 1663. He was his own architect, aided by the mason *Samuel Marsh*, of Welby, near Grantham. His mansion passed to the Pelham family, Dukes of Newcastle by a new

28. Nottingham Castle, east front before the fire, etching of *c.* 1750

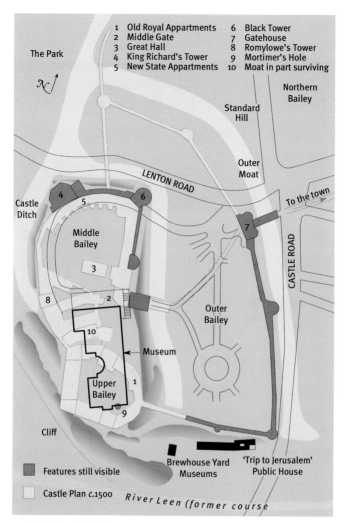

1	Old Royal Appartments	6	Black Tower
2	Middle Gate	7	Gatehouse
3	Great Hall	8	Romylowe's Tower
4	King Richard's Tower	9	Mortimer's Hole
5	New State Appartments	10	Moat in part surviving

The Park

Northern Bailey

Standard Hill

Outer Moat

LENTON ROAD

To the town

Castle Ditch

Middle Bailey

CASTLE ROAD

3

8

2

10

Outer Bailey

Museum

Upper Bailey

1

9

Cliff

Brewhouse Yard Museums

'Trip to Jerusalem' Public House

■ Features still visible

□ Castle Plan c.1500

River Leen (former course)

29. Nottingham Castle, plan

creation, but declined in importance after 1770 after they built Clumber, 20 miles N. It was gutted in the Reform Bill riots of 1831, the N and w fronts damaged severely. A model held in Brewhouse Yard shows this post-fire state. The castle was finally restored, with remodelling, by *T.C. Hine*, 1875–8, as the first local authority funded art gallery [16], conceived in conjunction with the Victoria and Albert Museum.*

*This account is indebted to recent research and corrections by Trevor Foulds, the Castle's archivist, in particular in *Thoroton Society Transactions* 106, 2000; also to Christopher Drage, *Nottingham Castle, A Place Full Royal*, Nottingham Civic Society/Thoroton Society, 1999.

30. Nottingham Castle, Gatehouse, commissioned 1251

The Medieval Castle

The **medieval castle layout** [29] is known from plans, chiefly that by
John Smythson, 1617. As built in 1067–8 it comprised the Upper Bailey,
a Middle Bailey and an outer enclosure that included Standard Hill to
the N. King John defined the present Outer Bailey. Henry II concentrated
expenditure on just six of his castles, including Nottingham. In 1171–89,
contemporary with work at Newcastle and Dover castles, a stone curtain
wall was thrown around the Middle Bailey, a new inner keep and state
apartments were built in the Upper Bailey, and the Middle Bailey gained
a great hall and perhaps a chapel, requiring repair in 1237. The NE tower
of the Middle Bailey was built early in the C13, probably by Henry III,
who from 1251 gave the Outer Bailey a stone curtain wall, with a
gatehouse. Basford sandstone rather than the castle rock was preferred,
but even this was an indifferent material. Edward III's works on the W
side of the Middle Bailey, 1362, included Romylowe's Tower and a new
chapel. But it was Edward IV who transformed the Middle Bailey into
what the poet John Skelton described as 'a place full royal', remodelling
the NE tower and adding state apartments running N to the new
Richard's Tower (named for Richard III). The apartments were a
curved line of canted bays with timber upper works, similar to those by
the Earls of Shrewsbury at Wingfield, Derbys, 1455–70.

Fragments of **Richard's Tower** survive in private grounds behind
Castle Grove, leased separately in the 1650s, and part of the Park Estate
developed in the 1850s (p. 118). It was a multi-angular, prestigious
design, comparable in size to the Upper Bailey keep, of three storeys
with a square side chamber served by a separate stair, in which Civil War
graffiti have been recorded. Remains may be glimpsed from Lenton
Road, cut through the Outer Bailey c. 1817–20.

Gatehouse

The **gatehouse** [30] is the principal medieval survival. The 1251 brief demanded 'a good stone gate', with flanking towers and a guardhouse over. There remains a gate passage between two D-shaped towers, approached over a stone bridge. Medieval fabric, concealed by refacing above bridge level, survives almost to first-floor height; below are contrasting bands of sandstone and magnesian limestone. Stylistically the gatehouse sits between square examples of the late C12 and the fully towered gates of Harlech or Caerphilly. The contemporary middle gate at Corfe Castle, Dorset, is perhaps the closest comparison, while the portcullis arrangement emulates that at Warkworth, Northumberland, c. 1240. The two arches of the bridge are still visible from the s, but N the ditch was infilled early in the C19. The rounded w arch, of sandstone blocks with a large keystone, replaced a pointed arch c. 1679. The pointed E arch has three chamfered ribs within. The tunnel-vaulted gate-hall is divided by an intermediate arch into two unequal sections. A portcullis operated within the outer arch. Behind the middle arch stood inward-opening gates; brick and stone patches indicate the positions of the hinges. The N tower is entered through a narrow doorway in the w wall with a pointed chamfered arch; other doorways are C20. Reduced to a lodge in 1651, the gatehouse deteriorated until 1908, when it was shorn of accretions and remodelled, with a ticket office and gates added to the N, by *T.G. Jackson*.

In the **curtain wall** s of the gatehouse along Castle Road survives more medieval fabric including three small bastions, mostly covered by the City Architect in ashlar, *c.* 1908. A small buttressed area has the oldest exposed fabric, then concealed by the Nottinghamshire Rifles' drill hall, 1799, demolished 1926. On its footings *James Woodford*'s **statue** of Robin Hood, erected 1952, with smaller groups of Merry Men and romantic reliefs depicting scenes from his life set in walling refaced by *T. Cecil Howitt & Partners*.

Little medieval work elsewhere above ground. Some remains in the Middle Bailey gate behind *T.C. Hine*'s rebuilding, 1874, best seen as the grounds are entered. The carriage drive, NW beyond the obelisk, leads to a length of exposed rubble walling including the round C13 NE **tower**. A **bust** commemorates Major Jonathon White, Robin Hood Rifles, 1891 by *Albert Toft*. Turn left at the C17 **gatepiers**. The line of the E wall of the Middle Bailey and its C13 apartments has been marked out on the greensward N of the castle – its high embankment incorporating C11–C12 earthworks – following excavation, 1978–86. Thence steps lead up to the C17 mansion, whose clifftop **terrace** has spectacular views across the city and Trent valley. On Christmas Day 1996 the terrace's sw corner collapsed, exposing sections of medieval curtain wall. This was consolidated and a new deck built across by the *Gibson Hamilton Partnership*, 2004–5.

Associated with the Middle Bailey are man-made **caves** (the Western Passages) reached down stairs from the carriage drive. The so-called

The Duke of Newcastle

William Cavendish (1593–1676) was created Duke of Newcastle in 1665 as a mark of his loyalty to Charles I and Charles II. He was an exceptional horseman, and published *La Méthode et invention nouvelle de dresser les chevaux* in Antwerp, 1658, with illustrations by Rubens's pupil Abraham van Diepenbeke. So Cavendish had impeccable artistic connections. He already owned castles in Northumberland, Welbeck Abbey in Notts and Bolsover in Derbyshire, where his additions survive. But although a member of the great building family begun by Bess of Hardwick (d.1608), he had never built a house entirely of his own devising. Moreover, the purchase of Nottingham fulfilled a long ambition of his beloved father, Charles Cavendish, who may have commissioned Smythson's survey, 1617, and agreed a lease from Katherine Manners in 1641. Nottingham was to be an occasional residence and symbol of power. The Duke may have sought continuity with the medieval remains, sweeping away vestiges of the Upper Bailey in creating a platform for his castle, but retaining Edward IV's work in the Middle Bailey, only later demolished.

King David's Dungeon was remodelled with lancet arches as part of Henry III's enclosure of the adjoining ditch, while the adjacent Romylowe's Cave relates to Edward III's eponymous tower. Whether Nottingham Castle's most exciting moment – Edward's capture of Roger Mortimer and Queen Isabella in 1330 – followed a surreptitious entry through the underground passage of Mortimer's Hole is doubtful. This was a goods entrance to the Castle from the River Leen, offering the easiest access to water and the castle's five mills. Medieval accounts suggest Edward III entered the Middle Bailey from the w. Hine opened up the spiral stair connecting Mortimer's Hole to the s terrace in 1864. From the 1930s the Thoroton Society and Peverel Research Group restored the Western Passages, with the Water Cave and Mortimer's Hole (part opened up in the Civil War as a gun platform), and in 1954–5 a new tunnel was dug to make a circular tour for visitors.

The New Castle

The Duke of Newcastle died on Christmas Day 1676, aged 83, but left instructions for the completion of the castle. William Benoist, or more probably Mark Anthony Benoist, Newcastle's important London servant, recorded in 1678 that 'his directions . . . are still so diligently observed, that this greate house, so lately begun, and all of free stone, will be leaded this Summer, and in all probability ended next yeare.' It was duly finished in 1679, at a cost of £14,000, built of Mansfield limestone and Derbyshire gritstone. It reflected Newcastle's exile in Antwerp, where he rented Rubens's house, built in the latest Italian style.

31. Nottingham Castle, detail of the east front, by William Cavendish, Duke of Newcastle, with Samuel Marsh, 1674–9

There seem to be references to the styles of Michelangelo in Rome and of Galeazzo Alessi in Milan and Genoa (as published by Rubens), so it is an Italian palazzo as filtered through Flanders and embellished with English symbols. The low, rectangular silhouette and Baroque references at Nottingham Castle were novel in England, anticipating the Office of Works' designs for Hampton Court and Talman's for Chatsworth. Architectural details have been renewed, but some on the E front can be trusted, i.e. the first-floor windows and the almost square upper ones surrounded by fleshy strapwork, typical of English mid-C17 style, here done with ducal grandeur.

The plan is a broad U, nine bays long on its principal (E) front facing the town, with short wings of three by three bays on the rear (W) elevation around a courtyard. The E **front** is approached up steps from the Middle Bailey, between high 1670s rusticated **gatepiers** with ball finials. The façade itself is a congestion of features, everything done to increase life and movement in the manner of the Continental Baroque [31]. The bays are broad, the outermost defined by pilasters, coupled at the ends, while those between are separated by engaged Composite columns carrying impost blocks. The heavy modillion cornice breaks forward over these. The columns and pilasters sink into the stone mass of rustication, large and chamfered on the basement, scaled down above. The basement doorway and window keystones also rusticated. A similarly excessive rustication is seen in the Duke's terrace range at Bolsover, developed with *Samuel Marsh*. The *piano nobile* is heavily stressed, its tall windows with alternating broken triangular and segmental pediments, and balustraded balconies. Steps (removed 1861) rose to a central door, with above it a mutilated equestrian statue of the Duke by *William Wilson* set against a recessed panel. Busts in the broken pediments were destroyed in 1831. The attic windows contain heraldic emblems surrounded by Cavendish's Garter. Crowning all is the ducal coat of arms. An indication of Newcastle's modernity is that the E and s fronts may have had sash windows from the first, and certainly by 1698 when illustrated by Knyff. In 1719 alterations were made by *Sir John Vanbrugh*, or more probably the joiner *John Smallwell* and cabinet-maker *James Moore*, including lowering the basement windows to light new family rooms. In 1875–6, *T.C. Hine* installed mullions and transoms, with arched tracery to the second-floor windows, which he blocked; a high parapet partly conceals skylights over his painting galleries. For Hine remodelled three storeys as two, the ground floor now partly lit by the bottom halves of the first-floor windows.

The other façades are plainer, with rusticated quoins and surrounds. The s **front** was the most ambitious. Awkward junctions to its neighbours – a pilaster at the right, quoins at the left – suggest the Duke's amateur hand. A rusticated ground-floor loggia, glazed by *Hine* as additional gallery space, is now the café. A single-bay projecting porch appears not to bond with the rest but is shown on early drawings. The W **front** is even more modest, and has the only evidence for pre-C19 stone mullions and transoms, indicating its lower status. The s wing is broader, reflecting the plan of the state bedrooms within. External stairs to the central first-floor doorway, removed in 1875, probably suggested by Vanbrugh; the segment-pedimented doorcase with its acanthus decoration may have served only a prospect balcony before the ground-floor remodellings demanded a separate entrance to the *piano nobile*. Hine installed a colonnaded exedra, filled with memorial **busts** to local poets installed 1901–4, including William and Mary Howitt by *George Frampton* and Lord Byron by *Alfred Drury*. D.H. Lawrence by *Diana Thompson* added 2007. Alterations by *Derek Latham Associates*, 1994–7, included a prominent disabled entrance and **education room** on the NW front, incorporating artworks. *Richard Perry* sculpted the (dated) terracotta balustrade, and *Maggy Howarth & Diana Hoare* the pebble and slate mosaic in the courtyard, its texts devised in an exchange programme with Jamaica.

The N **front** is devoid of ornament. Below it is a two-storey kitchen block set into a sunken courtyard linked to the Middle Bailey bridge by a tunnel, C18 and C19, with some medieval fragments. Carriage accommodation within the courtyard leads back into the caves, the one part of Newcastle's building relating to older survivals. *Herbert Walker* rebuilt the N kitchen block wall, 1889–91, with regularized fenestration. Cross-walls were eliminated to create a large textile gallery supported on steel and concrete, with stores and workshops below. By comparison, Hine's work was conservative.

The **interior** was not completed until 1683. It was noted for its cantilevered S staircase, under construction in 1675 and arguably the first in England, and marble fireplaces and cedar panelling noted by Celia Fiennes. The lack of enriched plasterwork was unusual in England. An inventory of 1717 describes seven 'very magnificent' state rooms, mainly in enfilade across the E front, with state bedrooms on the W and a private chapel on the S.

The interior today reflects the castle's role as museum and gallery [16]. The ground floor must have been very low before Hine's modifications, which retained three levels only in the curator's house (now offices) in the NW wing. His high Baroque doors are an insistent motif. In 1994 the E entrance was reopened and the interior remodelled by *Derek Latham Associates*, with the cabinet-maker *Nicholas Pryke*; *Michael Johnson* devised the tree-like security grilles. Hine's personal style is revealed in the stairs to N and S, no pastiche attempted; mosaic floor, S, by *Joanna Veevers*. On the first floor, Hine threw four rooms together to create the long E gallery, interrupted only by a screen decorated with medallions depicting Old Masters, by *Mr Shepherd* of Bristol. The S exhibition gallery was originally intended for watercolours.

The Castle Grounds

The first lease to the Corporation (1875) was for the Middle and Upper baileys. The lower grounds became a public park only in 1887 after the Newcastle Estate had proposed redevelopment. The military monuments reflect its C19 use as a parade ground. Near the gatehouse an **obelisk** commemorates the Afghan campaigns of 1878–80. The centre is dominated by the **monument**, unveiled 1921, to Capt. Albert Ball V.C. (1896–1917), son of a former Mayor who in 1916 shot down more German planes than any other fighter pilot. The sculpture, depicting Ball preparing for flight, a figure of Air resting on his shoulder, was by *Henry Poole*, the plinth by his regular collaborator *E.A. Rickards*, executed posthumously by *Brewill & Baily*. The octagonal **bandstand**, with cast-iron decoration, by *Arthur Brown*, Borough Engineer, 1894, the site chosen after tests around the ground by the local police band.

Council House

Old Market Square

The landmark of Nottingham's commercial centre, with its portico, dome and sonorous bell, Little John, the Council House was built by *T. Cecil Howitt*, 1926–9. It is a rare example from the early c20 of a Corporation commissioning its chief building from a staff architect. Its centre is a shopping arcade, and shops run along the ground floor, N and S. The council offices are stacked along the w front.

Rebuilding the old Exchange was ventured in 1899, but was seriously pursued only after 1920, when Nottingham's proposed boundary extension was rejected because of its poor record in health and housing. New offices were integral to its improved services, both practically and symbolically. In 1923 Herbert Bowles, Chairman of the Estates Committee, found the young City Housing Architect *Howitt* working late one night. They smoked and chatted, and Bowles offered Howitt the chance to set out his ideas. Howitt's initial scheme of 1923–4 anticipated recovery of the council's buildings for University College (Shakespeare Street, p. 132). He therefore proposed rebuilding the Exchange as a superior shopping arcade, modelled on Milan's Galleria Vittorio Emanuele, with top-lit arcades meeting under a dome akin to St Paul's, and incorporating at its E end an existing bank and offices. However, councillors demanded a chamber and mayoral suite, while architects protested that there had been no open competition. Howitt's more aggressively classical design of November 1924 included a public hall, council chamber and committee rooms overlooking the square, w, with a shopping arcade and council offices to the E. It is thus a building of two halves united by a common frontage and dome. It was formally opened by the Prince of Wales on 22 May 1929.

Exterior and Arcade

The ascending tiers of Renaissance arcade, Neo-grec portico, Palladian drum, Greek Ionic w portico and Wrennish dome have become so familiar that their incompatibility is rarely challenged. Indeed, a glory of the Council House is that its detailing reflects all the classical tastes of its day [32]. The old Exchange had a clock in its pediment; here it is set in the dome, with a 10-ton bell. The pediment was filled with Grecian figures by *Joseph Else*, Principal of the Nottingham School of Art; one, prostrate, clutches a model of the building. The dome is 200 ft (61.5 metres) high, compared with 360 ft (111 metres) for St Paul's. It is

32. Council House, Old Market Square, exterior, by T. Cecil Howitt, 1926–8

topped with sculptural groups by Else (Commerce, sw) and his students: *Charles Doman* (Civic Law, nw), *James Woodford* (Prosperity, ne) and *Ernest Webb* (Knowledge, se).

The shops are set between a giant order that also defines the offices. Within is a T-shaped **arcade** [33] with a dome at its junction. Murals in Eastman-like colour by *Noel Denholm Davis*, assisted by *F. Hammersley Ball*, show the Danes capturing Nottingham in 868, William I's visit of 1068, Robin Hood, and Charles I raising his standard. Howitt is depicted as William's surveyor. An inscription above records the purposes of the building as 'Merchandise, Welcome, Counsel and Crafts'. The upper offices have curiously domestic Georgian detailing. A lift on Cheapside lowers vehicles into a basement service yard.

To the ne, the National Provincial **Bank**, rebuilt in 1927–8 by *Bromley & Watkins* to fit the new building. Ground floor and staircase tower, right, are rusticated; voussoirs to the round-arched windows below, giant Ionic order above. The **banking hall** has a shallow-domed central lantern below a light well, on more Ionic columns. Howitt had served his tutelage under Bromley and the composition is more taut than the pupil was to achieve. At the se corner, facing High Street, Howitt incorporated Commercial Union **offices** of 1922 by *Evans, Cartwright*

33. The Exchange, murals by N. Denholm Davis and F. Hammersley Ball, 1928–9

& Woollatt, thin pilasters and a tiny pediment set over shops, without rustication and with a lower cornice. Its form must have nevertheless influenced Howitt's approach. The stylized **lions** at the Council House entrance are by *Joseph Else*.

Interior

The major interiors and their furnishings survive in exceptional condition, still maintained by income from the shopping arcade.

The Council House has a low entrance under the portico, between columns of French *stuc*. From this an imperial **stair** leads to a *piano nobile* of reception hall and dining room. Immediately striking is the bright colour, contrasting with the formality of the architecture. The amber glass over the stairwell, highlighted with blue, red and gold, illuminates a sculpture, *William Reid Dick*'s *Spirit of Welcome* and another mural by *Davis*. In the tight plan the principal rooms are piled behind the portico, with offices, mayoral parlours and committee rooms to the sides. The double-height **Reception Hall** [34] with giant Greek Ionic order and minstrel gallery reflects the tradition of the Egyptian Hall established by Lord Burlington at the York Assembly Rooms and developed at London's Mansion House. Again the colour contrasts and gilding against the white *stuc*, plus the quality and completeness of furnishings, make the space impressive. To the s the **Dining Room**, with figured Ancona walnut panelling and Pavonazzo marble fire surround, materials repeated in other high-ranking rooms. The **Lord Mayor's Suite**, N, includes a palatial bathroom tiled by *Carter*'s of Poole complete with colossal brass fittings. The **Private Meeting Room** and third-floor **Members Room** contain panelling from Aston Hall, Derbyshire, a house of 1735, but this work more likely related to its 1898 remodelling. Between them, the Sheriff now occupies the **Lady Mayoress's Suite**, with a bathroom like the Mayor's but a delicately Adamesque parlour.

The third-floor **Council Chamber** is semicircular and compact. Sliding doors serve the rostrum seats for the Lord Mayor, Sheriff and principal officers. Above is another frieze by *Else*, and a ceiling partly glazed, partly coffered. Acoustic treatment by consultant *Hope Bagenal* included deadening the sound with panels of dry seaweed behind fabric. Walnut panelling under the curved press and public galleries to the sides, and walnut fixed seating.

34. Council House, Reception Hall, by T. Cecil Howitt, 1926–8

St Barnabas's Cathedral (R.C.)

Derby Road

St Barnabas's was built in 1841–4 by *A.W.N. Pugin* at the behest of Robert William Willson, local priest, who chose the site and dedication. It cost £15,000, of which the 16th Earl of Shrewsbury provided £7,000. Pugin also designed the clergy house, s, and Convent of Mercy, sw. Father Willson supervised St Barnabas's construction, but in 1844 was made Bishop of Hobart. A distinguished penal and asylum reformer, he died in Nottingham in 1866, and is buried in the undercroft.

Exterior

Though begun before the restoration of the Roman Catholic hierarchy in 1850, St Barnabas was designed with cathedral status in mind. It is 190 ft (58 metres) long – Pugin argued hard with Shrewsbury to get something this big and lavish – and was noted in 1844 as the largest Catholic church built in England since the Reformation. It is cruciform with single-bay transepts and a square-ended E ambulatory. The style is Early English in a conscious re-creation of local medieval survivals, Pugin turning away from late English and German sources; particularly influential was the ruined Cistercian abbey of Croxden, Staffs, founded by one of Shrewsbury's ancestors. Its rusticity and severe gritstone sit oddly among Nottingham's red brick villas. The proud crossing steeple, 164 ft (50.5 metres) high, dominates the building. The robust spire is of a South Midlands type, based on Pugin's first (discarded) design for St Giles, Cheadle, in 1840, with a cluster of lucarnes and pinnacles half-hiding the broaches. From N and s the tower is asymmetrical, with cut-back buttresses at the E angles only. The transepts too are buttressed only at their E angles – presumably because of the fall of the land. Pugin used this to include a vaulted undercroft (St Peter's Chapel) below the sanctuary. The church looks its best from the E, where a family of gables clusters below the steeple, appearing much flatter from the garden, s.

Interior

St Barnabas was one of Pugin's more historicist designs, recognized at the time. It is now impossible to appreciate Pugin's original intentions, since so much of his furnishing and decoration has been eliminated. The **nave** [35] has five-bay arcades, with rather coarse octagonal columns and double-chamfered arches. The clerestory has two windows per bay in the standard Nottinghamshire Perp manner, with

35. St Barnabas's Cathedral, interior looking east, by A.W.N. Pugin, 1841–4

deeply splayed reveals and flattened two-centred heads. The roof, starved-looking as many of Pugin's appear, has a collar purlin and crown-posts on widely spaced principals. That in the **chancel** is richer, with arched trusses and one tier of curved wind-braces. More startling is the rough treatment of the lantern stage of the **tower**, with its unmoulded lancets and machicolations. Pugin's toughness here, the quality Butterfield so admired, strikes an odd note. Details in the E **chapels** include wall arcades of two-light blank arches with ballflower. The choir E wall under the rose window is pierced with a two-bay arcade with its central column behind the site of the original High Altar; this, with the undercroft and square-ended ambulatory, suggests Glasgow Cathedral as the model.

Furnishings

The choir was designed to be wholly enclosed, but only the **parclose screens** to N, S and E survive. The chancel screen, rood and High Altar were removed in the late C19. *F.A. Walters*'s restoration of some Pugin features in 1927 was undone in 1961–2, but partly restored by *John Smith* of *Smith & Roper* in 1992–4, with painted **roundels** between the arches of the nave arcade. Pugin's decorative scheme was never completed. All that remains from the High Altar is the original **Crucifix**, now hanging from the chancel arch. Of the seventy-six **stained-glass windows** designed by Pugin and made by *Wailes* (cheaper than his previous favourite, Willement), only the aisle windows survive. At the time, Pugin seemed satisfied. But later he made *Hardman* alter the windows to admit more light. The survivors contain numerous Shrewsbury shields, and a dedication to the 16th Earl runs through them. A post-war replacement campaign included three-light w windows of 1953 by

John Hardman Studios (*Donald B. Taunton* and *Patrick A. Feeny*), N and S transepts *c.* 1948 by *Joseph Nuttgens*. The **High Altar** under the crossing and the **retrochoir fittings** are by *Smith*, as is the **font**, in Mansfield stone with oak salvaged from the former pulpit. The flooring was also renewed. The result exaggerates Pugin's starker qualities, not his intended richness. But the E chapels have Pugin decoration, with **sedilia** (central chapel) and a **piscina** (in St Hugh's Chapel, right), and relocated chancel stalls. A **statue** of St Hugh attributed to Eric Gill is perhaps by his pupil *Laurie Cribb*, *c.* 1950.*

The highlight of the Cathedral today is the **Blessed Sacrament Chapel** [36] (S of the chancel aisle), restored by *J. Alphege Pippet* in 1933 and reworked *c.* 1974. With red, gold and green stencilling and a richly worked timber screen, it looks Puginian and splendid, if not strictly authentic. The glass is by *Pugin* and made by *Wailes*. The culminating feature is an outsize **ciborium** with marble piers and a cusped arch, similar in general form to that by Pugin at Grace Dieu Manor, Leicestershire, with a saddleback tiled roof on thin columns.

Subsidiary Buildings

The **clergy house** SE of the cathedral was also by *Pugin*, 1841–5 in Tudor style. It has a residential W wing, offices to the S and E and chapter house to the N. Pugin described it as 'simple and convenient'. A felicity of the

---

*I am grateful to Ian Wells for this suggestion.

36. Blessed Sacrament Chapel, by A.W.N. Pugin, restored by J. Alphege Pippet in 1933 and reworked *c.* 1974

internal planning is the corridor that leads right from the hallway into the sacristy and the E end of the church, representative of Pugin's evolving ideas on circulation. The s access to the Cathedral was opened up with the building of the **Cathedral Hall** in 1976–7, a neat brick octagon by *Eberlin & Partners.*

Pugin's former **Convent of Our Lady of Mercy**, 1845–7, SW, was converted to flats by *Wilkinson Hindle Halsall Lloyd*, 2002. Pugin's romantic Catholicism identified strongly with the revival of the religious orders, though the Sisters of Mercy were a 'modern' order and sought practicality in their buildings. Nottingham is perhaps the most impressive. It was first built in the form of an L, to which Pugin designed substantial additions, realized piecemeal. A two-storey **cloister** was quickly added to the inside of the L, and extended across the s entrance screen wall. The blind s wall and the wagon-vaulted upper cloister behind are among the building's most imposing elements. A rambling cloister became a feature of Pugin's convents, marking a processional route on two levels because of the first-floor chapel. The NW **range** served St Mary's Elementary School, while the W **range**, added shortly after 1862, may have accommodated a 'House of Mercy' for fallen women, founded in 1857.

The building is best understood from the N, standing in the car park behind modern flats in Derby Road. There are three floors above a basement. The chapel is on the first floor, above the refectory and at the junction of the original L. Its Dec tracery contrasts with the lancets of the refectory below and high schoolroom windows to the W, and with the more domestic E range. Its decoration includes a fine rosary window by *Hardman* to Pugin's designs, and stencilling [37]. It can be hired by the residents for dinner parties.

37. Former Convent of Mercy, by A.W.N. Pugin, 1841–5, chapel, with glass by Hardman

Nottingham Playhouse

Wellington Circus

The Playhouse is central Nottingham's most important c20 building, and the most imaginative post-war theatre in the country. It was built in 1961–3 by *Peter Moro*.

In 1948 a Civic Theatre Committee took on the former Goldsmith Street Picture House and secured an Arts Council grant for a professional company. It was a phenomenal success, largely due to its dynamic artistic directors. Hugh Willatt led the campaign for a new building and secured Moro as its architect. Funding came from a windfall compensation paid to the City Council on the nationalization of its gas undertaking, granted to the Playhouse after a long and acrimonious debate that delayed building for most of 1960.

Perhaps only Moro could have produced such a sophisticated theatre in England. He made a detailed study of European theatres, particularly in his native Germany, but found them too expensive, too technological and inflexible for English repertory. The strongest influence was perhaps Walter Gropius's geometric 'total theatre' design of 1928. Moro had been the job architect on London's Royal Festival Hall, whose 'egg in the box' plan is repeated: Nottingham's shapes are simpler, with a nearly-round auditorium. Moro had also to incorporate a flytower and workshops, which he set on several levels at the rear where the land falls steeply. The main **elevation** shows the three elements well. The square foyer has a clean-cut rhythm of vertical slit windows, typical of Moro and effective at night, when the pattern of light and dark is reversed. Behind it rises the drum of the auditorium, with the rectangular flytower forming a dark backdrop.

The round **auditorium** [38] is the key to the Playhouse's flexibility, developed with *Richard Southern*, technical consultant. It is not, however, a theatre in the round. The stage is conventional, but a large apron can be raised from the orchestra pit and front stalls to create a large thrust stage. A separate lighting rig suspended over this apron is a sculptural feature in the predominantly black space, looking impressive from the steep gallery. The vertical slits found in the façade reappear as acoustic slats and lighting troughs. Actors and audience are brought close together, but there is not the loss of theatrical illusion as occurs in theatres designed in the round. It was his ability to design flexible auditoria that were both technically and architecturally successful that makes Moro's work exceptional.

38. Nottingham Playhouse, auditorium, by Peter Moro, 1961–3

Foyer and ancillary spaces. The auditorium drum dominates the two-level foyer [21], decorated with a heavy aluminium relief by *Geoffrey Clarke*. The space was refurbished by *Marsh Grochowski*, 1995–6, when the concrete was painted and a lift installed. *Grogan Culling Macaulay Sinclair* in 2004–5 restored the foyer's lightness and sophistication.

Projecting from the front of the building is a long, low block containing rehearsal rooms and a bar. This was to have included a small bedsit storey for the actors, cut when the project was delayed. A second-storey **restaurant** was eventually added in 2000, by *Marsh Grochowski*, with a remodelled pavement area including granite benches and steps. Its climax is *Anish Kapoor*'s 20-ft (6-metre)-high Sky Mirror, a carefully crafted and polished stainless-steel dish. Its upside-down reflections encourage passers-by to study their environment. A larger version was installed in Manhattan's Rockefeller Center in 2006.

Central Nottingham

Walk 1.

City Centre: West and South

Nottingham's c18 buildings survive in two main groups w and e of the centre, linked by the streets along the s edge of the sandstone ridge, which enjoyed open views across the river. The principal streets radiated from the castle gatehouse, until severed by Maid Marian Way [20] in 1958–66.

This Walk concentrates on the larger w group, the first part leading from the Market Square towards the Castle, the second heading e along the ridge. (For the e group see Lace Market, Walk 4, p. 96). Comparing Nottingham's surviving c18 town houses reveals similarities in their liking for symmetry, while shared stylistic motifs suggest the handiwork of *Samuel Stretton* and his son *William*. This walk also contains Nottingham's handful of earlier buildings – mainly pubs.

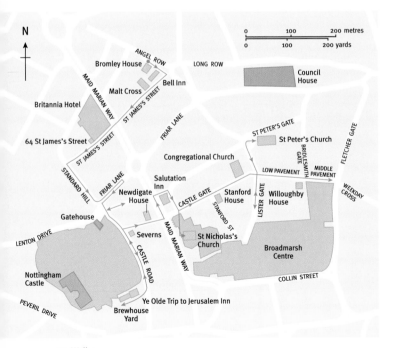

39. Walk 1

40. Bromley House, Angel Row, Drawing Room, 1752–*c.* 1754

From the Market Square to Brewhouse Yard

Standing at the sw corner of the **Old Market Square** on **Angel Row**, where the Nottingham-born artist *Thomas Sandby* drew the view, *c.* 1742 (*see* topic box, p. 76), there is nothing he would recognize. But turn through 180 degrees and c18 work survives above modern shopfronts.

On the s side, Angel Row boasts Nottingham's finest c18 town house, **Bromley House**, built by George Smith, grandson of the founder of Smith's Bank. Two stones in the rear garden walls, incised '1752 GS' suggest the building's date. It survives because in 1820 it was bought by the Nottingham Subscription Library, founded in 1816.

The five-bay front has an unobtrusive entrance under a fanlight between shopfronts – first inserted in 1929 in a conversion by *Evans, Clark & Woollatt*. Three storeys and attics. To the rear elevation a central doorcase with prominent cornice (door and fanlight altered 1929); at the top a clerestory and skylight added for Nottingham's first photographic studio, in 1841. A reference of 1752 to a 'lately erected' brewhouse suggests that the rear range, with its Gibbs-surround door-case, predates the house; cellars include the remains of a malt kiln and well. The **garden**, on two levels, is a rare survival.

Entering from the street, engaged Ionic columns (right) formed an open screen to a banking hall, which had a Rococo fireplace with family crests, sold in 1929. The **stair hall** behind is magnificent, an

Bromley House

Bromley House's authorship has long been debated. Carpentry details resemble others in Nottingham, e.g. at St Nicholas's church, but there is much that is not provincial. Holland Walker recounted in 1932 that the house was 'erected by Taylor'. The lost reference may refer to a noted local builder, but *Sir Robert Taylor*'s employment in banking circles and his clever plans with top-lit stair halls have encouraged speculation that he was the architect. Richard Garnier has now made close comparisons with features in early London houses he has attributed to Taylor, especially No. 1 Greek Street and No. 33 John Street. They include the construction of the stair in wood to resemble ogee-undercut cantilevered stone, the patterns of the plaster ceilings and the principal chimneypieces. A circular glazed cellar light is very reminiscent of Taylor's at Gorhambury, Hertfordshire.

open-well staircase with three balusters per tread (two twisted), ramped handrail and corresponding dado. The treads were lined in lead in 1844, renewed in 1983. Pedimented doorcases on the first-floor landing; above is a second-floor gallery, square dome and c20 lantern. Vitruvian scroll and Greek key banding. From the landing, a curved-ended stair from 1827 served the library's tenants. The service stair, opposite the main one, survives only from the second floor, but demonstrates c18 Nottingham's symmetrical planning. All the principal rooms had closets tucked behind the stairs.

The first-floor rooms, combined and linked by Soanic segmental arches *c.* 1844, retain fielded panelling and panelled shutters, cornices and fireplaces, commensurate with their c18 importance. The **drawing room** [40], originally entered from the landing and now the reading room, has the most elaborate fireplace, its overmantel *Rawson Walker*'s painting of Clifton Grove. Vigorous plaster ceiling, part Tayloresque, with fine trails, part heads in naïvely high relief. c19 bookcases, painted cataloguing references instead of cartouches, are equally charming. The smaller front parlour is now the issuing hall. The **rear room**, adapted *c.* 1844 as a double-height library, has a balcony, given a spiral staircase in 1857 with matching cast-iron balustrades. A clock in the **Standfast Room**, sw, records local time, based on true solar noon.

To the SE, **Newcastle House** is also mid-c18. The **Bell Inn** (left), has a fragmentary timber frame claiming associations with the Carmelite Friary, *c.* 1276, to the E, and is set over spectacular caves. It was first recorded in 1638 when Alderman Sherwin willed his share to the three Nottingham parishes. The pedimented frontage of *c.* 1820 has exuberant lettering and a replica shopfront [41]. The shallow front range contains a crown-post roof, dendro-dated *c.* 1437. To the w a higher and later cross-wing over the Elizabethan Bar, an assortment of

41. Bell Inn, Angel Row, roof *c.* 1437, refronted *c.* 1820

timberwork and panelling bearing little relation to the structure. The central flagged passage led to an open yard – as the gnarled brick indicates – until in 1927–8 the rear bar was rebuilt across the plot. Partakers of the pub's occasional tours descend a ramp to caves under this area; smoke-blackened fireplaces under the present kitchens. Further back is the 53-ft (16-metre) 'Monks Well', excavated of early C15 rubbish in 1998, perhaps with a small brewhouse. More caves on two levels under Exchange House to the E, including an L-shaped C19 wine store. **Exchange House** itself is early C18, as shown in the gables and sill bands along its St James's Street return. Inside, a dog-leg stair with intersecting balusters. On the corner of Beastmarket Hill the weak **Market House**, by *Lloyds Bank Architects Department*, built in 1966 (when excavations revealed remains of the friary), a nine-storey office block over a three-storey podium.

St James's Street begins with an early C19 terrace (w side), Nos. 2–10. Nos. 14–16, the **Malt Cross**, was built by *Edwin Hill*, 1877, as a pub over a basement hall or skating rink, but opened as a music hall. Its three-sided gallery has cast-iron columns with decorative fish capitals. Laminated timber brackets to the glazed roof. No. 14 was three drinking booths, seen in the unusual tripartite fenestration between cast-iron columns. Nos. 9 and 11 (E side), 1780s, retains an oval stair hall: spiral staircase with stick balusters and swept handrail, modillion cornice, fan ceiling and niches. A rear bow in the vestibule behind.

42. Sheriff House, No. 64 St James's Street, 1767

Next door the former Imperial, built in 1903 by *Evans & Son*, with giant pub lamps; beyond it another house of *c.* 1770 origins.

St James's Street is severed by **Maid Marian Way**, with an overwhelming three-part development planned by *John P. Osborne & Son*. Phase 1, s of St James's Street, has a multi-storey car park (1962, with hexagonal pre-cast panels) above shops; then followed the fifteen-storey Britannic Hotel, 1966, elevations by *James Roberts*, linked by bridge to the car park; the N stage of 1968–9, a bus station and shopping mall, was demolished in the 1980s for offices, though its car park survives.

To the w on St James's Street lurk good C18 **houses**. The best, No. 64, **Sheriff House**, was built for Cornelius Launder, a prominent landlord and noted miser (a rear datestone inscribed C1767L has gone). The five-bay, three-storey front [42] with a projecting centre is reminiscent of James Paine: a first-floor window with outswept jambs and false balusters sits heavily on a pedimented doorcase, all topped by a Diocletian window and a pediment with ball finials. Behind, a Venetian window lights the staircase, below another Diocletian window. No rear garden; these houses had detached gardens or 'vistas' across the street. The interior, restored by Nicholas Forman Hardy on advice from *Gervase Jackson-Stops* in 1995, bears comparison with the earlier Willoughby House (p. 73): a symmetrical plan with rooms in each quadrant separated by a stair or vestibule. To the rear of the ground floor is a mahogany staircase – one twisted and one straight baluster per tread and turned ends – rising to the first floor. A service stair (closed-string, turned balusters) in the centre of the right side runs the full height of the house. Most decoration seems old-fashioned for 1767, with box cornices, but beautifully crafted, with elaborate modillion cornices and fireplaces to the principal first-floor rooms and a severe dentil frieze and buffet alcove to the dining room (ground-floor left).

Next door No. 66 is early C18: a central attic window and a gabled rear elevation reveal its urbane brickwork is a refronting. A dog-leg stair has intersecting strings. No. 68, later C18, has three broad storeys, its guttae frieze and Adamesque tripartite ground-floor window the principal decoration. No. 70, entered from the side, is earlier and plainer, while No. 72 is lavish, with rusticated ground-floor arcading, the tympana with plaster fan decoration and a pretty fanlight. A frieze with raised diamond metopes, first-floor windows set over balusters, all features suggestive of the *Stretton* canon. No. 74, early C18, has brick bands and exposed sash boxes; the slightly later No. 76 was occupied by Lord Byron in 1798–9.

At the top of St James's Street is **Standard Hill**, land owned by the Dukes of Newcastle (*see* The Park, p. 118). Turning s down the hill is **St James's Terrace**, early C19 with rusticated lintels and doorheads. At its foot is Friar Lane, with **BZR**, a drum-like bar by *Sutherland Craig*, 1992; then No. 100, bow-fronted with broad windows, first of a line of *c.* 1830s houses surviving above shopfronts. No. 84, set back, offices by *W.B. Starr & Hall*, 1910, satisfyingly understated. Grey stone, with end gables

43. Ye Olde Trip to Jerusalem Inn,
Castle Road, Rock Lounge

and bows, and an offset segmental porch. Across **Friar Lane** is **St Luke's House**, studios for the Nottingham Society of Artists, thinly moderne, 1933–4 by *Harry Gill & Son*, the sculpture of St Luke by *Joseph Else*.

For the Castle *see* Major Buildings, p. 38. On the corner of Friar Lane, **Castle House** by *T. Cecil Howitt*, 1930–1, brick classical, but with herringbone panels and timber windows. Round the corner, **Wyville House**, No. 2 Castle Place, bow-fronted early C19. The road continues downhill as **Castle Road**, with *Fothergill Watson*'s Mortimer House, 1883, picturesque houses and shops. Gables, hipped roofs, and a corner tower turning Hounds Gate that in 1980 became the Castle Inn. The smallest of the old streets radiating from the castle gatehouse, **Hounds Gate** has on the left No. 74, projecting offices by *James McArtney*, 1980, incorporating an early C19 gabled range; beyond it Nos. 70–72, with broad windows under keystones and an inset bootscraper by the high entrance steps.

Down Castle Road is **Severns**, *c.* 1340, until 1969 a restaurant on Middle Pavement, when displaced by the Broadmarsh Centre. The timber frame, reassembled by *F.W.B. Charles*, was the front range of a merchant's house, a three-bay hall over a ground-floor shop and workroom. On its original site there was a long rear service range, over cellar caves still visible at Broadmarsh. The restoration is partly conjectural. It is, however, the best opportunity in Notts to see a C14 crown-post roof [6], dendro-dated 1334, though with no capital to the crown-post. Charles used an Exeter model for his traceried first-floor windows. The rest of Castle Road was demolished for the People's College, now **Castle College of Further Education**, by the *City Architect's Department*, 1956–61, its slate facings and shell roofs now period pieces. Extended in 1964, 1970 and 1979; there are proposals for its replacement, by *Hawkins\Brown*, 2008.

On the w side of Castle Road thirteen premises were demolished in 1909. Rooms cut into the castle rock survive, notably of a pub, The Gate Hangs Well. Happily its neighbour remains, the similarly formed **Ye Olde Trip to Jerusalem**. The network of long, narrow cellars and a chimneyed brewhouse built into the rock, first mentioned in 1618, are thought to be medieval. The painted date 1189 is spurious. The name was first recorded only in 1799, although a late C17 two-bay timber box frame separates the pub's two courtyards, terminating in a higher cell of *c.* 1760 which was the publican's quarters until 1996. Behind, the Ward Room and Rock Lounge are set into rock [43], with C19 fronts and a passage to a third bar cut through a chimney vent in 1996.

The River Leen originally ran here, making a natural site for **brewhouses**, first recorded in 1609. In 1621 **Brewhouse Yard** was granted by the King to John Mitten and William Jackson from London. The row of four cottages [44] superficially seems of *c.* 1700 but incorporates earlier elements – the w cottage is slightly lower, without bands; its timbers have been dated to 1640. Its neighbour has an infilled arch over the ground-floor lintel, and reused timbers inside. This and its e neighbours have open-string staircases similar to those at Nos. 51–53 Castle Gate with intersecting strings at the junction of flights; the two groups shared common ownership, Mary Mitten, heiress of Brewhouse Yard, marrying Lawrence Collin of Castle Gate in 1671. Framework knitting at Brewhouse Yard was first recorded in 1689; broad side windows serve upper rooms floored in gypsum. A second range of cottages to the s was demolished *c.* 1875. To the rear individual caves were linked to form an air-raid shelter in 1939. Brewhouse Yard was taken over in 1975 by **Nottingham Castle Museum** for its social history collection; installations include Fitzhugh and Carr's chemist's shop from Long Row. Above it to the w is **Castle Rock Cottage**, *c.* 1675, one room deep either side of an open-string stair, and with long windows for framework knitting in the top floor, now blocked. **Waterworks offices** at the bottom of Castle Road, now offices to Brewhouse Yard Museum, by *Herbert Walker*, 1899–1900, for Nottingham Corporation. Hard red brick, with offices, workshops and stables set around a partly covered courtyard. In the sw corner the manager's house has a big-boned staircase.

44. Brewhouse Yard, C17 cottages, restored as a museum 1975–6

Castle Gate and Low Pavement

Back up Castle Road, and right into **Castle Gate**, a major street along the s edge of the ridge. The s side was largely built by the Collin family, who lived at No. 41 (demolished along with their c18 almshouses). On the s side, Nos. 43–59 were from the 1960s the City Architect's offices, and in 1974–2004 housed the costume museum. On the corner next to Severns, Nos. 57–59, rendered, c18, still vernacular; No. 57 with a vertiginous winder stair. No. 55 appears earlier, its large fireplace and corner staircase in line with the entrance. Nos. 51 and 53 c. 1700, two gables and just one room deep, but with rear towers whose stairs have the distinctive crossover strings between flights also found in St James's Street and Brewhouse Yard. No. 51 was refronted c. 1820; its fluted Greek Doric doorcase has an open hood. No. 49, a rendered c17 facade, retains second-floor workroom windows, but was largely gutted by the *City Architect's Department*. The suave classical terrace, Nos. 43–47, dated 1788 (rear plaque resembling that recorded at No. 64 St James's Street) by Cornelius Launder and his wife Mary, née Collin.

Opposite is **Newdigate House**, No. 64, now World Service restaurant. Marshal Tallard, the French commander captured at Blenheim in 1704, lived here c. 1705–11 in semi-confinement. The house was built by Thomas Charlton of Chilwell, perhaps by 1674 when he was recorded as owning a property with twelve hearths.* After Tallard it was bought by Thomas Newdigate, barrister son of Sir Richard Newdigate of Arbury Hall, Warks, then in 1790 by Mrs Thomas Wright. An imposing five-bay façade [7] with bolection-moulded window surrounds of grey stone; alternating segmental and triangular pediments to ground-and first-floor windows, eared surrounds to the second floor. The **interior** is puzzling: probably remodelled for Newdigate, it is only two bays and one room deep. The rear range shown in Kip and Knyff's plan of 1707 was absorbed in a three-bay addition by *William Stretton* in the 1790s, demolished in 1963. Today, two ground-floor rooms stand either side of an entrance hall, this with full-height moulded wooden panels and cornice, and a bolection-moulded door surround. The dining room, right, has plasterwork and a resited *Stretton* fireplace. Two fully panelled first-floor rooms with moulded cornices, the larger and more restored room absorbing a back stair and closet in the E bay and perhaps a small room over the entrance. The heaviest and earliest cornice is on the second floor. Restored and remodelled with a new stair in 1966 for the United Services Club by *Harry Mein*, who made a modest w addition. Also by Mein the eleven-storey office block to the rear that funded the restoration, **Castle Heights**. The house was famed for the formal garden created to the w by *London & Wise* under Tallard's direction, illustrated by Kip and Knyff and important as a genuine French parterre garden, but Defoe already noted in 1725 that 'it does not

---

*Information from Pete Smith. T. C. Hine gives a Mr Jallard as architect and occupant of the house pre-Tallard.

45. St Nicholas, Maid Marian Way, interior, 1671–8 and 1699, remodelled 1848, 1863 and late C20

gain by *English* keeping'. To the front a small **forecourt** with a wrought-iron screen and gates for Newdigate by *Francis Foulgham*, who also worked at Arbury.

Maid Marian Way's confounding of the transverse plan of streets is more apparent here. To the N, the **Salutation Inn** competes with the Bell and the Trip as Nottingham's oldest and most haunted hostelry. A messuage is recorded in 1414, but the oldest surviving part is the three-bay NE range on Hounds Gate, jettied towards **St Nicholas Street**, probably C16. A screen beside the hearth in the E bay suggests the position of a screens passage; on the first floor part of the truss-and-collar roof is visible, with bracing below the purlins. A fragmentary two-bay cross-range, long used as a passage, is now the heart of the pub. From this steps descend to impressive cellars, with ledges for settling beer. The St Nicholas Street frontage incorporates an C18 brick dwelling one room deep. The long, rendered range and cross-wing to Maid Marian Way are contemporary with the new road, 1958 by *M.W. Ofield*, architect to Tennant Breweries. To the N on Maid Marian Way the **Theosophical Hall**, 1956. The **Royal Children** pub on Castle Gate, s, was rebuilt in 1933–4 by *A.E. Eberlin* of *Baily & Eberlin*. A model 'reformed' pub, originally having a separate rear lounge without a bar.

St Nicholas's Church [45] was rebuilt in 1671–8. Its medieval site may have been on the NE side of the fragmentarily surviving churchyard. It existed as a parish church by *c.* 1109, when Lenton Priory was granted the endowments of Nottingham's three churches. On 18 September 1643 Royalists used its tower to harass the Parliamentarian garrison in the Castle, who duly levelled the church. Rebuilding began in straitened circumstances that give the exterior its austere charm. Brick, the tower partly in English bond with Restoration Gothic bell openings. The E end with its flat-headed mullion-and-transom window is dated 1699. C18 engravings show similar windows to the nave and stubby transepts. St Nicholas's became fashionable in the C18, and the s aisle was added in 1756 and the N aisle in 1783, with heavy round-arched windows. Inside, a four-centred arched opening to the chancel and C18 moulded ceiling with dentilated borders and roundels. The nave has four-bay Tuscan arcades and a round arch into the tower; a gabled timber roof from 1848. The chancel was largely stripped of fittings in 1979 and the nave in 1991. Panelled **wainscotting** in the chancel suggests the late C17 style, but the 1750s **altar rail** now lines the E end. Inlaid **pulpit**, 1783. The present **organ** is from 1848, resited to a new chamber N of the chancel in 1863, when the **galleries** (installed 1783) were removed save that to sw and the C18 **box pews** cut down. E window 1913. **Hatchments** and wall **monuments** – that with putti on the s wall to John Collin (d.1717) the finest – a skeletal reminder of St Nicholas's history as a society church, and what has been lost to waves of Evangelical reform.

Now along **Castle Gate**. On the s side, No. 33, early C18. Then Nos. 29–31, dated 1794, two interlinked L-plans, with broad depressed windows like those to No. 72 St James's Street, and a double attic storey. A third, central, entrance by *Evans & Jolley*, c. 1890, formed part of alterations for the Nottingham Hospital for Women, opened here in 1875; older entrances to either side blocked c. 1901. No. 27, **St Nicholas Court**, dated 1900, free Baroque by *H.E. Woodsend*. Back on the N side, Nos. 34 and 32 are early C18 houses with an entry between, the left house with dog-leg stairs inside; the right with three Venetian windows and an open-well stair with turned balusters.

On the corner of **Stanford Street**, a former warehouse by *S. Dutton Walker & Howitt*, 1880, refurbished by *Maber Associates* in 1987 over car parking. The w side of Stanford Street has C19 warehouses. First a red brick, four-storey, seven-bay warehouse of 1878–9, by *Evans & Jolley*. In the middle, **Stanford House**, now offices, c. 1854 by *T.C. Hine* for J. Lewis & Son, ten bays wide, with a tripartite doorcase (left) and round-arched windows. At the bottom a larger warehouse, 1874 by *R.C. Sutton*, later a hosiery factory.

On the NE corner, **No. 19 Castle Gate**, c. 1776, reputedly for William Stanford, hosiery merchant; converted to offices in 1928. On the site of one of Nottingham's largest houses from the C17, George Augustus, Viscount Howe, built a 'magnificent mansion' here in 1755. The present house shows the influence of *John Carr* of York, busy at Colwick Hall in 1776 (p. 154); his assistant *Samuel Stretton* was perhaps the architect here. The façade is dominated by its slightly projecting centre, with a Venetian window and large fanlight, and finely carved doorcase with bucrania frieze and fluted columns. Its severity is relieved by first-floor windows with false balconies and linking bands, Doric cornice and balustraded parapet. The garden elevation is livelier, with a three-storey semicircular bay; the windows have moulded stone surrounds and bands mark the floors. Pete Smith suggests this front may have survived from Earl Howe's house. Much original decoration and joinery. Central hallway with trophy frieze and fluted columns with anthemion capitals. The rear stair hall has a modillion cornice and dog-leg stair with ebony stick balusters and ramped handrail. The room left of the entrance has an Adamesque frieze and cornice, ornate doorcases and twin alcoves, and an inlaid marble fireplace with portraits and figure panel. The right room is smaller and simpler, while the rear drawing room has an ashlar fireplace.

No. 17 is mid-C18, with a doorcase in a Venetian surround and decorative stone lintels, string courses and dentilled cornice. No. 15 is a massive former warehouse and bakery, 1897 by *W. Dymock Pratt*, with two Flemish gables implying a symmetry not realized below; turret-like side finials. No. 13 is severe early C19. No. 6 was **Castle Gate Schools**, 1882–3 by *Parry & Walker*; now offices to the adjoining Congregational Church. Warehouse-like, yet lavish for schools. The **church** is dated 1863, blowsy Lombardic Romanesque by *R.C. Sutton*, striving for effect in massive motifs. It replaced a popular chapel of 1689, in commemoration of the bicentenary of the 1662 ejection. Converted to the headquarters of the Congregational Federation and divided horizontally in 1981, retaining the stepped gallery as a church. The arcade has double cast-iron columns and foliage capitals, a ribbed barrel vault on corbelled-out wall-shafts, and an organ loft carried on cast-iron columns.

Albert Street was cut through in 1846. **Marks & Spencer's** dominates, 1929–30 by *Albert E. Batzer*, chain-store classical with a giant order, bronze panels and a heavy cornice. An extension of 1998–9 by *NJSR* and *Latham Architects* includes offices and a community hall for St Peter's church. On the s corner on **Lister Gate**, a hosiery warehouse of *c.* 1854 by *T.C. Hine*, now **Topshop**, only the parapet motifs recognizable beneath mid-C20 render. In the 1930s Lister Gate became the centre for chain stores. On the right are British Home Stores (now **Neu**), 1936–7, a cinematic blind faience façade punctuated by inset black columns, and the futuristic Woolworth's (now Marks & Spencer's), 1937 by *Woolworth's Construction Dept* (Birmingham branch, Chief Architect *B.C. Donaldson*, architect in charge *J.T. Winhouse*), with Aztec pylons and swept-back moderne finials.

A short diversion N up Albert Street leads to **St Peter's church** [46]. If St Mary's is an exceptional church in the county, St Peter's might easily stand in any prosperous Notts village. Its principal appearance is C15, its w steeple with pairs of angle buttresses, and thin spire (much repaired and shorn of detail) rising above the battlements. Unusually elaborate w doorway with pinnacles, and niches to either side. Embattled nave, aisles, N transept and chancel. Inside, the nave is not high for its width, and length of five bays. The s arcade has C13 piers with four filleted shafts and four deep hollows; the source is Lincoln, e.g. St Mary Magdalene, and versions are found around Notts. The capitals are partly moulded and partly stiff-leaf, the arches double-chamfered. The N arcade of c. 1360, with castellated thin capitals and taller arches on E.E. piers. The clerestories were added and new roofs to the nave and s aisle installed at the behest of Sir Nicholas Strelley in 1501–9 (shield on NW corbel); the bosses on the nave roof bear Kempe and Strelley arms. The chancel was badly damaged in 1644, but nevertheless the church was shared with the congregation of St Nicholas until 1682–3. Brackets along the N aisle suggest the position of a gallery. The N clerestory was renewed simply in 1699, the s aisle in 1800 based on an early C16 model. The chancel and organ chamber (N), with the N and s porches, and s buttresses, though not the chancel window tracery and vestry, were rebuilt in 1875–7 by *Evans & Jolley*, who simultaneously removed the W and N aisle galleries. The chancel was repaired, 1951, by *Stephen Dykes Bower*, who stencilled the wagon roof. In the SE corner, **piscina** and **sedilia**.

Fittings. The chancel has a Dec-style wooden **screen** dated 1897, with restored loft openings, s. – Bold altar **triptych** by *Tiffany Groves*, 2003. – The N side has a traceried wooden **screen** and **organ console**, 1898. – **Organ case** by *Snetzler* with bulbous acanthus scrollwork, 1770, brought to St Peter's in 1812 and now in the N aisle. – **Font**, s aisle. An octagonal C17 bowl, with a rosette in each bulging panel, on a C14 base. **W door** with ironwork by *Richard Bentley* of Derbyshire, 1977.

Stained glass. E window, 1878 by *Ward & Hughes*. s windows (Almond c. 1858 and Howard c. 1866) by *Heaton, Butler & Bayne*. s aisle, E end, 1881 by *Burlison & Grylls*. sw pair (baptistery) by *Margaret Trahearne*, 1976, garish compared to her work at Coventry and Liverpool Metropolitan cathedrals. Tower w window by *Powell, c.* 1906, inspired by Morris's teachings. N aisle: w window by *Julian Cole*, 2008; N windows by *J.S. Bucknall* to *Ninian Comper*'s designs, with figures and grisaille medallions of local views set in clear glass, 1963–9.

Monuments. On the chancel wall inside the sanctuary rail are alabaster monuments to Margaret Saunders d.1633 and Jane Ellis d.1639, wives of Sir John Locke. – Lady Gardner above the N porch (d.1811) is by *John Bacon Jun.*, her sorrowing husband holding her portrait. – N aisle, brought in 1933 from St James, Standard Hill: war memorial, c. 1921, angels supporting a supine figure; a bronze figure, arms raised, to Catherine Carey Wallis by *Albert Toft*; plaque to Lawrence Wilkins, his name in a sunburst, by *Sir George Frampton*. St Peter's war memorial in the centre of the church is by *F.E. Howard* of Oxford, 1922.

Continuing the line of Castle Gate, **Low Pavement** is one of Nottingham's most rewarding streets. On the s side, Nos. 4–6, to plans by *Lawrence L. Bright & William C. Thoms* dated 1915, but not executed until 1920. Arts and Crafts classical. No. 8 is **Café Uno**, baby Bruges Gothic by *A.R. Calvert*, dominated by an over-scaled stepped gable shielding a large roof, dated 1903. No. 10 [47], dated 1876, is by *Alfred Smith*, architect and builder, unsqueamish Gothic Revival with granite shafts and foliage capitals to its dominating oriel, a wild version of William Burges. No. 12 is a four-storey, five-bay stuccoed house, mid-C19,

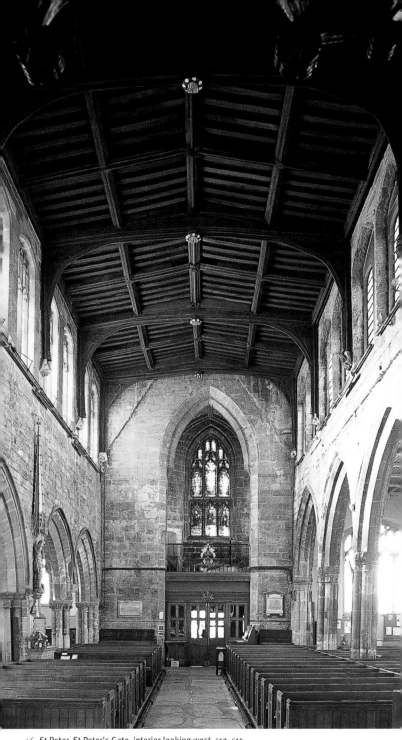

46. St Peter, St Peter's Gate, interior looking west, c13–c15

47. No. 10 Low Pavement, by Alfred Smith, 1876

with projecting centre incorporating a porch with paired Corinthian columns. Nos. 14–16, **Enfield Chambers**, 1909–10 by *Calvert & Gleave*, has a rich modillion eaves cornice, dressings and low ground floor all in alarmingly yellow stone. A central entrance leads to a separate office block. It was all converted to apartments, 2006–7, in a scheme including No. 18, **Enfield House**, *c.* 1755. One of the distinctive houses unique to that time, with six chirpy Venetian windows battling for supremacy across three storeys; a light modillion cornice. Rear wing, dated 1760 on a rainwater head, an addition. Two small front rooms on each floor with modillion cornices, those on the ground floor linked by an arched opening, with a staircase behind – full-height with turned and twisted balusters, three per tread, ramped handrail and dado panelling. The rear wing is simpler, retaining a severe stone kitchen fireplace.

Opposite, No. 9 was the **Assembly Rooms**, built in the c18, altered by *John Carr* in 1776–8 and 1790, and repaired and enlarged in 1808. It was refronted by *Thomas Winter* in 1836, which is all to survive conversion into offices in 1902 and subsequent denudations. Giant

Corinthian three-quarter columns of neo-Roman design, and Italianate Renaissance balustrading. No. 11 is **Lloyds TSB**, a severe Grecian design of 1836 for Nottingham Savings Bank; alterations by *Calvert & Gleave*, 1903, include the stone entrance porch with bold pediment and Ionic columns. Also part of Lloyds is No. 13, an early C19 house.

Back on the s side, Nos. 20–22, **Willoughby House**, now **Paul Smith**, *c.* 1738–43, for the Hon. Rothwell Willoughby, brother of Lord Middleton of Wollaton Hall. One of Nottingham's best C18 survivals, and an interesting comparison with No. 64 St James's Street [42]. Three storeys and five bays, set back and raised over a basement and front enclosure with high walls and contemporary railings, reached through cast-iron gates and overthrow. Central door to front and rear; a further door in a single bay (left) was probably added in the 1820s. The details are strong and rich rather than decorative; Ionic doorcase with a segmental pediment. Rear door with frostwork. The parapet to Low Pavement shields a transverse M roof with a central flat offering prospects over the river. The plan was once symmetrical, as survives on the second floor, with a room in each corner and smaller rooms over the doors to front and back. On the left is the staircase; the right side has no surviving features and is now mostly occupied by changing rooms. In the middle is a square vestibule, domed in brick on the top floor.

The **staircase** is a puzzle, small and cramped. That the basement stair is underneath, and the upper flights appear undisturbed, with double newels at the turns and a single turned vase baluster to each tread, shows there was nevertheless always a stair here. The main flights in between have alternating turned and barley-sugar balusters, with a C19 handrail; there is an awkward junction on the first floor. Over the half-landing below, a renewed C19 roof-light in the side bay. Above the changing rooms is an open flat roof. Perhaps the main stair was on this lost side, serving principal floors only, and we now see fragments of this grander stair grafted on to the service one.

The principal floors retain some 1730s cornices and dado panelling. The rear rooms have ceiling roses, friezes and dados from the 1820s, when some partitions were removed. The first-floor rear room has particularly frilly mouldings. An exemplary restoration in 2004 by *Franklin Ellis* for Paul Smith Ltd includes touches of panache, like the ruler markings on the stair treads, indicative of the locally born designer's trade. The restrained shop fixtures are designed like library shelving. Willoughby House retains a rear garden, originally with two summerhouses framing the view over the river.

Nos. 24–26, **Jass**, has a garden café from which something of this view over the Trent valley can be appreciated. On this site was Vault Hall, purchased in 1733 by Francis Gawthern and named for a vault hollowed out of the sandstone. He built two houses and moved into the eastern one in 1734. The regular front conceals two L-shaped interlocking plans, No. 24 having five bays to the front and No. 26 five to the rear. No. 24 is gabled to the rear, late for its date. It has a fine turned and twisted baluster stair, set behind the entrance hall in its own space marked by pilasters. In 1783 No. 26 was taken by Gawthern's great-nephew, also Francis, on his marriage to the diarist Abigail Frost, who lived there until her death in 1822. Abigail records that in May 1792 she sent for *William Stretton* and the builder *Mr Taylor*, and between June and December that year the garden front was rebuilt with its piecrust fluted lintels [9] and the front façade was re-sashed. The drawing room itself was remodelled in 1793–4 – the heightened first-floor room overlooking the garden with a fluted dado and swags to the frieze; anthemion mouldings to the ground-floor frieze and fireplace, also characteristic of the Strettons. A fragment of C18 stair at the side, now concealed. Both houses have fine bolection-moulded panelling and cornices to their first-floor front rooms. The wrought-iron outer gate to No. 26 bears the Gawthern coat of arms.

On the corner of **Bridlesmith Gate**, No. 19, three storeys with a big cornice, dated 1859 on first-floor keystones and extended in 1909. Next to it, Nos. 54–56 Bridlesmith Gate, substantially C18, and No. 52, **Oxfam**, *c.* 1700, smothered in render; a dog-leg closed-string stair at the rear. Nos. 48 and 50, **Fred Perry**, early C18, has tie-plates dated 1842 but perhaps modern. The N part of Bridlesmith Gate belongs in the C19 walk (p. 94). On the E side late C18 shops, the first-floor windows enlarged. **Jones** is dated 1890 above the parapet; by *W. Dymock Pratt* as a bakery, and surprisingly still Gothic. Next to it two more shops were rebuilt in 1896 by *Heazell & Son*, two storeys with high dormers. The exceedingly narrow estate agents was built in 1897–8 by *Sidney R. Stevenson*. On the W corner with Middle Pavement, No. 51, a curved three-storey, mid-C19 house with a big cornice and rusticated doorcase.

Of **Middle Pavement** little remains save No. 1, four-storey C18, with tie-plates again dated 1842. No. 15 is of 1907 by *Child & Watts*, a seven-bay frontage with alternating oriels on huge brackets, the central one also serving as an entrance hood, with a winged cherubic head. Opposite was the site of Severns, now the **Broadmarsh Centre**, developed from 1964 by the City Council with Town and City Properties, incorporating the Arndale Property Trust, and using their designers *Turner Lansdown Holt & Partners*. Opened in 1973, it was always more downmarket than the Victoria Centre, and obstructs the city centre from the S. In 2008 there are proposals for rebuilding by *Hawkins\Brown* in smaller units with routes between – the approach adopted at Birmingham's Bull Ring Centre. Models show blocks clad in concrete and glass with strong horizontal louvres.

Middle Pavement leads E to Weekday Cross, the start of the Lace Market, Walk 4 (p. 96).

Walk 2.

Commercial Nottingham: North and West

This Walk is centred on Old Market Square and the streets N, where Upper and Lower Parliament streets mark the boundary of the medieval town. Walk 3 (p. 88) covers the areas E and S.

The starting point is the **Market Square** in front of T.C. Howitt's Council House of 1926–9 [32], i.e. the opposite end from that beginning the w and s parts of the French Borough (Walk 1). A view by Thomas Sandby, 1740, emphasizes the vastness of the square, with the C18 Exchange [49]. It was known as the Market Place before it was laid out

48. Walk 2

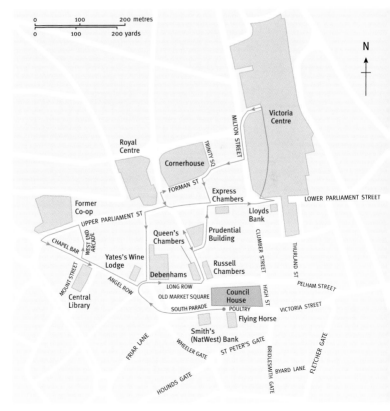

by *Howitt* as a formal quadrangle of walled gardens. But by 2003 the council wanted something more flexible and easily policed, and a limited competition in 2004 was won by *Gustafson Porter*. *Neil Porter*'s controversial £5 million design opened in 2007 is spare, emphasizing quality materials and bold shapes [50]. Steps down from a traffic-free Long Row serve as seating, with further steps to South Parade. The w side has asymmetrical water terraces, with waterfalls and fountains. This minimalist elegance makes the square seem smaller than before; it is also easily spoilt by clutter, as the utilitarian floodlights show.

One distinctive feature of the streets around the Market Square is the partial survival of **alleyways** behind many buildings, reflecting the historic burgage plots. Rebuilding in 1870–1920 was mainly in pairs, with central entries into these yards, and many disappeared only with

Old Market Square and the Exchange

49. Old view of the Market Square from Beastmarket Hill looking towards the Exchange, drawing by Thomas Sandby, *c.* 1742

The first record of a market here is from 1155. It served both the French and English boroughs (*see* pp. 5–6), which may explain its size, though used only for Saturday markets. By the c18 it was the town's centre, admired by the German traveller Carl Moritz in 1782 as 'hardly less handsome than a London square'. It was also noted for rallies and riots, and, until 1928, Goose Fair. Buildings grew up on its E side, and overlooking the square an Exchange was erected in 1724–6. This red brick classical structure was supported on stone pillars, which corresponded to the colonnades along Long Row and Poultry. It housed offices for both borough and market, and a public meeting room over shops. In 1814–15 it was refronted and rendered, and given a more sophisticated pediment. By mid-century this refacing was condemned as 'fake', and more offices were needed. *T.C. Hine* designed a replacement in French château style in 1857, which was rejected as too lavish. Instead courts and modest offices were built on Burton Street, as the Guildhall (p. 136).

50. Old Market Square from the Council House, looking towards Beastmarket Hill, square remodelled by Gustafson Porter, 2004–7

the merger of premises in the C20. They ran from Long Row N to Parliament Street, and several still link Poultry s to St Peter's Gate. **Arcades** sheltering the ground-floor shops, developed in emulation of Inigo Jones's Covent Garden piazza, were first noted by Celia Fiennes on one side in 1697. They survive extensively in rebuilt form.

The modern panorama begins on the s side at the **Flying Horse Hotel** on **Poultry**, now shops, its quaintness deceptive. Of its five gables the E three comprise the original inn, of which the westernmost projects on supporting columns. The two w gables are C19, the E of these rebuilt by *W.F. & R. Booker*, 1875, as a smoking room, the other a subsequent remodelling of older premises. That the whole elevation appears C16, with its jetty, carved bargeboards and pargetted panels, owes most to *D.G. Millet*, architect to Trust Houses, 1936, inspired by his native Essex. A little genuine timber framing in the E wall. The legend 'Est in year 1483' is another fantasy – the first record is early C18. E addition by *William Stretton*, c. 1782–8, its glazing perhaps 1830s, supported on columns and originally with stabling behind; later the Poultry Hotel.

51. Queen's Chambers, Long Row, by Watson Fothergill, 1897

A **shopping arcade** by Colchester's *Stanley Bragg Partnership*, 1987–8, replaced the pub additions and related properties. To the E, on **Peck Lane**, a genuine C18 gabled former pub, the **Punch Bowl**. Below are cellars serving the Flying Horse, Punch Bowl and, S, the Blue Boar (demolished 1915).

w of Peck Lane is a modern take on the oriel, extending down **Exchange Walk** (cut 1868), by *Turner Lansdown Holt & Partners*, 1972–3. Poultry then becomes **South Parade**, with the NatWest Bank, inscribed

'*Geo. R. Isborn* Arch^t 1878', a rebuilding of Smith's Bank, England's oldest provincial bank, founded in 1658 by Thomas Smith. Most of Isborn's work actually dates from 1871, a stone palazzo with entrances in projecting end bays, the w one the 1878 addition. The interior remodelled in 1968 when National Westminster took over. Nos. 10–12, the lumpy blue **Norwich Union House**, by *Evans, Cartwright & Woollatt*, 1957–9. The adjoining **Woolwich Equitable Building Society**, 1936–7 by *T. Cecil Howitt*, with giant engaged columns. Then a Northern Renaissance-style house and shop, one gable wide, 1889 by *Evans & Jolley*. Theirs, too, the similar tall corner block with Wheeler Gate, dated 1888. The **w side** of Old Market Square is **Beastmarket Hill**. The corner block is one of **Burton's** stores, distinctive for the detailing of their giant pilasters and between-floor panels, by the in-house architect *Harry Wilson*, 1923. Next is *W.A.S. Lloyd*'s **Bank**, designed 1959 as Barclays Bank, delicately classical, and then the bulk of Lloyds Bank, included in the largely c18 walk (p. 61).

The w part of **Long Row** is picked up later. For now, consider that part along the N **side** of the square, which in the early c20 became Nottingham's premier shopping street. **Debenhams**, long Griffin & Spalding, has grown haphazardly, with older properties and infilled yards behind new frontages. The oldest part is on Market Street, 1872 by *T.C. Hine & Son*, rock-faced with alternating projecting bays and round-headed dormers. The monumental stone classical block on Long Row was built in two phases by *Bromley & Watkins*, the E phase 1919–20, the centre and w half 1927 with the Market Street return. The centrepiece is a cartouche 'est.1846', set over a pedimented window aedicule and nonchalantly supported by two cherubs. Also part of Debenhams is an asymmetrical brick block built in two phases by *W. Dymock Pratt*, 1893–*c*. 1896, its offset oriel marking a rear yard, bookended by meagre 1950s rebuildings. Nos. 34–35 (**Pizza Hut**) has a five-bay front by *W.A. Heazell & Sons* dated 1910, the first floor with triangular, round and upswept pediments. No. 33, with striped green gables and copper-cheeked bows, was a cinema for Provincial Cinematograph Theatres by *Naylor & Sale*, 1912, replacing Caldwell's Photographic Studios, home to Nottingham's first regular film shows. The basement incorporates two medieval barrel-vaulted caves. Nos. 29–31 are a rebuilding of the **Ram Hotel**, by *Brewill & Baily*, 1899, with elaborate shaped gables. No. 27, also Renaissance but smaller and stone-fronted, 1902 by *J.W.J. Barnes*. Next door is **Queen's Chambers** [51], among *Watson Fothergill*'s most prominent works: shops and offices, 1897, rampant Tudorbethan Gothic combining elements of Norman Shaw and William Burges. The terminus to Long Row's historic arcading is a massive granite pier supporting an octagonal tourelle with a spire and lucarnes. A cacophony of gables and gargoyles up King Street.

The Y-planned **Queen** and **King streets** were cut in 1891 and 1892 respectively. On Queen Street the **Head Post Office** by *Henry Tanner*, the Office of Works' architect, 1895–8, loosely connected Caroline

52. Prudential Assurance, Queen Street and King Street, by Alfred Waterhouse, 1893–8, restored, 1991

classical elements in buff stone stepping up the street. Rebuilt behind its façade. At the streets' intersection the former **Prudential Assurance** [52], 1893–8 by *Alfred Waterhouse*, restored and converted in 1991. Waterhouse's favoured liverish brick and *Burmantofts* terracotta are sombre despite their Flemish Renaissance decoration, rising to a square tower whose turrets grasp a spire over the apex. The ground-floor public clerks' office, originally top-lit via a central light well, has tiled columns and strapwork ceiling panels; now a restaurant. A round stair-well to the rear, with a pretty iron balustrade, and tiling in the NE fire exit. **King Street** was mainly developed by *Turpin & Ball* with the architects *Frederick Ball & Lamb*, working in a Hanseatic mercantile style with high timbered gables, as on the E side at No. 8, 1894–6 between two 1950s rebuilds. On the SE corner is a tall block, **Russell Chambers**, a corner turret countered by a large gable to Long Row, 1895

53. Elite Cinema, Upper Parliament Street, by Adamson & Kinns, 1919–21

by *Marshall & Turner*. The w side has a more strongly horizontal composition, 1895–6 by *A.H. Goodall*, with **Grosvenor Buildings**, next door, 1896 by *Frederick Ball & Lamb*. The E side is dominated by the five-bay store built in 1895 for **Jessop & Son** by *Watson Fothergill*. A single gable with a red stone oriel on brackets, then a broad, two-stage tower with half-timbering and a finial, and three big gables each topping oriels. Round-arched windows and balustrading to the first floor. The third floor originally housed workrooms, with bedrooms for the girls above; their lounge and dining hall were in the basement. Iron columns on the ground-floor showroom, with concrete floors here and for the workrooms; other floors of lighter cinder construction.

Between King and Queen streets, fronting **Upper Parliament Street**, is the former **Elite Cinema** [53], 1919–21 by *Adamson & Kinns* (with Adamson also a financial backer). One of the earliest in Britain inspired by America's grandiose movie palaces. Vibrant faience frontage with figures under aedicules around the attic. Large auditorium, now largely hidden beneath a nightclub structure, inserted 1994–5. Three floors of tearooms and intimate dining rooms in Jacobean (one with a painted frieze), Georgian and Adamesque styles; converted to bars since 1995.

On the NE corner of King Street, offices from 1899 by *E.R. Sutton*, in Renaissance style, entered in Upper Parliament Street under a squashed dome and oriel. Next door is the earliest major surviving work by *Fothergill Watson*, Nos. 17–21, 1876 for the ***Nottingham Daily Express***.

Two gables, then a symmetrical three-bay centre flanked by stacks. The building was raised with new gables and attics in 1899, dated below the pentice roof. The E corner [54] is Fothergill at his most Burgesian Gothic, a colonnaded tower over an entrance decorated with heads of Liberal politicians; more commemorated on tiles inside the entrance, along with Queen Victoria and Prince Albert. Above are a balcony, a little colonnade of windows and a dormered tourelle. Graham Greene was a sub-editor here in 1926 (Nottingham inspired Nottwich in *A Gun for Sale*, 1936). Rebuilt behind the façade by the *John Madin Design Group*, 1982–3. Across the alley is the **Coach and Horses**, 1904 by *Heazell & Sons* for Allsopp & Sons, with an offset Jacobean gable and pedimented doorcase. Next, *Heazells'* insurance offices, 1900, with tall asymmetrical gables, now the **Nottingham Building Society**. At the corner with Clumber Street, the low C18 Corner Pin pub, rebuilt 1990–1. Clumber Street is one of Britain's most sought-after shopping locations, to its architectural detriment. Cross it, and Upper Parliament Street becomes **Lower Parliament Street**. On the corner, another **Burton's** store by *Harry Wilson,* of 1927–8 with giant pilasters. Then **Brown's**, perhaps *c.* 1885, with broad oriels in Venetian style. Nos. 12–16, **Lloyds Bank**, dated 1896, built for Furley & Co., provision merchants, on land cleared for the Great Central Railway, by *Watson Fothergill*. The corner has an angled entrance flanked by bartizans, and dormers above its pentice roof infilled with timber and brick nogging.

54. Nottingham Daily Express, Upper Parliament Street, by Fothergill Watson, 1876, east corner

55. Victoria Station clock tower, Milton Street, by A.E. Lambert, 1898–1900, set against the flats of the Victoria Centre, 1965–72

On the Lower Parliament Street façade terracotta reliefs by *Benjamin Creswick* depict colonial labour harvesting tea and sugar.

Lower Parliament Street is crossed here by a pedestrian bridge serving the **Victoria Centre** (for buildings further E, *see* the Lace Market and Sneinton walks, pp. 96, 146.). On the site of the Victoria Station of 1898–1900 for the Great Central and Great Northern railways, this was Nottingham's first indoor shopping centre, and one of the first in Britain: 1965–72 by *Peter Winchester* of *Arthur Swift & Partners*. It is five times bigger than Birmingham's demolished Bull Ring, its length matching that of the old town centre from N to S. Three layers of car parking built into the railway cutting below two storeys of shops, a bus station (rebuilt in the NE corner in 1997) and five slabs of flats on top, linked to resemble a giant toast rack. An example of the 1960s fascination for multi-purpose complexes or 'megastructures'. Reeded *in situ* concrete to the shopping area, not sustained through the development. Inside the malls have been sanitized, but *Rowland Emett*'s revolving **clock** or 'Aqua Horological Tintinnabulator', 1973, still tinkles on the quarter hours. The problem is that the Victoria Centre has severed the NE quadrant of the city from the hub.

Outside the NW entrance on Milton Street are old mementos amid the concrete. The Victoria Station **clock tower** [55] by *A.E. Lambert*, 1898–1900, is Baroque like his Midland station (p. 166), with balconies and heavy cornices. The Victoria Hotel (now **Hilton**), S, dated 1901, is

56. Cornerhouse complex, Forman Street, by Benoy, 1998–2001

by *R.W. Edis*, with variegated gables and terracotta window surrounds. Opposite, more shops, offices and flats replaced **Trinity Square**, by *Haskoll Architects*, 2006–8. On the corner, a tall gabled block by *John Howitt*, dated 1903 on its apsed corner. Nos. 7–11 Milton Street, **Halifax House**, is a remodelling for the Halifax Building Society, 1936–7 by *Cyril F.W. Haseldine*, stripped classical.

w of Trinity Square, **Forman Street** marked the N boundary of the pre-C19 city; still a taggle of shops and bars. The newspaper offices, N, that gave the street its modern name were replaced in 1998–2001 by *Benoy*'s brazen **Cornerhouse** entertainment complex [56]. Better is **Trinity Buildings**, s, dated 1923 by *H. Alderman Dickman*, mixing fashionable Greek and Egyptian motifs with the lions of Empire above an original shopfront. Turn left down the next alley, **King's Walk**, an early pedestrian arcade of 1901 by *W. Dymock Pratt*, the two sides linked by iron signs and lamp brackets, and incorporating in Nos. 6–10 houses of *c.* 1800 and *c.* 1840. w along **Upper Parliament Street**, No. 32 is by *Arthur Marshall*, 1913–14, rendered with a timber gable and oriel. The **Blue Bell** has a joyous frontage rebuilt by *Hedley J. Price*, 1904, with a green faience ground floor, a shell-hood over the entrance and oriels either side, rising to a broken pediment. More severe to Forman Street, by *W.B. Starr & Hall*, 1925, with blue faience bells and a large projecting one of glass. Nos. 52–54 are rendered and altered, but *c.* 1700. **Capocci** is pure 1950s, a grid of orange timber panels interspersed with sketches of Italian comestibles. On the corner of **South Sherwood Street** is the **Turf Tavern**, rebuilt by *W.B. Starr & Hall*, dated 1923 in faience.

The w side of South Sherwood Street has the **Royal Centre** (*see* p. 134), its portico fronting Theatre Square, and a **sculpture**, Carmen, by *Hilary Cartmel*, 1989. On the NW corner is **Westminster Buildings**, between Upper Parliament and Wollaton streets, by *A. Harrison Goodall*, dated 1909 in its broken pediment, bold but coarse. On the curved SW corner, Nos. 30–31 Market Street, now **Reflex**, is *T. Cecil Howitt*'s Martin's Bank, 1930, with giant Greek Ionic columns; one of his finest buildings before being crudely altered into a club.

Market Street was cut through on the line of Sheep Lane in 1865, and filled with tall red brick shops and offices from the 1870s. On the E corner, No. 36 is a former pub by *Evans & Son*, 1895, with Northern

Renaissance-shaped gables. No. 34, dated 1879 over brick-filled second-floor tympana, is by *S. Dutton Walker*. He also designed No. 32, auction rooms of 1878, Gothic with his distinctive tile-clad gables. No. 30, dated 1875, perhaps by *John Collyer*, has a very elaborate machicolated cornice and parapet. Nos. 26 and 28 are the Flemish Renaissance-style former **Constitutional Club**, dated 1897, by *A.R. Calvert*; now a bar. Stone, with a balconied first floor topped by the city crest. The side entrance leads to a stone staircase with bulbous pilasters. More red brick Flemish Renaissance buildings on the w, many by *John Jackson & William Heazell*, some with cast-iron balconies or projecting bays; all topped with an elaborate cornice and dormers, or by a decorated gable. Nos. 13–19 (the latter dated 1877) gently Gothic, Nos. 3–5 particularly florid.

At the bottom of Market Street, on **Long Row West**, is **The Talbot**, a Yates Wine Lodge since 1928–9, built for Charles Cox, 1876–8, as a gin palace. *W.A. Heazell & Sons* converted a Palace of Varieties to the rear (demolished), and they or *Evans & Jolley* were probably architects for the original pub. Restored and remodelled by *Stewart Riddick & Associates*, 1985, including the lamentable conservatory to the front. The interior – reminiscent of the Malt Cross (p. 61) – more sensitively refurbished, retaining a gallery on cast-iron columns; an open truss roof lined with lincrusta and topped by a skylight.

Next door, three c18 houses on Long Row [57] survived as part of Pearson's department store from the 1900s to 1990. All have ground floors set behind cast-iron columns. Nos. 50–52, late c18, the two-bay No. 52 slightly at an angle. Then No. 56 (**Habitat**), *c.* 1720, with prominent dormers and continuous bands; two panelled first-floor rooms. The adjoining four-storey house is *c.* 1740. The oldest, **Boots**, 1705, has sharp gables, large oak beams to its ceilings, and a splat-baluster stair.

57. Early c18 houses on Long Row west, Boots, 1705, Habitat, *c.* 1720

58. Nottingham Co-operative Society headquarters, Upper Parliament Street, from left to right, by John Howitt, 1906 and W.V. Betts, 1914–16 and 1925–6

All were extended by *J.W. Dawson*, 1929, and altered *c.* 1991–2; cellars carved out of the rock, with c17 brick barrel vaults; a round pillar with a capital is reputedly medieval. **Hurts Yard**, w, still runs all the way through to Parliament Street. Then more c19 frontages on Long Row. The broadest incorporates the entrance to **Cannon Court**, where the **Alley Café** is a homespun c19 warehouse. The **Dragon** (No. 67), formerly the George and Dragon, was rebuilt 1879 by *John Henry Statham*, though some c17 work survived until 1910. No. 70 Long Row and Nos. 2–6 Chapel Bar (to the right) are four lively if battered early c20 façades, including No. 2 Chapel Bar, by *W.B. Starr*, and No. 4 by *John Howitt & Son*, both 1908. Between Long Row and Chapel Bar is **West End Arcade**, this end from the 1920s, but leading N to an extension of 1966 by *Feast Anderson Associates* with shops on two levels and a tackily tactile façade to Upper Parliament Street. Opposite here, **West Independent Printers**, dated 1883, is a rebuilding of the Rutland Arms on Wollaton Street with frontage warehousing surrounding a central courtyard, by *J.W. Keating*. Dominating **Upper Parliament Street** is the former central store of the **Nottingham Co-operative Society**, converted to smaller shops, offices and flats with a new attic storey by *Marchini Curran Associates*, in 2005–7. This is a complex building, the main façade of three phases [58]. To the E a range of 1925–6 by *William V. Betts* in terracotta. One entrance at the rounded corner below a cupola and copper dome, the other under a square block with painted sculptures of a sailor, seamstresses and railwayman; extensions by Betts and his son *A.H. Betts* to the rear into the 1950s. The store began with the central range of marginally paler terracotta, 1914–16 by *W.V. Betts* as three separate shops. The left corner was built for the Cahn family's Nottingham Furnishing Co., fierce red brick with a clock tower, 1906 by *John Howitt* and united with the Co-op after 1945.

Chapel Bar is often deserted save for Quartet, four life-size figures by *Richard Perry* typical of 1986–8. On the NW side a large glassy redevelopment of offices and restaurants, by *David Lyons & Associates*, 2001–6. Across Mount Street is **Angel Row**, with on the corner the former **Westminster Bank**, by *Baily & Eberlin* with *G.M. Aylwin* in typically flat bankers' Georgian, 1929. No. 2 was a shop and warehousing for Henry Barker, furnisher, by *Harry Gill Sen.*, 1898–9, much rebuilt when converted by the *County Architect's Department* (*Michael Tempest* & *Colin McIntosh*) into the **Central Library**, opened in 1977 – a fifteen-month project that united the city and county collections, and reflecting municipal poverty in the 1970s. The **Odeon**, lavish Art Deco, was built in 1932–3 by *Verity & Beverley*, with *A.J. Thraves*, as the Ritz Cinema. Remodelled in 1964–5 and derelict since 2001. Nos. 10–11 are early C19, with a projecting large C20 clock. No. 12 was refronted in mock-Tudor style for Pearson and Pearson, with a high timber gable, 1915 by *P.H. Dawson*. Next to it, Bromley House is in Walk 1, p. 59.

Walk 3.

Commercial Nottingham: East and South

This Walk begins on the Old Market Square at the corner of King Street and Long Row, and explores the area to the E and S.

Long Row resumes, E, with a late C18 pair bridging Greyhound Street, its centrepiece a broken pediment over a devilish keystone, an upswept architrave and third-floor *œil de bœuf*, its modillion cornice continued in the remodelling of the right half in 1905–6 by *Heazell & Sons* as **Oriel Chambers**; wings of respective dates down Greyhound Street. Next door, Nos. 17–18 were refronted, 1924, by *Alexander Ellis Anderson*, C.R. Mackintosh's Scottish assistant in Northampton; Scottish vernacular in its over-scaled bartizans. The **HSBC Bank**, softly Baroque, by *T.B. Whinney*, 1911, for the London, City & Midland Bank. Then comes the site of *Fothergill Watson*'s Black Boy, its loss in 1970 aggravated by the insensitivity of its replacement, by and for Littlewoods, now **Primark** and **Poundsave**.

Quickly up **Clumber Street**, to the former **Lion Hotel**, built *c.* 1730 as the White Lion, remodelled 1846 (dated at rear) and given its green-

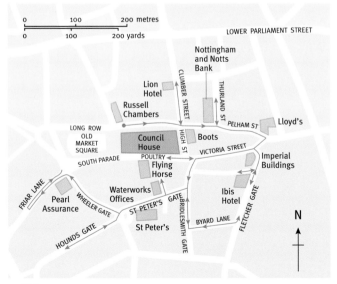

59. Walk 3

60. Boots, former headquarters branch, High Street, by A.N. Bromley, 1903

glazed tile frontage by *Frederick Ball*, 1910. The first floor has early C18 plaster decoration and a dog-leg stair. On the E corner with Pelham Street are offices for the **Alliance and Leicester Building Society**, by *Crampin Pring*, 1987–9, Postmodern.

Opposite, on the NE corner of High Street, is the former headquarters of **Boots** retail chemists, by *A.N. Bromley*, dated 1903 within the corner entrance porch. A lavish terracotta front [60] with Art Nouveau detailing, putti sheltering under the cornice brackets and a high balustrade with finials. The corner with Pelham Street has a small dome, a clock supported by more figures, and balconies. Boots filled the premises with a maze of tiny departments, a restaurant and subscription library, swept away in 1974 by the *Architects Design Group*; refitted by *CPMG Architects* for **Zara**, 2002. On Pelham Street, Nos. 5–7, N, *c.* 1810, No. 5 (**Gray and Ball**) with a jeweller's shopfront and pedimented doorcase by *Sutton & Gregory*, 1913. The W half of Pelham Street was widened in 1844, and rebuilding duly followed. Thurland Street was laid out in 1838, following the demolition of Thurland Hall, a C15 mansion rebuilt *c.* 1633–4. This passed in the C18 to the Dukes of

61. Nottingham and Nottinghamshire Bank, Thurland Street, by Fothergill Watson, 1878–82, detail of the monkey chained to his mortgage, capital

Newcastle, who preferred it to the Castle until it was sold by the 4th Duke in 1832 with the surrounding land between Lincoln and Pelham streets (good Newcastle names). Against this framework of early-to-mid-C19 houses, much altered, later C19 commercial buildings stand out.

Thurland Street has a stand-off between Hine and Fothergill, with early works facing across the road. The w side is dominated by *Fothergill Watson*'s **Nottingham and Nottinghamshire Bank**, now **All Saints**, the main elevation 1878–82, extended in keeping to Pelham Street by *Basil Baily*, 1924–5, for the Westminster Bank (described as 'a considerable improvement in the design of the original building' by the *British Builder*). Fothergill's work revolves around a full-throttle Rhenish tower, gables and paired stacks to either side, and stepped staircase windows on the right. The lower parts are largely Gothic, linked lancets contrasted with plate-traceried roundels around the round-arched entrance and stairs. A band of shields to the first floor, in a frieze carved with the locations of the bank's branches (many also by Fothergill). The gables and tower have three Portland stone friezes depicting farming, textiles and mining. More sculpted figures on the roof including dramatic eagle gargoyles, reptilian cats and a stork. Inside, the banking hall has a top-lit dome above a triforium supported on twelve granite columns, each capital carved with an animal, some stylized, others unsettlingly real like the monkey chained to his mortgage [61]. Stained glass to the offices. Opposite, the **Nottingham Corn Exchange**, now a bar, 1849–50 by *T.C. Hine*, the building which established his late classical Anglo-Italian style, with heavy quoins and window pediments, yet at the top a playful Jacobean brick frieze and his favoured encaustic tile band. Adjoining is the single-bay former **Artisan's Library**, 1854 by *Robert C. Clarke*, Italianate with fluted Corinthian window surrounds and a heavy cornice; it became Nottingham's first public library in 1867. The **Thurland Hall** pub on the corner of Pelham Street, 1898–1900, is by *Gilbert S. Doughty*, grey ashlar with a corner turret and high gables (one dated). An original bar back, which with the lincrusta cornice and ceiling makes for one of the area's few historic pub interiors.

62. *Nottingham Journal* offices, Pelham Street, by R.C. Clarke, 1860

On the s side of **Pelham Street** are the offices of the *Nottingham Journal* [62], now shops and offices, by *R.C. Clarke*, 1860. Gothic, its lancets linked by crisp foliage capitals and sculpted heads. The author J.M. Barrie worked here in 1883–4. Then comes **Ormiston House**, three grey bays with tripartite windows, 1872, the fourth, right, a careful addition of 1937 by *Evans, Clark & Woollatt*; three gables (dated 1872 with initials MIP) are repeated in Victoria Street. The N side of Pelham Street is now mainly bars. The Durham Ox was rebuilt as the **Bodega**, 1902, by *G.D. Martin* of London, with a curly segmental pediment and a large arch to the rear yard. From the first a single bar on the ground floor with a song room above. Pelham Street meets Victoria Street in a C19 temperance hotel, latterly a restaurant, round-fronted to Swine Green. Lloyd's Bar forms part of the Lace Market walk (p. 114).

Fletcher Gate, right, widened in 1971, marks the divide between the Lace Market and modern retailing districts. To the right again is **Bottle Lane**, 2006–8. Bildurn Properties and their consultants, *Lathams*, held an invited competition, won by *Benson & Forsyth*. They lined the alley with shops and a hotel, a largely glazed grid (smart and Swiss-like) at the base but with larger retro-Modern blocks superimposed for the hotel and roof garden [63]. The development incorporates the façade of *A.N. Bromley*'s solicitors' offices, 1898–9, and behind it a warehouse by *John Howitt*, 1888–9. On Fletcher Gate, s, are red brick offices of *c.* 1885, and a higher warehouse of 1883, both by *W. & R. Booker*.

Victoria Street, opened in 1863, retains sobriety and grandeur through the consistently palazzo-like buildings on its s side. But consider the N side briefly. The **Pit and Pendulum**, showrooms of 1870 by *Robert Evans*, extended by *Evans & Jolley*, 1873 – a pilaster at the junction. The bracket clock with automaton figures of blacksmiths and panels over ground-floor pilasters recall the clients, ironmongers Lewis and Grundy.

On the s side, **Imperial Building** was originally the General Post and Telegraph Office, by the Government architect *James Williams*, 1868, raised by *Edward G. Rivers* for the Office of Works, 1883. Italianate, a turret to Fletcher Gate. Nos. 16–18, now a casino, was built for the **Imperial Fire and Life Insurance Co**. in 1869–70 by *Robert Evans*, with a French tower and delicate capitals; altered for the Nottingham Liberal Club by *W.B. Starr & Hall*, 1912–13, including the porch and a bedroom storey. No. 12, by *Evans & Jolley*, was a club, 1872, now the **HSBC**, entered between granite columns under stone pediments; very refined for these architects. The adjoining bank by *Evans & Son*, 1895–7, is now **French Connection**, five bays with first-floor pedimented windows over a rusticated base, door to left; two matching bays, right, 1920–1, by *T.B. Whinney*, the Midland Bank's architect. On the corner is the **Nottinghamshire Club** by *Hine & Evans*, 1868. Tile bands over the first floor.

Before heading left down Bridlesmith Gate, two buildings at the E end of **Poultry**, ahead. Nos. 10–11 by *Ernest R. Sutton*, 1905–6, faience, free classical; cherubs contemplative between giant pilasters. No. 6 has

63. Bottle Lane and Ibis Hotel, by Benson & Forsyth, 2005–8

a bronze relief depicting the Exchange replaced by the Council House. It was the street entrance to The Exchange Pub, largely rebuilt by *W.B. Starr & Hall*, 1931.

Left into **Bridlesmith Gate**. The medieval thoroughfare has spawned smart fashion chains since the 1970s. On the w side, three buildings erected following road-widening. No. 4, its Italian Renaissance brick-work matching Hine and Evans's opposite down to the decorative bands, 1875–6 by *F. Williamson*. No. 6, rock-faced, was built in 1874–6 by *John Collyer* as the Dog & Bear pub. Shops since 1993, but animal heads survive over the ground floor. Next door, No. 21 St Peter's Gate, by *Heazell & Son*, 1895–6, Renaissance style.

More C19 buildings on the e side. Nos. 1 and 3, **Waterstones**, 1873–5 by *Lawrence Bright*; s bay in similar pilastered style by *A.N. Bromley*, 1927. A moulded cornice denotes the 1875 part; glazed rear extension by *Mark Stewart Architecture*, 1999–2000. Nos. 5–9 by *Gilbert S. Doughty*, 1895, massive, feisty red brick and Jacobean gables. It dominates the diminutive No. 11, early C16 and timber-framed. Jetties to the first floor and attic; C18 rear wing. Then **Bridlesmith Walk**, tall and gabled, half-timbered, by *John Howitt*, 1882. A long rear range, originally two warehouses reached via a carriage arch. Extended by another timber front, right, by *John Lamb*, 1911, remodelled 2006–7 by *Tan Gani*. Across **Tokenhouse Yard**, a shop and offices by *Harry Allcock*, 1907, timber-fronted, and two shops by *F.J. Architects*, 2000. **Hobbs** was Morris and Place's Auction Mart, an emaciated giant order and high attic, 1900 by *A.R. Calvert*. Then a bolder composition, symmetrical Jacobean with a projecting central bay and a high balustrade. Built by *Evans & Jolley*, 1884, for Hart Fellows and Co.'s Bank (**Café Rouge**), to which they added a projecting shop, N, 1887. This brings us to the narrow **Byard Lane**. On the N side, No. 5 was the working-class New Dining Hall by *Thomas Simpson*, 1865–6, with Gothic lancets. A Baroque composition next door, 1902 by *Hedley J. Price*, set back. On the corner of Fletcher Gate, the **Cross Keys** pub, by *Evans & Son*, 1899, an early example of a plain, 'improved' pub designed for easy supervision. Next to it is a lace warehouse by *A.H. Goodall*, 1895 and 1898, pink terracotta façades.

Back to Bridlesmith Gate, and return N towards **St Peter's Gate**. On the left, No. 30, by *A.R. Calvert*, 1906–7, sham timber. On the corner of St Peter's Gate, **Rutland Chambers** by *Lawrence Bright*, 1888, curved towards Bridlesmith Gate. Central entrance under a projecting two-storey oriel. On the s side, Nos. 4–6, 1898–9 by *Evans & Son*, a single gable: respectful of its neighbour, No. 2, with regular gabled bays and central oriel. This extends left down **St Peter's Church Walk**; by *Evans & Jolley*, 1887.

N towards Poultry is **Bank Place**, its buildings' status heralded in stone. **Hugo Boss** was the County Court, by *J.G. Sorby*, c. 1875. Italianate, with a rusticated ground floor; round arches to the *piano nobile*. The arcaded stone attic added by *Edward G. Rivers* of the Office of Works, 1883–4. The w side counters with Waterworks offices, 1874, a palazzo with refined mouldings, including a badge in the first-floor tympanum and motto 'Pure and Constant'. Attributed by Ken Brand to *Charles Hawksley*, son of Thomas, engineer to the Water Company.

At the bottom of St Peter's Gate Nos. 31–33 **Wheeler Gate**, by *W.A. Heazell*, 1887, modestly Flemish with strapwork gables. Opposite, No. 1 **Hounds Gate**, with a timber gable, 1883 by *Arthur W. Brewill*. Nos. 3–11 alongside are mid-C18 houses with wedge-shaped lintels and double keystones. No. 13, a warehouse of 1921–2 by *John Howitt & Son*, with tripartite windows, then No. 15 by builders *G. Bell & Sons*, 1886–7. Beyond is massive C19 warehousing, the s range by *Evans & Jolley* 1894–5, the bridge over the street of 1920–1 by *Brewill & Baily*. The N side similar but earlier, probably by *Thomas Wright*. He added the four w bays in 1881; stone surrounds to the ground-floor openings. A gap, then a warehouse by *Ernest R. Sutton*, 1895, reusing an earlier ground floor that was itself entirely remodelled by *James McArtney*, 1991, with a set-back entrance and rear additions.

Retracing our steps, **Wheeler Gate** has, w, a half-timbered survivor, **Morley's Café**, a 1908 refronting by *John Armitage* of an older building. The E side was entirely rebuilt following street widening, 1885–6, with shops and offices. Nos. 25–29, for long Sisson and Parker's bookshop, 1885–6 for E. Swann (E.S. in gable) by *Evans & Jolley*. Northern Renaissance with gables, two-storey oriels and pediments. Nos. 9–23, **Premier House**, 1894–5 by *John Howitt*, is curved, its bays defined by pilasters, volutes making the leap to the five-storey centrepiece. The w side is C20 save for No. 18, mid-C18, its ground floor remodelled *c.* 1868 probably by *Robert Evans*, who built his offices to the rear in **Eldon Chambers**. The façade has, right, a canted wooden bay with a Venetian window containing Gothick glazing. Its C18 rear wing has segment-headed sashes. Beyond, **Pearl Assurance** dominates, by *Evans, Cartwright & Woollatt*, old-fashioned for 1960–2, a grievous replacement for the C17 Oriental Café and bomb-damaged Moot Hall. Back on the E side, Nos. 1–3, **Cavendish Buildings**, by *John Howitt*, 1894, stone with a rusticated first floor and shallow central bay.

Left into **Friar Lane**. **Granby Chambers** on the NW corner, 1929–30 by *Calvert & Jessop*, domestic-styled shops and offices, the name a reminder of a street Maid Marian Way replaced. The N side of Friar Lane was redeveloped following road widening *c.* 1925. **Friary Chambers** is Spanish-style, by *H. Alderman Dickman*, 1927–8. Nos. 20–24 for the **Nottingham Permanent Building Society**, by *W.B. Starr & Hall*, 1928–9, its entrances emphasized by quoined projections. **Vernon House**, long Tobys, an elegantly understated frontage with metalwork panels and no mouldings, 1930 by *Calvert & Jessop*.* We are thus back at Old Market Square, with the start of the C18-dominated Walk 1 just to the N in Angel Row.

*Information from Ken Brand.

The Lace Market

The Saxon or English town is the oldest and densest part of the city, but save on its s thoroughfare, High Pavement, its character is C19, when it became the world's first centre of machine-lace production and distribution. Pre-1800 maps show substantial houses with large gardens and orchards [10], as dense post-medieval growth was concentrated in the French Borough. This changed *c.* 1800 as the gentry were replaced by the lace industry, and by the building of cottages with attic workshops, most set down small courts and cleared by 1914. Some larger houses became factories, making St Mary's Gate the industry's centre by 1840. Thence warehouses spread E and N. Imposed on a medieval street grid, momentarily on Stoney Street they have the quality of Manchester or Chicago's Loop – the effect miniaturized but intense.

The Lace Market buildings survived because the Market Square became Nottingham's commercial district. It was then detached from the rest of the centre, first when the Great Central Railway cleft Middle Hill in 1894 (its gap s of Weekday Cross filled only in 2007–8), and then by the widening of Fletcher Gate, 1971. A proposed E–W route, 1966, led to more demolition on Pilcher and Barker gates, which revealed Saxon and post-Conquest fortifications; it was abandoned and the Lace Market declared a Conservation Area in 1969. Cheap rents attracted arts venues, nightclubs and housing associations, but commercial development came only after 1989, when the Lace Market Development Co. began to sort out land-holdings. The area remains a beguiling mixture of the haphazard and run-down with the slick and new.

The Lace Market can be split into three E–W sections, an C18 streetscape along High Pavement, continuing that of Low Pavement; the central lace warehouses; and a mix of commercial and institutional buildings N of Carlton Street and Goose Gate.

High Pavement

We begin at **Weekday Cross**, reinstated by the Civic Society, 1993. Here was Nottingham's daily market, and its Guildhall until replaced by the Great Central's tunnel. Building began in 2007 on Nottingham's **Centre for Contemporary Art** by *Caruso St John* [22]. The immediate surprise is the exterior, the most representational of their buildings to date, clad in verdigris scalloped panels pre-cast with a traditional lace pattern, over a pre-cast terrazzo base and capped with bands of gold anodised

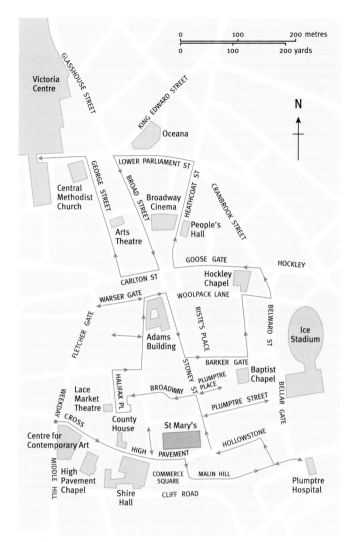

Scale: 0 — 100 — 200 metres; 0 — 100 — 200 yards

N

Victoria Centre

GLASSHOUSE STREET

KING EDWARD STREET

Oceana

LOWER PARLIAMENT ST

GEORGE STREET

BROAD STREET

HEATHCOAT ST

CRANBROOK STREET

Central Methodist Church

Broadway Cinema

People's Hall

Arts Theatre

CARLTON ST

GOOSE GATE

HOCKLEY

Hockley Chapel

WARSER GATE

WOOLPACK LANE

FLETCHER GATE

RISTE'S PLACE

BELWARD ST

Ice Stadium

Adams Building

BARKER GATE

STONEY ST

Baptist Chapel

HALIFAX PL

BROADWAY

PLUMPTRE PLACE

Lace Market Theatre

WEEKDAY CROSS

County House

St Mary's

PLUMPTRE STREET

BELLAR GATE

Centre for Contemporary Art

HIGH PAVEMENT

HOLLOWSTONE

MIDDLE HILL

High Pavement Chapel

COMMERCE SQUARE

MALIN HILL

Plumptre Hospital

Shire Hall

CLIFF ROAD

64. Walk 4

aluminium. The source is Louis Sullivan's Guaranty Building in Buffalo (near Caruso's native Montreal), the colours a counter to Nottingham's red brick. Entrances re-establish Middle Hill and Garnier's Hill on the map. One top-lit steel-framed floor of galleries at the level of High Pavement floats over two sunken floors of overscaled concrete entirely filling the vertiginous site. It is a mix of delicate spaces, their roof lights based on those of Malmö's Konsthall, with one that is quite brutal, using materials as found and exposed services. Weekday Cross gives its name to a typical c21 Lace Market development of shops and flats, red brick and grey metal windows, by *Benoy*, 2001–3.

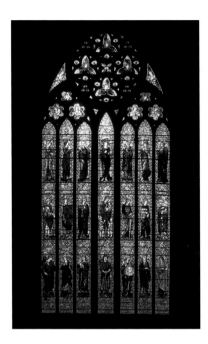

65. High Pavement Chapel, High Pavement, east window, by Morris & Co., 1904

On the SE corner of Weekday Cross, **Piccolino** comprises two mid-C19 warehouses. **La Tasca**, with a central oriel inscribed W. Cotton, milliner, by *W.A. Heazell*, 1874–5. Nos. 17–19, with oriels, by *William Jolley*, 1880–1, who added No. 1 **High Pavement** in 1884–5, a stone ground floor. Nos. 3–5 are C18, with canted bays and gabled dormers. No. 7, **The Living Room**, is by the builder-developer *G.S. Fish*, a plaque commemorating Queen Victoria's Diamond Jubilee. No. 9 is an C18 house with remnants of a shop by *Watson Fothergill*, 1898, while No. 11 was refronted by *George Attenborough* (1877).

High Pavement Chapel opposite, by *Stuart Colman* of Bristol, 1874–6, has fabulous **stained glass**. The Unitarian congregation built a chapel here in 1691, and its fashionable status through the C19 prompted a competition for its rebuilding. It was converted to a lace museum in 1987–9 and to a bar and restaurant by London's *Design Solution* in 1998. The stepped W tower, with boldly chamfered turrets and octagonal spire, complements St Mary's (p. 30) as a landmark. That the church's rock-faced body, with steeply gabled aisles and transepts, is also immensely high is most apparent internally, extraordinarily tall column shafts opening into the single-bay chancel. The church is also narrow, transepts no wider than the aisles. Four-bay arcade, the W incorporating a narthex and organ loft. The highlight is the seven-light E window [65], 1904 by *Morris & Co.*, reusing figure designs by *Burne-Jones* (top and middle tier) and by him and *J.H. Dearle* below. By *Morris & Co.*, too, the central N aisle window, 1907. N aisle W, 1919 by *Kempe & Co.*; N aisle E, Sunday School memorial window of 1906 by *Henry*

Holiday. s aisle centre, by *Leonard Walker* using extraordinary hues, 1934. Large transept windows: N, German, designed by *H. Enfield*, 1890; s, servicemen survey the ruins of Ypres and Mons, a war memorial by *Clayton & Bell*, 1920. Behind, on the cliff edge, **High Pavement School**, founded 1788, rebuilt in 1846, remodelled 1874, 1881, and now offices. E, No. 14 High Pavement is an C18 house with a pedimented doorcase and writhingly patterned fanlight.

On the N side beyond a gap (once typifying the area) is **County House**. Its oldest parts are late medieval, its plan suggesting a hall and cross-passage with wings to either side. It was much rebuilt for William Hallowes, *c*. 1728–33 (from which a staircase survives), and remodelled in 1833 by *Henry Moses Wood* and *James Nicholson* when it became the Judges' Lodging; theirs, too, an E wing. Converted 1922 for County Council offices; later additions. The main façade still has its original proportions, but the detail – including a delicate segmental iron balcony – was added by Wood and Nicholson. In contrast their E extension (on the site of stabling) is robust: massive two-storey sash windows imposed on squat Neo-Greek Doric columns of cast iron [66], the consequence of keeping a consistent *piano nobile* on rising ground. It looks like an Athenaeum or Literary Institute and in fact housed the judges' dining room. Inside, Greek Revival architraves and bracketed cornices; a Baroque Revival stair. The original house had a vista across the street overlooking the Trent valley, suggesting there was an C18 *piano nobile*.

66. County House, High Pavement, additions by Henry Moses Wood and John Nicholson, 1833

The **Shire Hall**, s side, with the County Gaol behind, were two distinct units on the same site, isolated elements of the county within the city. High Pavement is dominated by *James Gandon*'s frontage of 1770–2, important as the first public commission by a London architect in Nottingham. Some older work survives in the gaol, though its only elevation – s, perched high above the cliff – is of the 1830s, raised and extended after 1888.

The Shire Hall was first recorded in 1375–6 and was extended in the C17. The floor collapsed during the 1742 Assizes, but rebuilding was agreed only in 1767. Five architects submitted plans and the one Londoner, *James Gandon*, a pupil of William Chambers and friend of Nottingham born Paul Sandby, was commissioned. His first scheme, published in *Vitruvius Britannicus* in 1771, was thought 'too magnificent', and his cheapest alternative chosen. In 1833 wings were added and alterations made by *Henry Moses Wood* and *James Nicholson*. A Grand Jury Room was added by *R.C. Sutton* on the first floor in 1859. *W. Bliss Sanders* extensively altered the Governor's House and Crown Court, 1876, but that December a fire destroyed both Courts, sparing only the façade and Grand Jury Room. The Crown Court was restored immediately, while the Civil Court was enlarged, by *Hine*, 1876–9.

As built, *Gandon*'s façade [67] was a refreshingly severe composition of Ionic half-columns with unadorned semicircular niches and rectangular panels. These details and the ample expanse of bare wall show the influence of French Neoclassicism as well as William Chambers's Casino at Marino outside Dublin. Gandon's name is inscribed in the entablature. Above are carved an axe, cap and rods (fasces), the Roman symbols of authority. *Hine* busied Gandon's front, making round-headed windows and doors out of his niches. This façade is now flanked to the E by *Sanders*'s frontage of 1875–6, with entrances at basement level to either side – that to the right was inscribed GOAL and poorly corrected to GAOL. To the w is Hine's elaborate extension to the Civil Court, surmounted by a French dome. w on High Pavement a gateway and police station (a drastic remodelling with additions) were added in 1905 in a heavily rusticated Baroque style under *E. Purnell Hooley*, County Surveyor.

Interior. The **plan** was typical of contemporary courthouses, and was repeated by Gandon for courts in Dublin, where – again through Sandby – he later made his reputation. The two courtrooms were entered through colonnades directly off a grand central hall. Hine enclosed this entrance hall. His **courtrooms** were more practical than Gandon's, where proceedings were reputedly inaudible. They survive down to their gas lamps, each with a hierarchy of benches for jury, barristers and their staff to the sides and for public and press at the rear. In the centre is the 'dock', that for the Crown Court with a staircase to the cells below. The Crown Court is the grander, with a balcony on three sides; the smaller Nisi Prius Court has arcading to the sides.

THIS COUNTY HALL
WAS ERECTED IN THE YEAR MDCCLXX
AND IN THE TENTH YEAR OF THE REIGN
OF HIS MAJESTY GEORGE THE III

67. Shire Hall, High Pavement, by James Gandon, 1770–2, altered by T.C. Hine, 1876–8

A **County Gaol** in High Pavement was first mentioned in Nottingham's Great Charter of 1449. It was rebuilt *c.* 1618 and greatly extended in 1833. The County Justices having purchased County House, *Wood* and *Nicholson* built a new men's gaol on its vista, open land adjoining Shire Hall. Their work is supported on retaining walls well seen from Cliff Road (reached down Garner's Hill), where the date 1832 is boldly displayed. A new women's prison followed to the E, with a laundry and small exercise yard. Closed in 1985, the Shire Hall was adapted as a museum by *Hayley Sharpe* of Leicester, working with *Maber Associates* and opening in 1995. Further work for the Prison

Service Museum was carried out by the *Pearl Studies Design Co.* and *EDM Architects* in 2005. Visitors today see a series of dungeons cut into the rock, the women's quarters and the repetitive cells of the men's block, now the Prison Service Museum.

N, next to County House is a mock-timber pub, now the **Cock and Hoop**, rebuilt by *Baily & Eberlin*, 1933. No. 27, early C19 with a mid-C19 warehouse behind, is shared between the pub and the **Lace Market Hotel**. No. 29 is late C18, No. 31 refined early C19; inside, restaurant and bar installed by *David Collins*, 2004. Churchyard walls were erected in 1804–6 after homes facing High Pavement were demolished in 1774 and 1792. Up **St Mary's Gate**, left, Nos. 48–50 is a warehouse by *S.J. Cargill*, 1883, a rock-faced ground floor with lancets above. No. 46 was built as warehousing by *Evans & Son & J. Woollatt*, 1907, red and severe. Opposite, two early C19 houses, No. 49 with a large recessed doorway, and No. 5 Kayes Walk, its windows separated by neat brickwork. **Kayes Walk** was taken in 1806 off the N side of the churchyard, when the rest was enclosed; now lined with red brick mid-C19 warehousing. No. 1, *c.* 1853, raised in the late C19, was restored by *Cullen, Carter & Hill* as their offices, 1981.

E of Shire Hall, C18 houses opposite St Mary's establish **High Pavement**'s character of a genteel market town. Two large houses: No. 26, mid- and late C18, central ashlar doorcase and balustraded parapet; No. 28, late C18, with vermiculated keystones surrounding a yard entry. Then five small late C18 houses, with a central entry. No. 42 was built as an entrance warehouse to Commerce Square. Smaller C18 houses beyond, including No. 44, early C18 with a dog-leg stair, their rear gardens infilled by late C19 warehouses, the best No. 54a, by *W. & R. Booker*, a bold stone doorcase, more floors descending to Malin Hill behind.

Commerce Square is an ensemble of well-proportioned early-mid C19 warehouses. The largest descend eight storeys to Cliff Road S, unified by their suave red brick with later warehousing W and N, converted to flats and offices 1990–1 by *HLM* with the engineer *Ward Cole*. The two-storey E range by *Thomas P. Steath*, 1883, leads to Malin Hill, a steep route down the cliff, past small warehouses converted to architects' offices, that of **Marsh Grochowski** (1886) remodelled by *Alan Mulcahy*, 1986, Mackintosh windows; Mulcahy's own (No. 15) largely by *W. & R. & F. Booker*, 1897–8, heavily glazed.

At the bottom, across the busy ring road, **Plumptre Hospital**, almshouses rebuilt in 1823 by *Edward Staveley*, Surveyor to Nottingham Corporation. Cemented Jacobethan front, with high stacks and big hoodmoulds; the central pediment records the long history of the foundation established by John de Plumptre in 1392.

Short Stairs, lined with flats by *Grogan Culling Architects*, 1996–9, is another cliff route. It ascends from Malin Hill to Short Hill, raised over cellars, its retaining walls and stairs of *c.* 1740 restored 2007. Two mid-C18 houses here were extended as warehousing in the C19–C20: No. 1

with a stone Venetian door surround; No. 2 with a central Venetian window over a pedimented doorcase with fanlight and brackets. Warehouses along **Short Hill**. Nos. 8 and 9, 1860s; a rusticated ground floor and carriage arch to No. 8 and L.O. Trivett's initials on No. 9. The derelict No. 10 is an 1850s palazzo in orange brick. Opposite, **Hollowstone**, widened in 1740 as the town's principal SE entrance. Imposing warehouses on falling ground, earlier stone cellars exposed on the Bellar Gate corner, SE. No. 1, by *Sutton & Gregory*, 1908, has stone entrances with faience wreaths and the Plumptre coat of arms. The gabled block alongside has brick piers on stone heads; by *W. Dymock Pratt*, 1904 for the family firm, an extension to the plain, twelve-bay No. 53 Stoney Street, by *F. Williamson*, 1873 with a chimney. Short Hill has another gap before **High Pavement** resumes with No. 56, formerly St Mary's vicarage. C18, wide, extended as a warehouse in the C19. w again, No. 54 is mid-C18, two storeys of Venetian windows topped by Diocletian ones; more Venetian windows behind an exceptionally deep plan. The second part of the walk begins back at No. 53 Stoney Street, opposite.

The Nineteenth-century Warehouse District

Stoney Street was the N–S spine of the Saxon town, where the medieval grid is most assertive. Its w side was dominated by Plumptre House, rebuilt by *Colen Campbell*, 1724–30. It was demolished in 1855–6 for lace warehousing.

To the E, Nos. 49–51, warehousing now offices, 1883 by *R.C. Sutton* for an American entrepreneur, Philo Mills. Italianate, arched windows linked by hoodmoulds; the corner entrance with a bulging pediment and curved doors. Beyond, **Plumptre Street** was cut in 1797 through Plumptre House's paddock. On its s side, No. 4 by *Truman & Pratt*, 1884, two stepped ranges, its corner doorway with a bearded keystone and granite pilasters. Nos. 6–8 are three houses, *c.* 1800 and *c.* 1820; quickly altered to warehousing and doorways blocked. Nos. 10–12 (now **Stoneyard Apartments**), by *T.C. Hine* for E. Steegman, dated 1861; *c.* 1600 style with an E-plan and ES monogram. The central gable bears a pediment while the others are Flemish; more stilted than Hine's other warehouses. Then **The Point**, flats by *Church Lukas*, 2001, warehouse-style with gunmetal glazing. On the N side, **Lexington Place**, flats by the *William Saunders Partnership*, 2000–2, incorporate two warehouses by *W.H. Higginbottom*, linked over a covered way, and with prominent pilasters – the E of 1911–12, the w, with tripartite top lights of 1903. Next door, the white-tiled **Mills Buildings**, entered from Plumptre Place. No. 3, by *William Knight*, 1879, now houses the **High Pavement Unitarians**: Italianate with linked arched windows under keystones, and encaustic tilework. No. 1 Plumptre Street, a pair of *c.* 1800, doors again blocked in a factory conversion.

Returning to Stoney Street, **Mill House** (No. 47), from 1883, mirrors *Sutton*'s Nos. 49–51 opposite, suggesting he is again the architect. w, No. 34 (**Eastgate House**), 1850s: rusticated basement, carriage arch with

68. Broadway, warehousing, by T.C. Hine, 1855–6

lion's head; rounded corners add tautness and apparent height. E, No. 39, by *W.H. Higginbottom*, 1908, entered between banded columns on the corner with **Plumptre Place**. There, *Gilbert S. Doughty*'s **Mills Buildings**, dated 1906 on a segment-pedimented doorcase; heart motifs in its gates. At the end, in a courtyard, the former **General Baptist Church**, 1799, doors at either end, extended in 1834. Meetings ceased *c.* 1888, and the building later became **St Mary's Schools**. In the angle between Plumptre Place and Duke's Place is the blunt-ended **Swann House**, by *John Howitt*, 1889, a long, narrow extension by *Harry Allcock*, 1903. (For the rest here *see* Barker Gate, p. 110).

Returning to **Stoney Street**, No. 32a, w, is the **Broadway Business Centre**, an 1850s warehouse restored following a fire by *W.A. Heazell*, 1885. Keystones, tiles in the cornice entablature. It marks the entrance to the showpiece street **Broadway** [68], built on the site of Plumptre House by *T.C. Hine*, 1855–6, and serpentine in plan. Hine's brick is slightly orange, the details more delicate, and the balance of classical balusters and quoins with floriate shafts more considered than other architects' work. On the N side, No. 5, with a topshop by *Sidney R. Stevenson*, 1882, turns a recessed, rounded corner, with a projecting four-bay front to Stoney Street. On Broadway it presents a complex 4–3–3 composition with a canted bay to an otherwise set-back centre-piece. On the s side, **Birkin Building** for Richard Birkin, lace manufacturer, dated 1855. A bee and many initials over the carriage arch – including T.C.H. with an architect's dividers and square. Within the arch, a re-set two-light window, C12, from St Mary's, and the Plumptre arms. The carriage arch is flanked by balustraded, stone canted bays with round-arched glazing, the smaller lights voussoirs in glass; round-arched windows to the adjoining brick façades. The frontage makes a picturesque Italianate curve nearly closing the street, with another canted oriel and balcony. A continuous attic floor and eaves cornice bind the composition. No. 3, opposite, contorts round the concave (N) side of the curve with a three-storey prow at the apex. Its centrepiece is a large flat staircase window of unmoulded tracery. The simpler Nos. 2–4 have an oriel over the left-hand entrance and Birkin's initials in the door keystones.

Broadway returns, w, to **St Mary's Gate**. w, Nos. 5–47 Halifax Place, flats for the Bridge Housing Society by *Peter Hill* of *Cullen Carter & Hill*, 1981–3, admired then for re-creating the street, now looking tame. Cut through the development and out the s end, where can be seen County House's extraordinarily tall staircase window, and, left, the timber-clad eco-house created by *Marsh Grochowski*, 2005–6, for Alan Simpson M.P. out of an 1840s backland workshop. Then into **Halifax Place** itself. Opposite, **Halifax House**, by *J. Bindon Carter*, 1883–4, has a castellated entrance and broad mullion-and-transom windows. The **Lace Market Theatre** was adapted in 1970–2 from an independent chapel, 1760; timbers in its kingpost roof may be earlier. Its rendered C19 front is overburdened by doors and windows.

Ahead, **Pilcher Gate**, largely demolished in the 1960s for road-widening. The corner warehouse, No. 16 by *T.C. Hine*, *c.* 1856, survives. Upper windows linked by hoodmoulds, imposing corner entrance, large staircase window with plate tracery. N, No. 33, **Milbie House**, by *Fothergill Watson*, 1889 incised into the stone. Despite granite columns to the ground floor and Fothergill's distinctive big-hatted dormers, it is relatively symmetrical and reticent.

Next door, No. 41 was built for the Sherwin family between 1689 and 1699, when it appeared on Kip and Knyff's view with three gables like those of Brewhouse Yard. These were remodelled *c.* 1807, and a NE wing added by 1820. When Pilcher Gate was widened *c.* 1884, No. 41 lost its front garden, the door was lowered and the steps transferred inside the entrance hall. A warehouse conversion, by 1886, added a wing in the rear courtyard and inserted a large window into the left front (original openings reinstated *c.* 1980). Central entrance with fanlight and Ionic pilasters. Square windows to the side elevations, those on the upper floors set progressively nearer the corners; evidence on the second floor suggests a similar pattern on the w elevation now blocked by Milbie House, and that the main rooms were in the corners. Inside is a magnificent late C17 staircase of four broad flights – all with heavy newel posts and thick turned and twisted balusters. Two secondary entrances front St Mary's Gate, *c.* 1820, one in a wing of that date.

To the s, No. 27 **St Mary's Gate**, for the Turner family, a late C18 house in the *Stretton* canon. Over-extended giant order of pilasters with acanthus capitals, balustrading beneath the first-floor windows, and round attic windows. A C19 carriage entrance inserted when converted to a warehouse (before 1880) disrupts the ground-floor arcading. A sumptuous interior. Large rooms to front and rear, separated by a top-lit staircase hall at right angles. A delicate stone service stair runs from basement to attic behind it. The stone cantilevered main stair, partly collapsed in 2007, has an intricate wrought-iron balustrade with medallions; the walls have dainty swags and arches; a fanlight lights the service stair. Arched overdoors incorporating plaster roundel reliefs. Fluted mouldings and a metope cornice in the front ground-floor room are similar to *William Stretton*'s at No. 26 Low Pavement (p. 10). The most elaborate room is the first-floor rear, with an Adamesque swag frieze and door surrounds. The bedroom floor is curiously low, with an old-fashioned trabeated ceiling.

N up **St Mary's Gate**, Nos. 14–18 retain early C19 domestic frontages, with a hosiery factory behind reached through the additional doorway. In **St Mary's Place**, left, No. 4, s, five low storeys, seemingly a pre-1850 warehouse, and a taller warehouse beyond (**Nottingham Buddhist Centre**), its centrepiece a double-height architrave with volutes. To the N, a development of flats, shops and restaurants, project planners *Maber Associates*. Built in two phases, the ambitious **Lace Market Square** by *Franklin Ellis*, 2005–7, landscaped by *Fiona Heron* with wire trees; behind it, w, **One Fletcher Gate** by *Church Lukas*, 2002–5. The square exposes views of the rear of the **Adams Building** [69], by *T.C. Hine* and perhaps his masterpiece (the main front on Stoney Street, p. 109). Seven bays of 1855 for Adams, Page & Co. to the left, matched by a longer range of 1865 that includes an off-set angled entrance and a doorway with lace edging cut in stone. To the right a set-back entrance arch under stone pediments on three levels. Converted for **New College Nottingham** by *Crampin Pring McArtney*, 1997. Brick arcading behind

69. Adams Building, by T.C. Hine, rear, detail of 1865 additions on Lace Market Square

The Lace Warehouses

The name Lace Market is apt, describing where 'brown' (undyed) lace and finished goods were sold. While London's Wood Street remained the national centre for textile trades, Nottingham developed a strong independent export market. In an industry dependent on fashion, marketing and finishing were critical. Warehouses assumed a common form based on that built for Thomas Adams in 1855, with a first-floor showroom (sometimes given an elaborate stair), and an attic finishing shop under continuous clerestories. These are shown as 'lanterns' in contemporary plans and today called 'topshops'. Little attention was given to fireproof construction compared with warehouses elsewhere; floors are of timber, occasionally lined in gypsum, supported on cast-iron columns.

The trade slumped *c.* 1908 and revived only with the arrival after 1945 of nylon. But finishing joined manufacture in Long Eaton, while the hosiery and garment industries declined in the 1970s.

70. Advertisement for Thomas Adams & Co., showing their showrooms in Nottingham and London, and factory in Sherwood Hill, 1856

the carriage entrance with cast-iron beams on brackets; otherwise cast-iron columns support timber floors. Hine's 1880 range, N, uses darker brick, with a curved corner and a carriage entrance; a tympanum vividly depicts trade and industry under Britannia's supervision.

Warser Gate has late C19 red brick warehouses on its N side, e.g. No. 7 by *Thomas Wright*, 1884–5, narrow with pilasters, and *Evans &*

Jolley's No. 11, 1890, with a high off-set gable, and Corinthian capitals to the ground floor. Bolder is No. 23, by *John Howitt & Son,* 1909–10. Baroque, with a rusticated ground floor rising to massive keystones around the right-hand entrance, double doors and pilasters. Then a lower warehouse by *W. & R. & F. Booker*, 1890–1, with an oriel perched over the office and carriageway entrances. Nos. 31–33 by *W. Dymock Pratt*, 1909, classical with rustication across doorcase and flanking pilasters. Finally, a puzzle. No. 35, inscribed '1879 RB' for Rogers & Black, is listed as one of Britain's earliest steel-framed warehouses. The present building was there by 1904, but the surviving 1879 plan, by *John H. Kent* of Chesterfield, shows a conventional brick structure, albeit for a rear extension and the staircase. The brickwork of the corner entrance is subtly different from that to Warser Gate, an elevation, along with the jack-arched concrete floors behind it, apparently of *c.* 1900.

Back into **Stoney Street**. The N spur has on its left Nos. 2 and 2a, early C19 houses, with typical wedge lintels. Opposite, on the corner of Goose Gate, No. 1 was the **Nag's Head** pub, mid-C19, rendered, with stone dressings. No. 3, 1887, designed 1884 as a warehouse by *R. C. Sutton*. The **Old Angel** pub, originally *c.* 1800, the Gothic stone entrance and four bays added along Woolpack Lane of 1878 by *Lawrence Bright*. The tall song-room windows may be his. Across Woolpack Lane, No. 15 by *Heazell & Sons*, 1910. Rusticated ground floor, oriel over the entrance. They also designed No. 17, 1901, its ground floor enlivened by giant openings and keystones, and No. 19, with round-headed windows, 1898. Nos. 21–27, by *W.D. Pratt*, 1910, is a complex composition – an earlier building on the left, made symmetrical around a new carriage arch, with a long extension, right, incorporating another entrance.

Left, the Italianate front of *Hine*'s massive **Adams Building**, this first phase of 1854–5. Described on opening as roomy and well-lit, it even had a basement chapel for the workforce. An E-plan, with a mainly Ancaster stone ground floor and centrepiece. Its canted bays repeat the round arches of the other windows, as on Broadway [68], though greater height and narrower width make a tauter composition. The ironwork doors have lace tracery. The interior, partly a public restaurant, has a spinal arcade and a stone stair with a cast-iron balustrade serving the first-floor showroom. The chapel retains one stained-glass window. Next door, No. 16 by *Evans & Jolley*, 1872, uses a dourer red brick. A canted bay and high gable. Additions, 1881, on King's Place, cut across an earlier town house at its end. Across the street, the 1960s road clearance site was filled by *James McArtney*'s **car park**, 1985–6. Beyond it, No. 30, *c.* 1890, with a raised ground floor, the first-floor central window in a stone architrave. No. 26 by *W. Dymock Pratt*, 1913–14, its glazing suggesting a steel frame behind giant pilasters. Rear range by *S. Dutton Walker*, 1878. Opposite, E, No. 37, **Price House**, fills the block S to Plumptre Street: by *John Howitt*, 1894. Nine paired bays, terracotta dressings articulating the end entrances.

On the NE corner, No. 29 Stoney Street and No. 1 Barker Gate are warehouses by *Watson Fothergill*, 1897, now **Nevilles Textiles**. Polychromatic banding with shafts to the windows and a corner oriel; bartizans rise through the pentice to flank a hipped garret. **Barker Gate** has the worst scars from the intended 1960s road, the s side cleared. Amorphous warehouses on the corner of Riste's Place, by *W. & R. Booker*, 1883, the corner elevation built or rebuilt 1895 (dated gable). The Barker Gate elevation follows the original plans, with a tall staircase window and carriage entrance.

The scale drops at the entrance to **St Mary's Burial Ground**, cleared and landscaped in 1907. **St Mary's Hall** began as St Mary's Boys' School and soup kitchen, the left portion by *T.C. Hine & Son*, dated 1874, domestic medieval, sideways to the street. The earlier gabled range, *c.* 1834, was rebuilt after it became the Institute (church hall), 1905, and much altered by *Maber Associates* as its offices, 1991. Opposite, an extension to **St Mary's Schools** links the former chapel in Plumptre Place with **Duke's Place**, by *John Howitt*, 1904–5, with stone mullion-and-transom windows. To the E another burial ground, 1742, part adapted as the boys' playground, denoted by railings and an archway. On the N side a crude 1980s block with green gables, remodelled as flats in 1999 by *Paul Gauguin*, incorporating Nos. 23 and 23a – houses of *c.* 1830 with attic topshops, a transitional stage in the lace industry between domestic and factory units.

Belward Street has the modernistic **Ice House** flats, by the *Raven Group*, 2001–6, and the **National Ice Centre**, by *Nottingham City Architect's Department* with *FaulknerBrowns*, 1999–2000, set behind **Bolero Square**, the nearest to a show front given this constricted lump. The main arena is designed also for concerts, holding up to 9,000 people; alongside is a public/training rink. Supremely practical but no way architectural. The **sculpture** by *Wolfgang & Heron*, Axel, 2003, should rotate. **Hockley Mill**, left, is a narrow mid-C19 range with a painted gable-end, and a prominent green corner apartment block by *Maber Associates* with the *Urban Design Forum*, simplified in execution, 2004–7.

Goose Gate and North

At the bottom of Belward Street, **Hockley** is the area's E gateway; redeveloped as a shopping area in the 1930s. To the w, **Goose Gate**, continuing the E–W shopping alignment, slowly reasserts a C19 character. At the foot, **Emmanuel House**, a former Burton's store, 1929 by *Nathaniel Martin*, in-house architect. Upper windows separated by pylons; Burton's name survives on Cranbrook Street. No. 60, s side, by *J. Rigby Poyser*, 1908, has a cut-down catslide roof. Then the white hulk of the **Hockley Methodist Chapel**, 1783. Next door, five shops by *Marshall & Tweedy*, 1938–9 with herringbone panels, the centre set forward with a giant order. No. 30, **Freewheel**, has blind stone gables, by *Booker & Shepherd*, 1913–14.

On the N side, Nos. 41–51, flats and maisonettes by the *City Architect's Department*, 1978–80. Balconies supported on steel columns. Shops by *A.N. Bromley*, 1883, with a hipped roof, turn the corner to Brightmoor Street. Back on the S side, Nos. 24–28, dated 1873, with tripartite first-floor lancets. Jesse Boot leased Nos. 16–20 (**Oxfam**) in 1878–80. Rebuilt for him by *R.C. Sutton*, 1882, they have a two-storey cast-iron shopfront with barley-sugar columns [71], the first floor (despite large windows) for storage, with staff accommodation above. No. 14, early C19, shows their previous form. Next to Angel Alley, No. 12, with a first-floor oriel, by *Thomas Wright*, 1881–2. On the N, Nos. 21–23 a partial C19 refronting, probably by *Walker & Howitt*, of a *c.* 1700 house with a hipped roof and dormers; staircase with moulded and ramped handrail and two balusters per tread, one twisted. The attic flight has single balusters. No. 23 has an early C18 panelled second-floor room with panelled overmantel. On the S side, Nos. 2–10, early C19 with wedge lintels, and exceptionally

71. Jesse Boot's original store, Nos. 16–20 Goose Gate, by R.C. Sutton, 1882

narrow rear staircase windows. The scale of Victorian building escalates on the N side, with blocks by *S. Dutton Walker & John Howitt*. Nos. 15–17, 1881, continue their corner range into Heathcoat Street, terracotta, 1879–80. Timber shopfronts with trefoil top lights, save No. 17 – a bar from the first. An entrance between granite shafts serves the upper chambers, **Heathcote Buildings** (the street's pre-1930 spelling). The courtyard elevations rebuilt.

Heathcoat Street, created by widening Beck Lane in 1874, has to the w **Carlton Buildings**, again by *Walker & Howitt*, 1881, continuing into Broad Street, massive and red. On the E side, No. 14, **Churchill House**, late C18, stuccoed but old-fashioned. One room deep, set over a raised courtyard and basement, perhaps a service range to Morley House, the abutment to which shows it must be later. Wrought-iron railings and arched gate, *c.* 1750, with openwork piers topped by jolly heads and an overthrow, moved from Morley House in the street widening.

Morley House was built in 1750 (date on hopper head), Charles and Mrs A. Morley having made their fortune manufacturing Nottingham's brown salt-glazed earthenware. Austere, with stone dressings. George Gill acquired it in 1854 for the **People's Hall**, a temperance centre related to his People's College (p. 128). Surprisingly rich inside. A dado-panelled entrance hall with a fine open-well staircase – triple-turned and twisted balusters [72], a ramped handrail paralleled by wainscoting – leading to a landing with pedimented doorcases. Panelled rooms on

both floors with box cornices, dado panelling, eared fireplaces and overmantels, details perfect for 1750. Morley House had a vista across the lane, but no rear garden. The N rooms were extended in 1854 to form a semi-basement women's hall (now shop), ground-floor snooker hall and a meeting room with a skylight over queenpost trusses. Gill's Trustees also built the adjoining shop, by *R.C. Sutton*, 1887, with three timber gables (those to the side topped by dragons) over oriels, as a crèche, shop and café linked to the women's hall. Behind is a terrace of four houses, by the Trustees *c.* 1860.

72. Morley House, Heathcoat Street, 1750, detail of staircase

73. Broadway Cinema, Broad Street, Screen One, by Burrell Foley Fischer, 1993

On the w side, across High Cross Street, C19 houses over shops, the oldest canted to the corner. At the end the former **Old Plough** pub, rebuilt by *W.B. Starr & Hall*, 1927–8, with sunburst gables. The E side has more C19 buildings: a house with oriels, 1882 by *W. & R. & F. Booker*, then shops and offices by *Lawrence Bright*, 1898–9, with – left – a Jacobean doorway, *œil de bœuf* gable and large stack. Sandwiched next door, a Queen Anne house and surgery by *Martin & Hardy* for two doctor brothers, 1883, with oriel, volutes and sunflower gables. At the end more shops by *Bright*, 1897–8, with further gables. Turning left, **Lower Parliament Street** was an improvement scheme, opened 1930.

On its angle with King Edward Street is the former Palais de Danse, the start of the Sneinton walk (*see* p. 146).

S, on the corner of Lower Parliament Street and Broad Street, is the **New Market Hotel**, rebuilt 1929 by *W.B. Starr & Hall* as the Plough and Sickle. White faience with pilasters, shallow broken first-floor pediments. Inside, a massive central counter and bar back, a lobby to the lounge hall, left, and a rear smoke room. Opposite, No. 34 is a curved block by *S. Dutton Walker & John Howitt*, 1883–4; then No. 43 **Broad Street**, a C19 house refronted by *F. Parker*, 1899, with an oriel; a classical **telephone exchange**, dated 1938, and early C19 houses and shops. On the E side, Nos. 26–30, three houses with weavers' workshops. Some late C17 chamfered beams inside, but largely C18. Then the **High Cross** pub, with an Art Deco fin, by *W.B. Starr & Hall*, 1936–7. Across High Cross Street is **Shaw's**, a warehouse by *John Howitt*, 1912–13 with stone keystones and voussoirs to the corner and ends.

Opposite on the w side of Broad Street a **Sunday School**, looking 1950s but dated 1819. Dominating the E side is the **Broadway Cinema**, built as a Wesleyan chapel by *S.S. Rawlinson*, 1839; a plaque commemorates William Booth, who committed himself to God here aged fifteen.

From 1959 it housed the Co-op Film Theatre. A study by *Burrell Foley Fischer* in 1990 resulted in its remodelling [73] with a 140-seat second screen and café bar, 1993; in 1997 they added a glazed link to a narrow 1950s office building alongside, enlivened by glass screens by *Martin Donlin* and *David Pearl*. The blue-glass frontage framing the giant columns of the classical chapel front, 2006; doors slide open in summer to create a balcony bar. Two basement screens opened 2006, interiors by *Leaf Design*, Screen 4 with double seats in *Paul Smith* fabric.

Opposite, Nos. 15–17, a warehouse by *S. Dutton Walker & Howitt*, 1883–4, has twin dormers and chunky brackets. Nos. 11–13 are *c.* 1860, with a rusticated ground floor. Then No. 9a (**Muse**), a chapel dated 1863 in its stepped gable. Converted to warehousing by *Hedley J. Price*, 1903, when he refronted No. 7 with a broad tripartite centre under a Diocletian window. No. 5, *c.* 1850–60, has a big cornice, Italianate, as has the earlier No. 21 Carlton Street, on the corner. Back on the E side the stuccoed **Nottingham General Dispensary** by *Nicholson & Goddard*, 1841–3, classical with giant Ionic pilasters. The bay window, right, was added by *Sydney Birbeck* of *Evans & Jolley*, 1883.

Carlton Street is the W continuation of Goose Gate. On the SW corner with Stoney Street very tall houses of *c.* 1800, with attic workshops. The houses then step down to four and three storeys, the upper floors with varied stone wedge lintels, many with keystones. No. 32 is late C18, a fan motif in the lintels repeated as metopes in the cornice frieze, Stretton-style. Most of the other buildings are arranged in pairs. No. 6, *c.* 1860, has bewhiskered faces to the first-floor keystones, and more realistic headstops and barley-sugar twisted columns to the second floor. On the N side, No. 15, *c.* 1840, painted brick, late Regency style. The street is dominated by the **George**, now **Comfort Hotel**, and its big French roofs. A weird confection: a tiled façade over shops to Goose Gate (*Heazell & Sons*, 1914); but the E two bays are separated by giant pilasters with giant heads squashed under broken first-floor pediments. An open-well C19 stair inside.

On the W corner of **George Street**, No. 3, C18, genial orange brick with curved corner sashes. A competition for Wright & Co.'s Bank next door at No. 1 Carlton Street, 1858, was jointly won by *Samuel Walker* of Nottingham and *C.H. Edwards* of London. Edwards's design was built, an L-plan to Carlton Street and a more dignified range on George Street with twin buttresses and a balustraded parapet. Now **Lloyd's Bar**. *Evans & Jolley* infilled the L in the late 1880s, but Edwards's tall, slightly Egyptian front can be seen behind their stone two-tiered entrance. The banking hall has a trabeated ceiling on Corinthian marble columns, the walls with pilasters and dentilled cornices.

On the E side of George Street, No. 4 is a gaily painted warehouse of *c.* 1870, its Venetian Gothic windows squeezed between high, narrow doors. No. 6 is stuccoed classical. No. 8 was Nottingham's first legitimate post-Reformation Roman Catholic **church**, now offices, *c.* 1825–8 by *Edward Willson*, Lincolnshire County Surveyor, a major Gothic

74. No. 15 George Street, panel by Benjamin Creswick, 1894–5, depicting Wollaton Hall under construction

scholar and friend of A.W.N. Pugin. The priest was his brother (cf. St Barnabas's Cathedral, p. 50). It resembles a chapel, a stone pediment with a cross and understated trefoiled lancets. Also by Willson No. 10, the **Presbytery**, dated 1827, with a canted bay. The **Arts Theatre** occupies **Staveley's Particular Baptist Chapel**, 1815. It has lost its detailing, save a porch with four Greek Doric columns; remodelled as a theatre for the Co-operative Society by *A.H. Betts*, 1946–8. Across Old Lenton Street, offices with moulded brick openings by *A.E. Lambert*, 1904.

Down on the w side, No. 15 was *Watson Fothergill's* office [17], 1894–5. The lower parts are Gothic, with trefoil-heads to the first-floor windows and the office entrance, set between engaged shafts, left. A first-floor oriel, high timber spire and double dormer. The decoration combines homage and advertisement, proclaiming 'Watson Fothergill Architect' over the door. Is it Fothergill who presides as the central statue, plans in hand and cathedral model at his feet? Busts of A.W.N. Pugin and G.E. Street, while G.G. Scott, William Burges and Norman Shaw are name-checked. Four terracotta panels by *Benjamin Creswick* depict classical and medieval buildings, and Wollaton Hall, under construction [74]. A side passage leads to **Brewitt's Place**, the best surviving example of Nottingham's yard housing (*see* pp. 12–13), *c.* 1845. More early C19 framework knitters' houses and workshops in **Lincoln Street**, but those fronting George Street were remodelled as **Leighton House** by *Hatfield & Co.*, 1934, rendered with a double-height centrepiece.

Opposite, the front of the 1938 **Telephone Exchange**, next to the original nine-bay exchange, 1898–9, extended N by two bays in 1907, both phases by *A.N. Bromley*. Paired windows in terracotta surrounds, a large carriage entrance with keystones, left, beyond a smaller door and a pediment containing a candlestick telephone in relief. Converted to flats by *Franklin Ellis*, 2002–4. At the end, shops and offices by *W.B. Starr &*

75. Central Methodist Mission, George Street, by R.C. Sutton, 1876

Hall, 1937–8, with a glazed staircase tower and a sharp corner to Lower Parliament Street.

On the w side, the stark **Viscosa House**, dated 1924, by *H. Alderman Dickman*. Next to it is *Dickman*'s Motor Auction Mart, 1922, with a garage entrance under a Diocletian window, extending in an L to a similar entrance on Lincoln Street. At the N end of George Street is the **Central Methodist Mission**, a rebuilding by *R.C. Sutton*, 1876, of an 1817 chapel. Cheap brick with a square corner tower and high basement schoolroom, the chapel with a pretty trefoil-fronted gallery and organ case [75]. Stained glass to the lower aisles and w end, mainly early C20. The adjoining schools and vestries were rebuilt in 1986 and extended 1999, forming a glazed front to Lower Parliament Street.

On **Lower Parliament Street**, N side, **Argos** was a wholesale fruit store by *A.N. Bromley*, 1900, using his favoured red terracotta. Finally, on the s side, the **Dog and Partridge** pub, early C19 (left), extended to the corner *c.* 1900 and remodelled by *W.B. Starr & Hall*, 1925, with a high parapet. We are now at the **Victoria Centre**, part of Walk 2 (p. 83).

Outer Areas

Walk 5.

The Park

The Park lies immediately w of the Castle Rock, high land forming a horseshoe round the N, making a steeply falling bowl of the estate. It developed from a royal hunting ground to become, via the Dukes of Newcastle – owners from 1663 – Nottingham's premier suburban estate and the most rewarding architecturally. It remains a gated, regulated enclave and a remarkable lung for any city.

Nottingham Castle's hunting grounds were first recorded in 1178, though they were perhaps a century older. Edward IV incorporated the monastery of St Mary de la Roche, sw. By 1609 the Park had 129 acres from the River Leen to Standard Hill. Development began on Standard Hill from 1780, when land was granted for a General Hospital. *William Stretton* laid out streets in 1807, and built St James's Church, 1808–9; demolished 1936. In 1822 the 4th Duke commissioned plans for the land N and W from *John Jephson*. But when building began in 1827 he employed *Peter Frederick Robinson*, fashionable architect of Leamington Spa. The Park was planned as a grid, although Park Terrace, The Ropewalk and Park Valley were threaded picturesquely

76. Walk 5

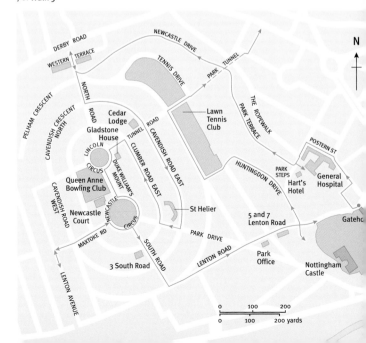

77. Park Estate, aerial view

around and below the ravine. Semi-detached villas were interspersed with eyecatchers. But the Duke concentrated on developments on his estates elsewhere. The design eventually realized was more striking and appropriate to the contours [77]; there was never a church (proposals for one in Newcastle Circus *c.* 1897–8 were roundly rejected by residents). Earth moving was undertaken from the 1820s, initially to relieve unemployment, without which today's gradients would have been still more extreme.

In 1851 the 4th Duke died. His son turned to *T.C. Hine* and in 1854 building began in earnest. Hine designed nearly 200 houses, mostly brick; though few are special, their overall effect is grandly homogeneous, thanks to The Park's scale, consistency of materials and mature planting. Hine's recognizable motifs are a distinct pierced star set in a roundel; plate tracery with round lights between transoms, as in his warehousing; single quatrefoils; and decorative tile bands, occasionally with elaborate door surrounds. Other architects worked

78. General Hospital, Standard Hill, left, by John Simpson, 1781–2, raised by T.C. Hine, 1854–5, chapel (extreme left); right, Jubilee Wing, by Alfred Waterhouse, 1897–1900

under Hine's scrutiny as the Duke's surveyor. Roads were embanked and high walls ensured privacy, as did coachhouses and service quarters fronting the street. Many houses present their show fronts to the gardens, overlooking the Castle, or falling steeply down the ravine; entrances are often at mid-level. This walk concentrates on the more rewarding E side of the estate.

As Nottingham's élite began to prefer commuting by car, in the 1930s many houses were converted to flats. From 1952 residents were permitted to acquire the freeholds, with covenants; coachhouses were converted and houses built over gardens. The area has Nottingham's best concentration of one-off modern houses, those following designation as a conservation area in 1969 of genuine quality. Ownership passed in 1938 to Oxford University and in 1986 to Nottingham Park Estate Ltd., run by residents.

This walk starts outside the Castle Gatehouse (*see* Major Buildings, p. 40), from which **Standard Hill** rises N. At the bottom, left, a double house, *c.* 1810, perhaps by *Stretton*, grand yet clearly suburban in character; adapted 1901 as St Mary's and St Peter's vicarages. Left, steps rise to **King Charles's Street**; a plaque commemorates Charles I raising his standard, 1642. It is dominated by the war memorial **nurses' home**, w, by *Robert Evans Jun.* of *Evans, Clark & Woollatt*, 1919–23, stylistically reflecting the C17 castle; converted to flats by *Maber Associates*, 1996–9. Standard Hill, right, has, E, the early C19 **St James's Terrace**, and, w, the **General Hospital**, the older parts surviving as flats and restaurants to a masterplan by *Hawkins Brown Maber*, 1998–2000. In 1778 a banker, John Key, left £500 towards a County Hospital; the site was jointly given by the 3rd Duke of Newcastle and the Corporation. Today the centrepiece remains *John Simpson*'s block [78], 1781–2, extended in 1787 and 1802, and raised a storey in 1854–5 by *T.C. Hine*, who supplied Italianate details and the present clock. Behind is his contemporary chapel and a wing of 1877. *Alfred Waterhouse* partly concealed the complex from Standard Hill with his **Jubilee Wing**, 1897–1900: circular, five storeys and recounted to Pevsner as 'a joy to work in'; remodelled as a restaurant by *Crampin Pring*, 1997. Housing by *Maber Associates*, **Arena Apartments** of 1995, forms a bowl around Simpson and Hine's work; **City Point** added behind in 2003–5. Hine's accident wing on **Park Row**, 1877–9, remains, remodelled by the *Harry Mein Partnership* as flats 1999–2002. Behind, **Hart's Hotel**, 2001–3 by *Marsh Grochowski*, followed the success of **Hart's Restaurant** in the adjoining hospital offices. Park Row was the site of the city defences' outer ditch, infilled 1777. On the corner of The Ropewalk, the lumpen **Outpatients' Department**, by *Robert Evans Jun.*, 1927, remains in health-service use. Beyond, the **Eye Hospital**, Queen Anne, by *Arthur Marshall*, 1910, now flats with ponderous penthouses by *Lewis & Hickey*, 2006. For the rest of the Ropewalk, *see* Walk 6 (p. 128).

At the s of Park Row, **Tower House** introduces the Park's stylistic protagonists in a single confection. Begun probably by *P.F. Robinson* and *William Paterson*, 1827–33, Italianate; porch, oriel and bands *c.* 1860 by *T.C. Hine*, going Gothic; given a timber attic by *Fothergill Watson*, 1880s. It marks the entrance to the **Park Estate**. The road curves, right, to Park Terrace while, left, **Park Steps**, 1829, plunge down the ravine.

Building began on **Park Terrace** with boxy stuccoed villas, Nos. 7–12, followed by three pairs, Nos. 1–6, and 'the Italian Villas', Nos. 15–17, by 1834. Between them is a 1960s–70s line hugging the cliff, their site cleared for a putative ring road, Park Way. No. 14a, **The Studio**, a mono-pitched house over garaging, *c.* 1967, addresses the street, its neighbours the view. The **Brown House**, 1973 by *Graham Brown* for himself, has a street façade of grey Kinton brick, with sliding windows in a steel frame facing the view. Extensions by *Marsh Grochowski*, 2007. **Abbot House**, 1966 by *Brown*, single-storey to the street with built-in planters, has three storeys behind. No. 14d is *Brown*'s current home, *c.* 1986 – a white concrete block frontage concealing a glazed, California-style braced steel frame on stilts, a striking contrast with the c19 Gothic gazebo alongside, which served Alderman Herbert's caves (*see* topic box, p. 6).

The Victorian Park Estate

The core of The Park was developed only from the 1850s, the 4th Duke concentrating on redeveloping Thurland Hall (p. 89). *Robinson* laid out North Road and Western Terrace, but built few houses save in Park Valley, 1838–9. Houses by *T.C. Hine* began in 1844.

Hine's style appears at Nos. 18–20 w along **Park Terrace**, Gothic, dated TCH 1881. Thence the centre is reached via **Newcastle Drive**, enormous houses whose principal elevations face s views: Nos. 1–13 (odd) by *Hine*, *c.* 1856–9, and Nos. 15–17 by *A.N. Bromley*, *c.* 1878, with stepped staircase windows and oriels. Opposite, a modern brick house inserted against the cliff by *Beckett Jackson Thompson*, 2006–7. The inner side continues with No. 19, dated 1886, Gothic; Nos. 21 and 23, pastily half-timbered, by *Fothergill Watson*, 1884; No. 27, 1884–5 by *Fothergill*, with sunflowers. By *Hine*, No. 29–33, *c.* 1856–9, and Nos. 35 and 37, slightly later, lugubrious Renaissance. No. 39 is by *Fothergill Watson*, dated 1886; following the curve into **Tattershall Drive**, it erupts into polychromatic banding, with a half-timbered square tower.

Newcastle and Tattershall Drives meet at **North Road**, on The Park's central axis. Right, it leads uphill past Western Terrace to **Derby Terrace** (p. 128). Robinson's stuccoed lodge (now **Walton's Hotel**) with bow windows and large sashes, completed by 1834; extended by *T.C. Hine*, his star on the retaining walls to Derby Road. **Western Terrace** followed. From the w, No. 11, **Lincoln Villa**, stuccoed, by *Robinson c.* 1840, canted bays to the garden, is followed by stuccoed pairs, pedimented to the gardens, 1844 by *Hine*. Across North Road, Nos. 5–6, 3–4 are more assertively his; giant Ionic pilasters on their s elevations. Beyond, **One Degree West**, by *Julian Marsh* and *Mike Askey*, 2004, its mechanized garage concealed below stepped mezzanines facing the view.

Hine developed the central area with concentric circles around the dumb-bells of Lincoln and Newcastle circuses; Duke William Mount is their linking arm. *John Loverseed* built much of **Pelham Crescent** (1869–74) and **Cavendish Crescent North**, including **Haddon House** for himself, initialled JL. Opposite, No. 9, Peveril Tower *c.* 1875 by *Hine*. Rendered exterior with an octagonal turret. Houses E of North Road concentrate their effects on the SE garden fronts. No. 14, attributed to *Watson Fothergill c.* 1896, has half-timbering and sunflower panels. **Cedar Lodge** is an intruding block of flats, 1964–7 by *J. Enness & Co.*

Across Tunnel Road, there are larger houses in **Cavendish Road East**, beginning with *Hine*'s **Cavendish Court**, No. 25, 1884–5 with gable stars. No. 25C, **Cavendish Cottage**, Arts and Crafts. Then a group with half-timbered gables: No. 27, the **Bishop's House**, 1883; No. 28 (**Gartree**) with stained glass, 1884; No. 31 with stained glass and Gothic tracery, 1884 for Marriott Ogle Tarbotton. Could he have designed this group? No. 33 (**Redcliffe**) by *Stockdale Harrison*, dated 1898 with heavy half-timbered gables. Beyond the squash club a group by *Hine* includes **Cavendish House**, 1881; **Overdale** and **Elmhurst**, both 1883, all behind coach houses. On the corner of **Park Drive** the grandiose **Ashley House** by *S. Dutton Walker*, 1877, with a Gothic porch and an octagonal corner bay facing the garden. Fine views of the Castle down Park Drive. Opposite, No. 1 **Cavendish Crescent South**, by *Hine*, 1877, has a tall staircase window and a corner office range under a glazed lantern. Uphill, right, into the inner ring, **Clumber Road East**. Here, **St Helier**, a stripped-down butterfly block of flats by *Cyril F. W. Haseldine*, 1950, replacing Jesse Boot's eponymous mansion. **Westwood**, Arts and Crafts, by *Ernest A. Sudbury c.* 1910, the sloping site incorporating a rear basement 'summer room', with a servants' yard to the front. Opposite,

Mevell House belongs on Newcastle Circus. **Jelenice/Hillside**, 1901 by *E. M. Lacey*, is also Arts and Crafts. Larger is **Adam House**, 1885 by *Arthur Marshall* for the photographer Samuel Bourne, with half-timbered gables and large stacks. **Edale**, by *Fothergill Watson*, 1883, Gothic with gabled porches, has a staircase hall at the side. At the corner of Tunnel Road, **Penrhyn House**, 1879, by *Hine* but with few tell-tale motifs save to the arched window surrounding the entrance; a fox in the gable and symmetrical garden front. On the NW corner with Tunnel Road, a single-storey house above a high rock-faced wall, by *Mike Sinclair*, 2002. An uphill walk returns to North Road.

79. No. 6 Maxtoke Road, by T.C. Hine, *c.* 1875

The largest houses follow the central N–S axis of North Road, Lincoln Circus, Duke William Mount, Newcastle Circus and South Road. They include **Claremont**, No. 7 North Road, by *Hine* for George Sparrow (monogram in gable), 1872. On **Lincoln Circus**, Lincoln House was replaced by thirty-two town houses by *Diamond, Redfern & Partners*, 1968, two curved terraces. SE, **Gladstone House**, by the builder *Edwin Loverseed* for himself, 1876–7. Its classicism contrasts with the Gothic Nos. 1 (*c.* 1875), 2 and 3 **Duke William Mount** of 1887, all *Hine*.

Newcastle Circus is more complete. **Mevell House** (No. 7), 1877 by *Hine*, is French classical. **Newcastle Court**, NW, the low rear service range by Hine, the rest seemingly rebuilt *c.* 1905. A canted entrance range echoing the curve of the street added *c.* 1926; a pedimented stone porch under a balustrade; gables to the S garden elevation alongside. The interior remodelled as flats 1962 by *Sutton & Pearce*, moving the staircase. **Linden House**, W, by *Hine*, *c.* 1875, has stonework bays and Venetian windows in the gables. W again, No. 6 **Maxtoke Road**, *c.* 1875, has a Romanesque cut brick doorcase and *Hine*'s star motif on its outshut [79]. On the edge of The Park in **Lenton Avenue**, Nos. 11 and 11a, two houses under a single tall gable by *Julian Marsh Associates*, in 1986 admitting his early admiration for Robert Venturi and Postmodernism, reminiscent of Jeremy Dixon's Kensington housing. Back along Maxtoke Road, the SW and SE quadrants of **Newcastle Circus** contain a gaggle of houses credited to *G. T. Hine*, but displaying many paternal motifs. **Burton House** has a richly moulded tile doorway, and a plate tracery stair-hall window with stained glass set between large gables. **South Road** is more upbeat thanks to No. 3, by

80. No. 3 South Road, by Fothergill Watson, *c.* 1881–97

Fothergill Watson [80], *c.* 1881–97, phases united by half-timbered attic storeys; a square tower topped by a pyramidal roof, and a further turret w. No. 1, **William House**, late 1850s by *T.C. Hine*, has a pyramidal tower over its central porch.

Lenton Road, running E–W across the bottom of South Road, contains an early *Hine* group, Nos. 13–33, dating before 1858 to 1862. Some classical and some Gothic, others in between, like the faintly Venetian No. 31; contrasting cornices and bands of square tiles, a little diaperwork on No. 23. No. 13/13a (**Fairholme**) was extended left, first with projecting bow by *Evans & Son*, 1910, then with staircase drum, oriel and bay, *c.* 1922 by *Evans, Clark & Woollatt*; Art Nouveau motifs to both extensions. There are later *Hine* houses down **Peveril Drive**, s, together with No. 2 **Kenilworth Road**, *c.* 1871. Nos. 2–8 and Nos. 5–13 **Hope Drive** were developed by *Fothergill Watson*, 1888–9. No. 7a **Lenton Road** of 1909 was the estate office, from designs by *A.R. Calvert*, a half-timbered lodge with big eaves and high stacks. No. 7 dated 1872 and No. 5 of 1873 are Gothic, by *Fothergill Watson* for the Misses Woods, his earliest surviving works. **Castle Grove** is one of the earliest and most complete of *Hine*'s groups, 1856–8. It is entered through the crenellated carriage arch adjoining No. 6, a muscular octagonal lodge. Nos. 1 and 2, semi-detached, set high behind walls that incorporate the remains of Richard's Tower (*see* Nottingham Castle, p. 40), with red brick diapering and Gothic shafts. No. 1 has an appropriate corner tower, No. 2 a defenceless balcony. No. 3 (concealed) has a corner turret. Nos. 5 and 5a are austere grey brick, with stone mouldings, entered at second-floor level for, behind, the cliff drops sharply.

The southern area was largely developed after the River Leen was diverted and Castle Boulevard cut through in 1883–4 – No. 1 **Clifton Terrace** by *Hine* an exception from 1851. Nos. 3–4 **Huntingdon Drive**, N, are by *Fothergill Watson*, 1888–9. Covered corridor entrances to the street; main façades to the gardens. On the corner of **Lenton Road** with Park Valley are seven-storey flats by *Cartwright, Woollatt & Partners*, 1969–70.

To finish the tour at this point, head E through the gorge of Lenton Road, *c.* 1818–20, back to the Castle Gatehouse. But there remains a curiosity for those prepared to turn N up **Park Valley**, part of the early development. Nos. 4 and 6, right, are stuccoed Georgian villas, while Nos. 8–10 by *Robinson*, *c.* 1828–9, is a *cottage orné*. Left, Nos. 5 (stretched), 7–11 and 21–23 are by *Hine* from 1844–51, still stuccoed but Italianate; No. 11 remodelled 1880s. Nos. 15 and 17–19 by *Robinson*, 1838–9, classical. No. 25 is dated 1878 on a corner turret, with sunflowers on its timber studio. Left into Clare Valley, and right into **Tattershall Drive**. This part of the Park was left open for sports use. A timber-clad **tennis pavilion**, by *Child & Watts*, 1911. Thence right into **Tunnel Road** and across Tennis Drive, through Langridge Homes' suburban **Tennis Mews**, 1996, and head straight towards the cliff.

The idea of a **tunnel** straight into Derby Road may have begun with *Robinson* in 1827. *Thomas Winter* prepared plans in 1839, and his 1847 plans survive. Boring began in 1844, but it was finally realized for the 5th Duke by *Hine* in 1855. He cut a tunnel through the rock some 135 yds (125 metres) long, with stairs in an open central section leading to The Ropewalk; Hine's Park Terrace housing perches picturesquely above. Deemed too steep for carriages, the tunnel is still used by pedestrians, emerging beneath Park Gate student flats halfway up Derby Road, the concealment only enhancing its fascination.

Walk 6.

North-west, with Nottingham Trent University

In this narrow segment began Nottingham's mid-c19 expansion for the middle classes, and in the mid c20 it was its prime office location. The walk heads NW from Chapel Bar, returning along Talbot Street before heading N to Nottingham Trent University and the Arboretum.

81. Walk 6

82. Albert Hall Methodist Mission, North Circus Street, by A.E. Lambert, 1907–9

Chapel Bar was Nottingham's last medieval gate, demolished 1743. It is now a traffic island surrounded by offices. **Byron House**, on the sw side, has Postmodern brickwork under a coved cornice, and behind, Barclays Bank, now **Cooper Parry**, both by the *William Saunders Partnership*, senior partner *Graham Brown*, 1987–9. On **Derby Road**, sw side, their **Royal Bank of Scotland**, 1994–6, Hine-like stars and trefoils. These developments were linked to the restoration of the Albert Hall, below. Opposite, N, **City Gate**, offices by *Ian Fraser, John Roberts & Partners*, 1973–6, a figure-of-eight plan stretched over the road. Clever, yet the fibre-glass fins screening the car park make an ugly streetscape for the pedestrian. On Wollaton Street, N, **Atrium**, by *Stuart Jackson* of *Crampin Pring*, 1989–91, brick classicism acknowledging Lambert's factory behind (p. 130), and originally for the Co-operative Society.

Up Derby Road, sw side, **Mia House**, by *Thomas Wright*, 1882–3, a doctor's house and surgery. In **North Circus Street**, left, the terracotta **Albert Hall** thunders at Pugin's cathedral opposite (p. 50). *Fothergill Watson*'s Temperance concert hall, 1876, became a Wesleyan mission in 1902, and burned down in 1906. *A.E. Lambert*, a Methodist, designed the replacement, opened 1909. It resembles his Midland Station [110]: terracotta and Baroque motifs to the tower; his Victoria Station tower has similar balconettes [55]. The façade has a central broken pediment and smaller side ones. Until 1982 this was Nottingham's principal concert hall. *Graham Brown* subdivided it for conferences at the level of its cantilevered balcony, 1989. It retains its segmental ceiling, curved seating, and giant organ [82], presented by Sir Jesse Boot, between fiery windows by *Mayer & Co.* of Munich, 1908.

The Corporation's first enclosure, in 1839, was 18 acres of Lammas land between Derby Road and The Park (p. 118). Planned as a smart residential area; the legislation prohibited industry. **Wellington Circus** is its centrepiece. On the E side, the Playhouse (p. 55). **Oxford Street**, sw, is lined with villas. No. 10 on the NW corner of Regent Street, by *T.C. Hine*, 1859, Gothic, with traceried porch and balcony. Opposite, No. 1, 1851, and Nos. 28–28a Regent Street, dated 1858, all by *Hine*, classical with tile decoration. **Regent Street** (left) has short terraces, now offices. No. 26, High Gothic, by *R.C. Sutton*, 1875–6. Nos. 2–24 are by *Hine*, *c.* 1854 and 1858, classically symmetrical but with Flemish gables and strapwork. The s side is more varied. Nos. 1, 3 and 5, 1840s, still Georgian; then Nos. 7–15 by *Hine*, 1850–4, Flemish gables; No. 17 symmetrical Jacobean, dated 1844; Nos. 19–23, classical. No. 25 by *Hine* for himself, 1845–6. The raised entrance has a Gothic doorcase under a square corner tower, a tradesmen's entrance counterpoised below. To the side, on Oxford Street, Hine's single-storey **drawing office** has a reticulated tracery window matching that to the house.

On **College Street**, w, No. 1 by *Hine*, 1851, and contemporary terraces: Nos. 3–9 classical, Nos. 11–15 Gothic, with arcaded entrances. The street is named for the **People's College**, founded 1846 by George Gill to give 'superior instruction to the working classes' regardless of sex or religion. By *Isaac Charles Gilbert*, refronted save for its imposing plaque. It was taken over, 1881, by the Nottingham School Board, for whom *Evans & Jolley* made additions, 1881, 1891–2, 1897.

Derby Road, N into commercial Late Victorian Nottingham at its assertive best, all fiery brick and terracotta. The sequence begins at **Regent Court**, Nos. 48–60 by *Samuel Dutton Walker & John Howitt*, 1878–83. Gables decorated with bands of tiles. Nos. 62–68 is an C18 terrace, well preserved above the shops, with stone lintels. Nos. 70–82 return to Flemish *fin de siècle*, 1899 by *G.S. Doughty*. No. 84, late C18, another remnant of earlier ribbon development. Nos. 88–94 by *Arthur W. Brewill*, 1884, stone surrounds. 1830s–40s survivals, left; then Nos. 83–85 by *F.M. Palmer*, 1886–7, narrow with double-height oriels, while Nos. 93–95 are olde English, by *Fothergill Watson*, 1884. Finally, right, Nos. 106–124 by *G.S. Doughty*, 1898–9, the pick of the Flemish crop for their scale; gables supported on heads and an *œil de bœuf* centrepiece. Nos. 124–132 turn the corner, by *R.C. Sutton*, dated 1877 over its apex clock.

On the hilltop, Derby, Ilkeston and Alfreton roads meet at **Canning Circus**, with the C18 **Sir John Borlase Warren** pub. Early C19 shops and houses linger within the traffic island. On the corner of Derby Road and **The Ropewalk** are more stuccoed pairs, *c.* 1827–31 by *P.F. Robinson*, their best elevations overlooking The Park. A grander pair face the corner to Derby Road, dated 1820. Gilded angels in its pediment. An intrusion, left, is the first of the Nottingham Waterworks Co.'s **pumping stations** for drawing artesian water [83]. By *Thomas Hawksley*, 1850, Gothic with lancets. Along Derby Road, **Clinton Terrace**, 1850s with polychrome bands, its centre houses rebuilt. Then the red brick and glass **Octagon**, offices of 1971–2, heavily remodelled as flats by *Crampin Pring McArtney*, 2000–1. Nos. 1–9 **Derby Terrace** by *Robinson*, 1830–1, part of his Park development. A high rusticated ground floor and some surviving cast-iron balconies.

83. Pumping station, The Ropewalk, by Thomas Hawksley, 1850

On the N side, **Herman Street Flats**, by *Boden Lloyd*, 2003–4. They incorporate Nos. 154–162, partly a late C18 house converted to Alton's cigar factory by *Frederick Ball & Lamb*, 1897–8. Across **Park Hill**, with early C19 houses and steps, are shops under a broad bargeboarded gable, by *Thomas Wright*, 1884, delicate next to the grandly Baroque frontage of the former **Territorial Army centre**, by *Brewill & Baily*, 1910–12. Nos. 180–182, late C18, painted brick, now serves the adjoining **Greek Orthodox Church of the Virgin Mary Eleousa**, the former Park Hill Congregational Church, 1882–3 by *James Tait & J. Langdon* of Leicester. Strikingly asymmetrical turrets above the double entrance. The interior retains its four-bay arcade and rear balcony, both levels with long pews, but enriched by colourful Greek Orthodox fittings, including an iconostasis at the (ritual) E end.

From here it is a short walk back to Canning Circus.

The General Cemetery, Clarendon Street and Nottingham Trent University

On the NE side of Canning Circus is the **General Cemetery**, founded in 1836 and beginning the arc of greensward through the former Sand Field that continues NE through the Arboretum into Elm Avenue (p. 139). The cemetery's coup is its concealment from Canning Circus, its gateway set within **Canning Terrace**, stuccoed almshouses of 1837–40 by *S.S. Rawlinson*. A central carriage arch, under a clock tower,

84.Lambert's Factory, now Stanley House, Talbot Street, by R.C. Clarke, 1863

has debased classical details familiar from J.C. Loudon's *Encyclopaedia*, 1833. The gates dated 1839 by *Falconer & Co.* of Derby. The cemetery is a wooded valley, enhanced romantically by All Saints and St Andrew (pp. 142, 140) on the skyline. Rawlinson's chapel, 1840, and a Dissenters' chapel, *c.* 1850, were both demolished in 1958. The **memorials** are subsidiary to the landscape. The best just E of the entrance, including that to Daft Smith Churchill of the Cemetery Co., shipwrecked 1838; a truncated obelisk.

In the angle between Talbot and Wollaton streets, E, commercial **stables** on two levels, by *Hedley J. Price*, dated 1902, stone plinths on falling ground and high E gables on both streets. Down **Talbot Street**, right, two pairs of stuccoed villas, *c.* 1840, Nos. 91–93 with a central bay and Nos. 87–89 with a pediment. Left, No. 116, **St James's House**, late C18 with deep dentil eaves and a canted bay, w. Beyond, bleak post-war offices conceal **Talbot House**, by *Dawson & Lambert* for Sir Julien Cahn, 1937, offices, garaging and a private flat. Art Deco front with giant columns; relief plaques between two rows of windows. Beyond Clarendon Street, left, **Russell Place** is an enclave of *c.* 1840 villas. **Lambert's Factory** dominates ahead, bleaching and dyeing works dated 1863, by *R.C. Clarke* [84]. Now offices (**Stanley House**). Vivacious skyline with three stone features, an arcaded centrepiece, and skewed towers at each end, w an Elizabethan open loggia, to the E a tall clock tower rebuilt 1991–3 following collapse. (An Elizabethan tower by Clarke designed in 1858 was not built.) The rear rebuilt, with **Government Offices for the East Midlands** behind, by *James McArtney*, 1990–4. The best thing the wavy external staircase, Beaux-Arts pastiche.

Now N into **Clarendon Street**, an oasis of 1850s town houses, most now offices. Nos. 9–11 with enclosed Tuscan porches; Nos. 13–15 with giant Ionic columns. Nos. 10–30, right, are a stepped terrace, Nos. 10–16 with reeded doorcases and tiny fanlights. Left, Nos. 17–19, 1860s with foliate capitals to a round-arched porch, now flats. The **Society of Friends' Meeting House**, N, is by *Bartlett & Gray*, 1960–1, on the site of their burial ground, 1852. Its novelty was a laminated timber dome (an elliptical paraboloid), engineered by *Hume & Tottenham*, creating an interior without orientation or internal ties. This was replaced by a double-pitched roof by *Peter Hill* in 2006–7.

Clarendon Chambers, E, was the Royal Midland Institute for the Blind, by *Aicken & Capes*, 1852–3. Five shaped gables each to Clarendon and Chaucer streets, the centre ones dated; stone ground-floor corner. Tower range on Chaucer Street by *A. N. Bromley*, 1888. Three E bays with carriage arch by *Harry Gill*, 1908–9, who added rear workshops, and a recreation wing on Clarendon Street, 1904–5, with high, straight gables. On **Chaucer Street**, E, the **Taylor Building** (**Nottingham Law School**) was the female House of Refuge, a regular classical villa, but its three-bay centre remodelled with a tiny entrance. Opposite, S, **High Pavement Sixth Form College**, by *Ellis Williams*, 2001–2. Now Part of New College Nottingham. Red brick disrupted by double-height glass panels: left, a skewed staircase; right, arched roofs over weatherboarding.

Ahead is Trent University, but first look right down **Goldsmith Street** to **St Andrew's Presbyterian Church**, now United Reformed, by *Robert Evans*, 1869–70. Rock-faced; semicircular transepts and a prominent porch, originally intended to have a tower; rear additions 1960. A lofty interior, transept openings spanned by double wooden pointed arches with traceried spandrels. Pews curve around the transepts; rear gallery on cast-iron piers. E window 1870; the rest C20, the best by *R. A. Milne* of *Parr & Pope*, 1948, in the war memorial at the entrance. Next door, the **Masonic Lodge**, by *John Howitt & Son* (*Claude E. Howitt*), 1928–31. Neo-grec; inside, an Ionic great hall and Corinthian small hall. Less formal drinking dens beyond.

A tour of **Nottingham Trent University** should start up Goldsmith Street, N, at the **Arkwright Building**, entered through *Hopkins Architects*' glazed atrium, 2006–9. This was Nottingham's original University College, 1877–81. The Corporation was offered £10,000 anonymously (presumed by Lewis Heymann, lace manufacturer) towards a college in 1874 following a successful lecture series organized by local businessmen and Cambridge dons. It was also pressured to build a public library, and to house the collection of the failed Nottingham Natural History Society. A competition in 1876 was won by *Lockwood & Mawson*. Opened in 1881, the Ancaster stone elevations are a scaled-down version of their Bradford Town Hall, three linked pavilions embellished with pinnacles, the centre originally with a lead flèche. Sculptures by *Farmer & Brindley*: from E to W, Shakespeare and Milton on the former library, Bacon and Newton on the College, with (above) panels depicting the arts; Watt and Cuvier on the natural history pavilion, W, were destroyed in the war. The central pavilion has an arcaded triple doorway, above which traceried windows light the double-height entrance hall. Behind was a 400-seat lecture hall, required by the donor but replaced by Hopkins's additions; a laboratory and Venetian chimney survive. The library and museum, entered separately, retain high cross-shaped upper halls with bracing tie-beams installed after structural movement was noticed in 1883.

In return for full university status in 1948, the college ceded the Arkwright Building to the Technical College. The **Newton Building** [85], S, by *Charles Hyde* of *T. Cecil Howitt & Partners*, 1956–8, was part of a scheme intended to replace it. A modern 'slab and podium', but stylistically American stripped Beaux-Arts classicism. The entrance has pilasters *in antis*, the eight-storey slab a vibrant rhythm of strip windows.

The College of Technology merged in 1970 with the College of Art and Design to form Trent Polytechnic, from 1992 Trent University. On the N side of Shakespeare Street, N, Art and Design's **Bonington Building** by *Peter Spring* for the City Architect's Department, 1967–9, with Students' Union and hostel (**Sandby Hall**, N). Red brick, chamfered semi-basement plinths and glazed roofs. Indebted to Stirling & Gowan's Leicester Engineering Building and similarly inspired by Midlands factories, but informal. Remodelled by *Dykes Naylor*, 2005–6. Opposite, **Boots Library**, by *ECD Architects* with *James McArtney*, 1995–8. A lecture theatre, classrooms and media lab surround a tear-shaped atrium library, surprisingly delicate after the exterior.

The College of Art and Design was founded in 1843 to stimulate lace design. The **Waverley Building**, right, in Waverley Street, by *Frederick Bakewell*, 1863–5, was its first purpose-built premises. Hollington and Bulwell stone. Italianate, with a colourful tiled clock tower; busts of architects and artists enliven the upper storey. A conservatory, 1881, supplied plants for still lifes. A theatre added c. 1900, and studios to the side and rear, c. 1950. In 1999–2000 *Robert Evans* of *Evans Vettori* converted the entrance into an exhibition gallery and added a glazed circulation link. On the corner with Clarendon Street, left, is **Terrace Royal**, now university offices, by *A. Wilson* and *S. Dutton Walker*, three feathers and the date 18 March 1863 commemorating the marriage of Edward and Alexandra. Gothic, remarkable for the quality of its carving by a *Mr Smith*, 'late of Oxford', the ground-floor lancets on Clarendon Street with regal heads; Shakespearean figures to Shakespeare Street. Figures support ballflowers around the doorhoods. Animals as label stops and gargoyles higher up; foliage in the gables. Beyond, the **Djanogly International Centre** (languages) incorporates the former Clarendon Street Board School by *A.N. Bromley*, 1889.

85. Nottingham Trent University, Newton Building, by Charles Hyde of T. Cecil Howitt & Partners, 1956–8, from the south

Waverley Street runs NW. It was laid out in 1852, when the **Arboretum** opened to the E. The Enclosure Act required a recreational area and these seventeen acres were chosen for their variety and salubrity. Realized to modified plans by *Samuel Curtis*, the Arboretum was free on Sundays, Mondays and Wednesdays – no refreshments on Sundays and no smoking. Pineapple-topped **gatepiers** and diapered s **lodge**, by *Moses Wood*, 1851. A **bust** to Samuel Morley M.P., by *Joseph Else*, 1928, adjoins the lodge. Left, a small lake and **aviaries**: the circular aviary, 1880, was moved here in 1891, the main aviary, N, 1955–6, whence the centre walk winds through a valley planted with alternating cedars and limes. Shrubs were planted in the alphabetical order of their botanical names, 'A' at the s lodge; today the dahlias are more famous. **Bandstand**, NW, 1907. E, a **memorial** to the 59th (2nd Notts) Regiment of Foot, by *M.O. Tarbotton*, erected 1862–3 around a bell looted from a Canton temple in the Anglo-Chinese war of 1857–61, and two cannon captured at Sebastopol in 1854–5. To the E, **statue** of the radical leader Fergus O'Connor, M.P. for Nottingham 1847–52; by *J.B. Robinson*, erected 1859. A **tunnel** under Addison Street, by *Wood*, then the park narrows to his E **lodge** and **gatepiers**, simple Jacobean. A short walk or bus ride down Mansfield Road (Walk 7, p. 138) leads to the city centre.

North, including Mansfield Road and The Forest

This walk starts at the Royal Centre N OF Upper Parliament Street. It zigzags N through the pre-enclosure Sand Field, whose rising sandstone terrain proved popular for smart villas and schools, to The Forest, open land retained in 1845 for recreation. The tram is convenient for returning to the centre.

The Corporation acquired land here under the 1845 Enclosure Act (*see* Introduction, p. 14), and in 1852 laid out Shakespeare and South Sherwood streets. The **Theatre Royal**, the city's lone surviving Victorian theatre, opened in 1865. By *Charles J. Phipps*, the first great theatre specialist, noted for practical planning. In 1895 an adjoining, undeveloped site was ceded to the entrepreneur Henry Moss, whose architect *Frank Matcham* built the Empire Theatre alongside (dem. 1969). In return the Theatre Royal was remodelled by Matcham in 1897–8. The City Council bought the Theatre Royal in 1969, and in 1976–8 it was restored by *Nicholas Thompson* and *Clare Ferraby* of *Renton Howard Wood Levin* and *Iain Mackintosh* of Theatre Projects. Their intended concert hall was realized to revised designs in 1980–2.

86. Walk 7

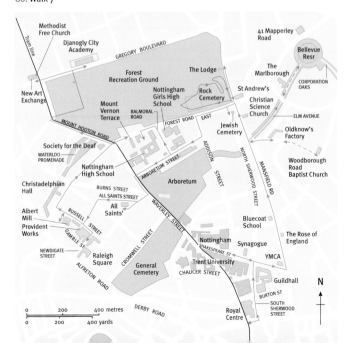

87. Theatre Royal, Upper Parliament Street, auditorium by C.J. Phipps, remodelled by Frank Matcham, 1897–8, restored by Nicholas Thompson of RHWL, 1976–8

The Theatre Royal was then a novel and ambitious restoration, later repeated by RHWL at London's Old Vic, and most sensitively at the Lyceum, Sheffield.

The **elevation** terminates the steep vista up Market Street – itself created in 1865 and initially called Theatre Street. It is still dominated by Phipps's splendid giant Corinthian colonnade, of Ancaster stone, fronting a stucco façade with a heavy blind parapet and (re-created) urns. The County Hotel of 1867 (formerly on the left) was sacrificed by *RHWL* for a new workshop and dressing-room block, a series of white mosaic ripples that physically as well as visually support the old structure shorn of its cross walls when internally gutted to create large, open foyers.

Interiors. New stairs linked the various levels, previously accessed separately. The backstage – all concrete block, red paint and bold stencilling in the exciting style championed by RHWL at Sheffield's Crucible – was planned for sharing with a new concert hall from the first. A higher flytower was built.

Phipps's **auditorium** was roughly circular, with three tiers of horse-shoe-shaped galleries on slender piers. He probably redesigned the proscenium, with paired Corinthian columns, in 1884. *Matcham* lowered the stage and replaced Phipps's balconies with steel cantilevers and curving fronts, giving improved sight lines and a new stack of boxes flanking the proscenium. His decoration was restrained: putti solely on the lowest boxes, other balcony fronts with cartouches, upper balcony with simple swags [87].

Mackintosh created a lower proscenium, with fibreglass columns modelled from those of the façade. Matcham's boxes, with wide arches, were replaced in sanitized form. Small bulbous-based columns, reused by Matcham at the sides, are characteristic of later Phipps work, and Mackintosh added more to create three rear boxes. He wanted 'to restore a "Phippsian" sense of unity and enclosure', but this work is controversial in preferring fake Phipps to the real palimpsest. Boudoir greens and gilding replaced pre-1977 red. The safety curtain was painted by *Henry Bardon*.

The 2,500-seat **Royal Concert Hall** was added in 1980–2, at right angles where the Empire had been parallel. The most elaborate elevation faces South Sherwood Street, wider than a pavement, yet not a square. The **grand stair** and **foyers** have a real Hollywood swish. The hall was designed for extreme flexibility, hosting classical and pop concerts, cinema and conferences. The very tall **auditorium**, developed with the American acousticians *Artec Consultants*, is faceted, giving volume and acoustic reflections while resembling a vigorously over-scaled Art Deco cinema. Banners increase absorbency when the sound is amplified; permanent finishes are designed to keep absorbency to a minimum. The resulting acoustic is loud, if short in reverberation – an unusual compromise, but suitable for a multi-purpose hall.

E and N the area became a focus for civic planning, from 1870s schemes by *Marriott Ogle Tarbotton* for council offices, courts and a university college (now Trent University, Walk 6, pp. 132), to *R.M. Finch's* 1943 plan for a civic centre that extend N to the High Schools.

Today the principal public building is the **Guildhall**, 1884–8, by *Verity & Hunt* following a competition. Their winning scheme was pared down on cost grounds to law courts, a police and a fire station. It is French Renaissance with pyramidal roofs, erected in dour Darley Dale and Coxbench stone (brick courtyard fronts). A projecting centrepiece and portico, Ionic columns over Doric, has figures of blind and seeing Justice; more delicate decorative flanking panels; a pediment on the left return, but jollity limited to a skyline of high dormers and acorn finials. Inside, an entrance hall lined with Derbyshire marbles leads to panelled **Police and Summons courts**, disused since the building of new courts (p. 167). Above, the C17-style ceiling survives of the subdivided **Grand**

Jury Room. On South Sherwood Street, across a carriageway, the scale drops to the former **fire station**; a billiard room over the engine house, and lodgings for eighteen firemen. To the N on **Shakespeare Street**, facing Nottingham Trent University's Arkwright Building (pp. 131–32), new **police** and **fire stations** were built in 1938–40. Relief figures over their respective entrances; Art Deco staircases within.

A line of mainly public buildings flanks the N side of **Shakespeare Street**. W of its junction with North Sherwood Street, the **YWCA** is a rambling 1850s villa given a corner hall and gymnasium by *W.B. Starr & Hall*, 1929–30, classical. Continuing W along Shakespeare Street, the **Wesleyan Reform Chapel** by *Thomas Simpson*, 1854, a **synagogue** since 1954; triumphantly classical pedimented frontage [88]; Wesleyan and Hebrew inscriptions. Inside, an oval gallery on iron Corinthian columns, and original pews. Granite and marble tabernacle, resited from the Chaucer Street Synagogue (*W.H. Radford*, 1889, Moorish, dem. 1991). Across Shakespeare Villas, the **Registry Office**, built for the Poor Law Guardians by *A.H. Goodall*, 1885–6, Italo-French Gothic with foliage decoration.

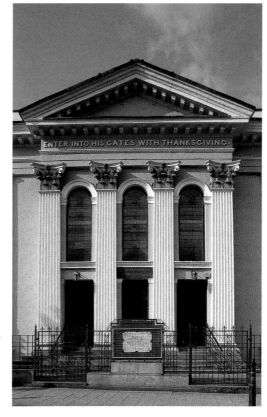

88. Synagogue, former Wesleyan Reform Church, Shakespeare Street, by Thomas Simpson, 1854

89. YMCA, Mansfield Road, by T. Cecil Howitt, 1937

E of North Sherwood Street, Shakespeare Street continues with the Italianate **Orange Tree pub**, *c.* 1850. Four terraced houses and shops by *William Holbrook*, 1906, projecting oriels, dwarfed by *CPMG*'s flats and shops, 2007–8. No. 22, *c.* 1860, has a tower, windows in Gibbs surrounds, contrasting with its classical neighbour, the **University of Nottingham Adult Education Centre**, *c.* 1853–4 as Angelo Terrace, classical with giant Corinthian columns. Perhaps by *Thomas Simpson*, a resident; four dwellings shared the central arched entrance. No. 12 is an 1850s palazzo. On the corner with Mansfield Road, the **YMCA** [89], 1937, ranks among *T. Cecil Howitt*'s best buildings, North German style with diapering, pylons to the squat pyramidal tower; vitrolite ground floor.

Mansfield Road is Nottingham's N artery, with continuous ribbon development to The Forest by the 1840s. The E side has **The Rose of England**, by *Watson Fothergill*, 1898–9, 'tap' pub to the Nottingham Brewery. Distinctive banded brick and stone, here contrasting mullion-and-transom oriels with timber attics. A fat entrance tower with rose finial. Extensive caves were discovered when the brewery was replaced by the miserable **York House**, 1961–2. Left, on the corner of **Peachey Street**, the **Peacock pub**, *c.* 1850, retains wainscoting and fixed benches with bell-pushes. Opposite, the YMCA has expanded into *Henry Sulley*'s warehouse, 1887–8; muscular with two tiers of dormers. Next door, a house and workshop by *Henry Daubney*, 1875, classical, and a Gothic range dated 1874, a niche over the door. N, Nos. 45–53 Mansfield Road, retain *c.* 1860 commercial ground floors. Above Bluecoat Street is *T.C. Hine*'s **Bluecoat School** [90], 1852–3; a plaque commemorates its foundation on High Pavement, 1706. Jacobean, with broad mullion-and-transom windows; the projecting corner range with scroll gables and niches housing two Bluecoat scholars, copied by *J. Stonehouse* from the old building. N of the school a battered **factory** of *c.* 1825, said to be

Nottingham's oldest warehouse; extended forward 1881–2 by *W.F. & R. Booker*, with bracketed and dentilled eaves, a central carriageway between shopfronts.

N, on **Egerton Street** (right) is **Oldknow's factory**, *c.* 1850, four storeys, extended *c.* 1855 on St Ann's Hill Road, taller and with a clock on its rear stair-tower. The view s overlooks *Watson Fothergill's* masterful former **Woodborough Road Baptist Chapel** (1893). An octagonal tower with a saddleback turret, with behind it a w apse to a long hall under a single, high roof. The interior has cast-iron arcades (elaborate capitals), now infilled with offices for the **Pakistani League of Friends**, and an arch-braced roof. *Fothergill's* Emmanuel (C. of E.) Church (1892–8) on Woodborough Road was demolished in 1972.

N again, right, is **Elm Avenue**, the E continuation of the Arboretum created by the 1845 Enclosure Act and planted 1850; entrances denoted by bulbous stone **gatepiers** found also on The Forest. It is crossed by **Cranmer Street** with, left, **The Marlborough**, retro-Modern flats by *Marsh Grochowski*, 2000–2, and right, the **Gordon Memorial Home** (high cupola), by *Ernest R. Sutton*, 1902–3. Elm Avenue leads to the **Belle View Reservoir**, by *Thomas Hawksley*, 1863–4, with twelve brick chambers, on the hilltop, continuing as **Corporation Oaks** and **Robin Hood Chase**, 1851. 1860s–70s houses flank Corporation Oaks; Robin

90. Bluecoat
School,
Mansfield
Road, by T.C.
Hine, 1852–3

Hood Chase rebuilt early 1970s. Beyond the reservoir, NE, **Mapperley Road** is dominated by No. 41, the tempestuous, be-towered Malvern House, 1874, probably by *Henry Sulley*, who designed the lodge and linked stables right, 1875–6, timber-framed over stone Gothic ground floors.

Further N on Mansfield Road, E side, **Neales** occupies a roller-skating rink by *Barnes, Booth & Richardson*, 1930. Across Villa Road is the Presbyterian, now **Christian Science Church**, by *Brewill & Baily*, 1898. Arts and Crafts. Ashlar blocks with a square tower, delicate tracery and ironwork. Inside, an aisled preaching box with a high balcony over an inner lobby between porches. Continuing N, **St Andrew's House**, by *Watson Fothergill*, *c.* 1893, timber and nogging to the squashed attic storey, a turreted corner and porch facing Mapperley Road.

St Andrew [14], back on Mansfield Road, is by *William Knight*, 1869–71, with a W baptistery of 1884 by *S.R. Stevenson*. Slightly later N porch; vestries by *Heazell & Sons*, 1905. Its tower is among Nottingham's greatest landmarks, rock-faced Bulwell stone with large bell openings, shafts, tourelles and a bulbous broach spire with two tiers of lucarnes. Sanctuary, chancel under tower, transept chapels (one the Sunday School), four-bay nave and aisles, W baptistery and porches. Lancet windows, roundels over the transepts and at the W end, and a clerestory. The interior height is dramatized by its narrowness. Round nave piers. Double rebated arches on imposts to the tower, under which *Heazell & Sons* made piecemeal additions, including **sedilia** (1918), **organ case** (1933, for a Snetzler C18 organ) and **choir stalls** (1934). **Rood screen** 1917, partly surviving in N aisle, W end. N **chapel** (1931, with screen) with a war memorial, 1921. Late C19/early C20 **stained glass**, including four by *Gibbs & Howard*, 1882. Sanctuary windows 1918. S aisle, 6th from E, David by *Andrew Stoddart*, 1932, the richest. Aisles, W, a sensitive pair of double windows with roundels, by *H.O. & Charles Powell*, 1902.

Racing had been held on **The Forest** since the C17. *John Carr* built an imposing grandstand in 1777. With the Enclosure Act, The Forest passed to the Corporation, who installed their distinctive chunky **gatepiers**. A **lodge** survives on Mansfield Road, N, by *Moses Wood*, 1857, stuccoed Greek Doric with porticos, comparable with Council House (p. 46). By the 1880s racing had declined, and Councillors worried about becoming drawn into a sport noted for accidents and betting, and opposed by local churches. Racing ended in 1890, and The Forest became home to recreational sports, and from 1928 to Goose Fair. Prominent timber **café and changing rooms**, 1927.

The **Church** or **Rock Cemetery**, on the SE corner of The Forest, was founded 1848. It occupies a steep N-facing hillside, laid out by *Edwin Patchett* in four parts. On the top terrace, *E.W. Godwin*'s chapel, 1878–9, was demolished *c.* 1958; footings survive. Early C20 monuments packed along one side, photogenic with St Andrew's behind [91]. Angels predominate, Italianate in their attitudes, but by local masons. Next, the central and NW hillside, terraced with stone retaining walls; then a near-

circular catacomb range set into exposed bedrock, the centre filled with
common graves. The NE corner is a romantic quarry valley, with cliffs
and caves, and the best Victorian **monuments**, to William Hannay
d.1862, a crocketed gable over a cave; the Sylvesters, 1877, granite, a
trefoiled canopy; and the Cutts family's baldacchino, 1882, with an
angel, by *W. Jackson*. A delicate iron cross commemorates T.C. Hine.

On **Forest Road East**, s, Nos. 1–4, oriels over original shopfronts;
converted from a pub by *Hedley J. Price*, 1901. Left, just into **North
Sherwood Street**, hidden behind a stone wall, the **Jewish Burial
Ground**, leased 1822, closed 1869. Some fifteen standing stones remain,
and a low obelisk to Berta Nathan Metz, 1821–1917, with German
inscriptions.

Villas in **Forest Road East** are mainly 1860s Italianate, with large
quoins and deep eaves. More pairs in **Addison Street**. On **Arboretum
Street** the 1860s–70s houses, s, belong to the **Nottingham High School
for Girls**, the second foundation of the Girls' Public Day School Trust
outside London. Opening in 1875 in Oxford Street, it moved in 1880 to
Clarence Lodge, No. 9. By *Emile Vandenberg* of Lille, 1875, for a lace
manufacturer. Lace-patterned ironwork; massed columns to the rear in
contrasting granites and Mansfield stone. A columned stair-hall, and
rococo ceilings. N of Arboretum Street the Girls' Senior School or
Milford Building, by the *GPDST Property Department*; curtain-walled

science laboratories of 1960–1 with brick additions 1973–84. w, a circular brick **dining hall** added in 2001–2 (*Gavin Nolan* the Trust's project architect). Across Baker Street, the Junior School occupies **Upnah House** in **Balmoral Road**, dated 1873, attributed to *Henry Sulley*, extended in 2007–8 by an addition to *Nolan*'s **sports hall**, 1997–8.

Nottingham (Boys) High School, immediately w, was founded in 1513 by Dame Agnes Mellers in Stoney Street, and refounded as fee-paying in 1855. The Arboretum Street site was bought in 1860 and a competition won by *Mr Wilson*, whose scheme was rejected by the Charity Commissioners. A design by *Thomas Simpson* with *Hine & Evans* was built in 1866–8, T-shaped, with wings for classical and English schoolrooms, soon reformed as Upper and Lower schools. Both were originally double-height, with Perp traceried windows. The mix of church and castle motifs must have been striking when all the parapets were castellated, as survives on the central tower. Inside the English school (w), the upper part retains Simpson's hammerbeam roof. His doorways have solid cusps, reminiscent of those at St Mary's. In 1910 *J. F. J. Clark* of *Evans & Son* split the classics room (E) horizontally with two tiers of traceried windows. Extensions levelled the ridge towards Forest Road, *Robert Evans* excavating a chemistry laboratory and lecture theatre below the school rooms, 1886, adding massive flights of steps to reach the entrance. Additions of 1872–3 over a N entrance, the linking spur raised by *R. C. Sutton*, 1876–80, including a rooftop drawing room.

Later additions rationalized the spine and added quadrangles to either side, by *Evans, Clark & Woollatt*, 1932–60.* Theirs too, NE, the **Player Hall**, 1935–6. Gothic, with copper cupola, and organ on a high gallery.

Later buildings are free-standing. Fronting the s gates, **war memorial** by *Henry Poole*, with *Brewill & Baily*, 1922. E, the **White House**, dated 1861. w, the **Lady Carol Djanogly Music Room**, Modernist, 1997 by *Maber Associates*, and the **Simon Djanogly Science Building**, 1982–3 by *Feilden & Mawson*, brick and concrete, spoilt by low ceiling heights. Behind, an over-scaled concrete structure of Y-arched cantilevers and pre-cast panels, the **Founder's Hall**, 1963–5, a ground-floor pool at right angles and a first-floor theatre.

Facing the end of Arboretum Street, **Waverley House School**, a stuccoed villa, *c.* 1850. On the corner of Raleigh Street are two semi-detached stuccoed villas by *Frederick Jackson*, 1858. Left, then right into **Raleigh Street**. On the apex between Raleigh and Burns streets a Gothic villa, **Lindum House**, with corner shafts and tympana to the windows. Raleigh Street gave its name to Frank Bowden's bicycle works in 1887, long gone. It is dominated instead by the splendid **All Saints'** church [92], parsonage and schools, now a community centre and workshops. By *Hine & Evans* for William Windley, 1863–4. Gothic, rock-faced stone

*A top-floor room containing a fireplace inscribed with the name D.H. Lawrence, an old boy, was added after 1910 – too late for the graffiti to be authentic.

92. All Saints, Raleigh Street, by T.C. Hine, 1863–4

with bands of red Mansfield and cream Little Eaton ashlar. Apsidal chancel, with N chapel and S vestry. Five-bay nave and aisles, their E bays transept-like with three-light E.E. windows; the W end with porches. W tower with baptistery, three-light belfry, and an elegant spire with lucarnes. Choir W vestry by *R.C. Clarke*, 1900. The interior, red Alton ashlar in the nave and Devonshire marble and alabaster in the chancel, has roll-moulded arches and shafts to the main windows. The chancel has marble shafts, a polychrome gable and an arched wagon roof. Caen stone and alabaster **pulpit**, cross-framed **benches** and traceried **stalls**, and a brass eagle **lectern**: a well-preserved ensemble. War memorial **reredos** and **altar**, S transept, by *Harry Gill* 1919–20. The **font** and **cover** also his. **Stained glass**. E window, 1864 by *Hardman & Co.*, over triptych by *Hammersley Ball*, 1938. N chapel E window, 1922 by the Misses *C.C. Townsend & Joan Howson*. Behind, **vicarage**, gently Gothic with gables, bays and porches. The rock-faced **schools** have lancets in unmoulded ashlar surrounds, paired chimneys, and a round turreted stair-tower. The **parish room**, NW, a wide timber gable, by *Frederick Jackson*, 1883.

To the W, lace manufacturing followed machine building in Russell and Newdigate streets, by 1870. The first works were multi-occupied as tenemented or 'flatted' factories. **Russell Street** has several on its W side, with lantern finishing rooms on top. From the s, Kirk's factory, later a cigarette factory and now **Liberty Square** (flats) 1872, additions 1879 and 1894. A rounded corner with dated clock, globe finial and curved corner door. Behind, **Russell Square**, the Z-planned former Foster's Factory, 1881, main ranges linked by a cupola; small gables facing **Newdigate Street**. Opposite, the **Provident Works**, c. 1870, fourteen bays; with behind it on Gamble Street, **Adcock's factory** of 1881. N on Russell Street, **J.H. Spray & Co.**, c. 1870, five storeys with topshops and projecting stair-towers. Its octagonal chimney is truncated, but behind in Gamble Street, a majestic survivor at **Albert Mill**, a rebuilding by *Arthur W. Brewill*, dated 1893; now flats. Red-brick twelve-bay front, white-brick rear.

Turning E on to **Forest Road West**, the **Christadelphian Hall**, former Wesleyan church, late 1860s, a gabled front inscribed like that on Shakespeare Street (p. 137) and perhaps also by *Simpson*. Interior with a trabeated ceiling, organ and choir gallery. Between Larkdale and Burns streets, SE, No. 111, Queen Anne, by *Sidney R. Stevenson*, dated 'R.C.C. 1884' for a Dr Chicken. A wrought-iron overthrow with lamp, and a high-gabled carriage house.

Opposite, on the W corner with Southey Street, No. 58 was the vicarage to Christ Church, Radford (dem. 1948). 1871, Gothic, with a corner tower. On the E side, No. 56, with big timber gables, the first of six houses by *G.T. Hine*, 1880–4. No. 48 has canted and straight bays. On the s side **Rob Roy Terrace**, early 1870s, entered from a terrace over a rock-faced service level. The s gables with stars, a T.C. Hine motif, but impossible to credit him with such a crude design. On the N side, No. 22, the **Nottingham Society for the Deaf**, built as Paton Congregational College, 1865–7, simplistic Dec tracery over a two-light hall window. Arcaded entrance hall. Opposite, **McIvor Terrace**, adjoining Waverley Street, 1883 by *T. Fish*, builder; diapered gabled bays.

Just s down **Waverley Street**, Nos. 19–25, **Mount Vernon Terrace**, c. 1840, with a tower added c. 1865, supposedly for viewing the racing on The Forest. Twenty yards E, off Forest Row E, up steps, **Mount Hooton**, a Late Georgian terrace at right angles, c. 1850.

To the w off **Mount Hooton Road**, **Waterloo Crescent**, semis set in an arc around a public walk, **Waterloo Promenade**, extending w behind Forest Road West; giant **gatepiers** with sunburst mouldings either side of Southey Street. The houses mostly by *R. Charles Sutton*, erected c. 1875–9 to a common design; restored by *James McArtney*, 1972–8. At the foot of Mount Hooton Road, **Gregory Boulevard**, running N along The Forest, boasts *Foster & Partners'* **Djanogly City Academy**, 2002–5. The light, glazed metal structure harks to Norman Foster's early minimalism [93]. Two tiers of classrooms line a double-height corridor, brises-soleil shading strip windows. The school specializes in computer studies; heat gain is absorbed by chilled beams and night cooling in the standardized upper classrooms. Larger

93. Djanogly City Academy, Gregory Boulevard, by Foster & Partners, 2002–5

specialized studios and laboratories on the ground floor. The open library forms a central feature. The building resembles a trainee office; fabulous when empty, it cannot absorb the noise made by 11–14 year-olds.

NE are two of *Watson Fothergill*'s most intriguing developments. Nos. 75–95 **Foxhall Road**, 1901, is a quirky terrace with blind gables, an indication of his modest speculative work demolished elsewhere. Right, and along **Berridge Road** his Norris Ladies' Homes are more playful, nattily detailed with projecting porches, high stacks and behatted dormers.

w of the forest, a red brick chapel on the corner with Noel Street, the **Hyson Green Community Centre**, built as the Methodist Free Church by *Frederick W. Dixon* of Manchester, 1895–6; Perp terracotta tracery. Next door, w, the **New Art Exchange** for black and Asian artists, intended as a focus for Nottingham's ethnically diverse Hyson Green, by *Hawkins\Brown* with the artists *Sutapa Biswas* and *Hew Locke*, 2007–8, grey brick with scattered square openings over a glazed ground floor. The tram stop on the corner of Mount Hooton Road and Gregory Boulevard serves the city via Waverley Street.

Walk 8.

Sneinton

Sneinton (Snotington or Notintone) was a subsidiary Anglo-Saxon settlement to Nottingham (Snotingham). Its hilltop retains a village identity, with the landmarks of its early C19 prosperity: St Stephen's church and Green's Mill. Between the two old centres, Sneinton Market was developed from *c.* 1860 outside the parish at the hill's foot, an area redeveloped by the Corporation in early C20.

The start lies a few streets E of the Victoria Centre (p. 83) where Lower Parliament and King Edward streets intersect. In the angle is the former Palais de Danse, now **Oceana**, by *Thraves & Dawson*, 1924–5, a frieze of dancers and a globe over the entrance. Refurbished by *Bignell Shacklady Ewing*, 2005, with a bar alongside. **King Edward Street** is overshadowed by **Litmus**, thirteen-storey flats by *Tim McArtney* of *CPMG*, 2004–8. Paired floors behind a brise-soleil lined with coloured glass panels – simplistic Le Corbusier. Ahead, the **William Booth Memorial Hall** [95], by *Oswald Archer*, 1914–15, giant engaged Ionic columns and a squat domed tower denoting the galleried meeting hall (large band platform); the office range in front later raised.

94. Walk 8

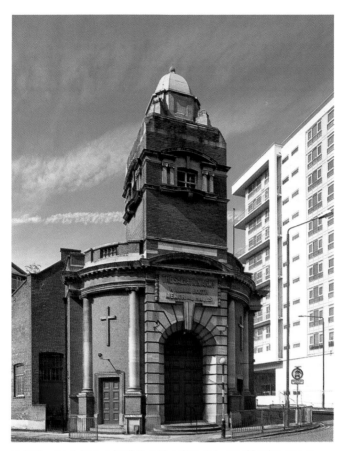

95. William Booth Memorial Hall, King Edward Street, by Oswald Archer, 1914–15, with behind it Litmus, by Tim McArtney of CPMG, 2004–8

Opposite begins **St Ann's Well Road**, Nottingham's NE artery, largely rebuilt in the 1970s. On the corner, a **power station**, 1900–2 by the *City Engineer's Department*; now partly a bingo hall, a high clerestory roof and entrance indicate industrial origins. The **mosque** beyond, begun by *John Laing Design*, 1981, much extended. **Victoria Hall**, student flats by *Harry Mein Partnership* on both sides of the road; left, Postmodern, 2003–4; right, smart gunmetal drums, 2006, replacing St Catharine's vicarage and Institute. Beyond them survives **St Catharine's church**, by *Robert Clarke*, 1895–6. Rock-faced, with a w bellcote over Dec lancets and rose window. Four-bay nave and two-bay chancel; Lady Chapel, s. Inside, an open truss roof. **Rood** by *F. E. Howard*, 1924. **Stained glass**: the s aisle damaged, the best of the N aisle by *Kempe*, 1899 (w), and St Catharine (*Kempe & Co.*), *c.* 1926. Lady Chapel E by *Curtis, Ward & Hughes*, 1908. Reredos (1908), organ and font were removed when the church closed, 2003.

96. Victoria Leisure Centre, Gedling Street, by Arthur Brown, Borough Engineer, 1895–6

Behind, St Ann's Cemetery opened in 1832, precipitated by cholera. Closed in 1906, it became **St Mary's Rest Garden**, cleared 1946, with slate tombs lined against the E wall. The worn **lion**, s, commemorates William Thompson, as 'Bendigo' twice prize-fighting champion of England, d.1880. To the E, a **ventilation tower** to the Corporation's Beck culvert, 1883. Turn s, and ahead are **Bath Street Schools**, Nottingham's first Board School, by *Evans & Jolley*, 1872–4. Right, a fifteen-storey **telephone exchange**, by *M.H. Bristow*, Ministry of Works, 1968–9.

Victoria Park began as a cricket ground under the 1845 Enclosure Act, becoming a park in 1894. On the N side is **Promenade**, a late 1850s paired terrace; restored by the council, 1975–6, a pioneering conservation scheme. E of the park, **Bancroft Buildings**, formerly William Windley's silk factory on the corner of Robin Hood and Roden streets. A corner gable with weather vane and date 'AD 1869 WW'. Converted to flats by *Church Lukas*, 2003, the topshop remodelled as penthouses. The **Bath Inn**, s, has fat acanthus pilasters over a ground floor with Egyptian faience columns (1928). Across Bath Street, masked by trees, **Park View Court**, Nottingham's first public housing (then called Victoria Dwellings), by *Bakewell & Bromley*, 1875–7, and among the first in the country after the City of London and Liverpool. Five-storey flats with Gothic polychromy and turrets; open stairwells on a U-plan.

Turning SE into **Gedling Street**, the **Victoria Leisure Centre** [96] is by the Borough Engineer *Arthur Brown*, 1895–6. A tall clock tower with balconettes and weathervane, the right-hand entrance formerly for women. Left, it incorporates an oval pool, 1850, overclad and remodelled as a gymnasium, 1975, when Turkish baths were installed. Rear pools by *T. Wallis Gordon*, 1927–8. Next door the **Town Mission Ragged Schools**, by a *Mr Edwards* of London, 1858–9, now the Notts Wildlife Trust, its rough stone and polychromatic brick gables punctuated by high stacks. Opposite, **The Exchange**, 1956 as the 'Archer' telephone exchange. Wavy shell concrete roofs. Converted into student flats and shops, with an addition on Lower Parliament Street, by *Franklin Ellis*, 2004–6.

On the left is the triangular **Sneinton Square**, from *c.* 1860 a general market. On the N side, shops terminate (E) at the former **Midland Bank**, 1911 by *T.B. Whinney*, one tall storey with a cupola. The **Wholesale Market** decanted in 1900 from Old Market Square; buildings by *R.M. Finch*, Borough Engineer, 1938. Steel-trussed roofs. Stalls following the old street pattern were preferred to a covered market by the tenants. One gabled survival, **Peggers** pub, between two streets, by *Evans & Son*, 1905–6.

Back down Carlton Road, ahead in Southwell Street is **Nottingham Corporation Tramways Depot**, now a bus garage, dated 1926. A stone pedimented centre and ends, eleven bays in similar style follow the curve into Carter Gate, their roof supported on radial steel girders.

SE into the bottom of **Sneinton Road**. The **Lamp** pub, by *W.B. Starr & Hall*, 1923, faience ground floor and original layout. Opposite, a gate leads into **Bond Street**, where lurks **St Alban**, since the 1960s a Ukrainian Catholic church [97]. An iron church, 1881, was replaced 1885–7 by *Bodley & Garner*, then working at Clumber. Brick with stone bands, tall but without a clerestory and only a modest bellcote; reticulated tracery windows, those to w and E ends of five lights set very high. Four-bay nave (designed for lengthening); chancel and aisles with tall arcades and wagon roof. Chancel and chapels separated from the

97. St Alban, Bond Street, interior, by Bodley & Garner, 1885–7

Tractarianism in Sneinton

Five churches were built or rebuilt in Sneinton between 1865 and 1935, when the parish was a centre of Anglo-Catholicism, led by the Rev. W.H. Wyatt (incumbent of St Stephen (p. 152) 1831–68, and friend of John Mason Neale) and Canon Vernon Wollaston Hutton (1868–84). A surpliced choir was formed as early as 1831. Stoles and coloured vestments followed in 1870–1, and incense, sanctuary lamps and sung mass in the 1890s. Wyatt oversaw the building of St Matthias, supported by the 3rd Earl Manvers, whose heirs gave land for the building of St Christopher's and St Cyprian in the C20. St Alban [97], by *Bodley & Garner*, was Hutton's personal venture, he and his trustees holding the living.

St Matthias, St Matthias Road, is of 1867–8 by *T.C. Hine*, acquired 2008 by the Coptic Church. Rock-faced with a high bellcote; small but not cheap. w, a single lancet and rose window, two lancets N and s, other light from the continuous clerestory below the barn-like roof. The chancel arch has massive foliate columns. The bomb-damaged apse rebuilt in 1950. Chancel **windows** by *Kempe & Co.*, Crucifixion 1913, and St George (war memorial) 1918. s transept glass by *Jones & Willis*, 1904. Further E is **St Cyprian**, Carlton Hill (Marston Road), by *Claude Howitt*, 1934–5, replacing his father's mission church. Chunky Byzantine; a five-bay nave with aisles, and a two-bay chancel; Lady Chapel never realized. Hanging **rood** by *John Heaps*, 2002. – Limed oak **fittings**, the choir stalls 1963. – **Font**, C13–C14, found in a field outside Gedling. E window, of St Cyprian holding building plans, 1935. Now Evangelical is **St Christopher**, Colwick Road, by *F.E. Littler*, 1910. Tall, red brick. Dec tracery the principal adornment; larger transept windows and higher ones in chancel, but the roof undifferentiated. w bellcote and porches. Gutted in 1941, leaving only the walls and (stone) arcades, the latter refaced in restoration by *C. Howitt & Partners*, 1952, job architect *C. Wooley*. **Stained glass** with 1950s figures by *Pope & Parr*.

nave by delicately carved **screens**, a rood above the centre, now serving as the iconostasis decorated with **icons** by *Mr Cholak, c.* 2000. s (Lady) chapel fitted out 1898; oak **sedilia** by *Heazell & Sons*, 1937. **Font**, **stoup** and pretty **offertory box** at w end. **Altars** by *William Potik*, 1960s. **Stained glass**: E (central) window by *Burlison & Grylls*, who may have designed the chapel E windows too; Lady Chapel s window, 1904; nave s window 1949 by *Pope & Parr*. SE vestry planned by Bodley; parish room, s, 1912, pinkish brick with Diocletian windows.

At the top of Bond Street, on the corner of Haywood Street and Sneinton Road, the **Wheatsheaf**, by *C. Howitt & Partners*, 1964, pavilion-like. Opposite, the **Albion Congregational Chapel** [98] by *Thomas Oliver* of Sunderland, with *William Booker*, 1855–6; classical,

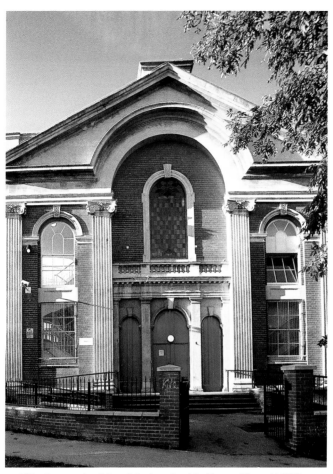

98. Albion Congregational Chapel, Sneinton Road, by Thomas Oliver, with William Booker, 1855-6

now flats. Sneinton Road was rebuilt in the 1960s; first plans 1957, three sixteen-storey Wimpey blocks built 1963–8. Concealed, left, the **William Booth Memorial Complex**, Notintone Place. Three houses survive from a stepped terrace, *c.* 1825, because in No. 12 (centre) was born William Booth (1829–1912), founder of the Salvation Army. His father was their builder. One window wide; centrally placed stairs renewed. Acquired by the Salvation Army in the 1930s as a hostel, in 1963 the houses were spared clearance, and restored within a development of care facilities by the *Army Architect's Department* under *Major David Blackwell* (project architect *David Greenwood*), 1969–71, in sympathetic red brick and concrete. Booth's **statue** is a copy of that by *G.E. Wade* at the Army Training College, Camberwell, South London.

St Stephen, Dale Street, answers St Mary's and the Castle on their summits. A church was recorded in 1234; an earlier foundation perhaps stood just E. Rebuilt 1790, 1810 and 1837–9, the latter by *Rickman & Hussey*, whose tower and part of the S transept survive. Lancet style, T.C. Hine considered it 'the first example of the revival of pure Gothic architecture' in Notts. The sooty tower appears stark since pinnacles fell in 1860; brick-lined with vast relieving arches under a mid-C17 bell-frame.

The E end (1908–9) is credited to *Bodley & Hare*, the nave and transepts (1910–12) to *C.G. Hare* alone. This rebuilding, sponsored by the Rev. the Hon. Robert Dalrymple, was conducted around the existing church, only then demolished. Blind E end, other elevations with two-light Dec windows, delicate tracery the only hint of internal richness. Internally, the chancel of ashlar, the rest mostly rendered. A large E end: light chancel behind a C15-style rood and screen [99] (partly of 1878); the Lady Chapel – its screen now carrying the 1872 organ – incorporating the S transept, and the narrower St George's Chapel, N. Dying responds to the lofty (four-bay) nave arcade, in the Bodley late Dec tradition. Raised sanctuary; the **reredos** designed by *Hare* and carved at Oberammergau in 1909 in high polychromatic relief. Magnificent C15 or early C16 **stalls** with misericords and canopies, salvaged for 10s., 1848, from St Mary's (p. 31), remodelled 1909 to back on to the screen. **Misericords** depict a lion, a donkey, a double-bodied cat with a mouse, and a bearded head (s), a monkey, a fox and hound, fox, and a green man (N). Hare's painted **organ case** has gilded pomegranate work. Eagle **lectern**, 1883. St George's chapel **reredos**, 1927, a film-star George, and **war memorial**; both by *Hare*. The Lady Chapel entered through a double arch, carved with a Madonna and Child. **Reredos** 1937 by *Heazell & Sons*. Font, w end, recast C19. **Stained glass** in the Lady Chapel commemorates Canon Hutton, reset 1912 and 1944, after war damage; SS Stephen and Laurence by *Alexander Gascoigne*, 1912, for Fr Dalrymple. Three nave windows, 1886–90 by *Hardman,* reinstalled without backgrounds. The churchyard walls incorporate stone from the earlier churches and are lined with slate **tombstones**, some made locally. Calvary **war memorial**, by *Hare*, 1920. **Monument**, NE corner, to George Green, 1793–1841, Sneinton's mathematician miller.

On the corner of **Dale Street** a sombre former vicarage, 1842–3, sashes but four-centred doorways. The **Fox** pub of similar date. Opposite, Nos. 4 and 6, early C19, handsome sashes and stone lintels. Nos. 1–17 **Perlethorpe Avenue**, left, dated 'WW 1902', workers' terraces. Nos. 9–13 Dale Street demonstrate Sneinton's distinctive 1890s tiled doorways and figurative hoodstops. Nos. 21–23, *c.* 1820, have attic workshops. Sneinton's manor house, owned by the Earls Manvers, was on the corner of **Sneinton Hollows**, right; replaced with Nos. 2–12, by *A.R. Calvert*, 1894. The surrounding streets were laid out by *W.F. & R. Booker*, 1888, but earlier houses survive to the s in **Castle** and

99. St Stephen, Dale Street, east end, by Bodley & Hare, 1908–12

Thurgarton streets. Left off Dale Street, up Belvoir Hill is **Green's Windmill**, rebuilt in 1807 for the mathematician's father, also George. A brick tower of five stages. Staggered sliding sash windows, and a wooden gallery on the first. Burnt out 1947; restored to working order in 1981–6, with two canvas sails and two shuttered 'spring' sails. Museum buildings follow the footprint of Green's outbuildings. Green lived at **Mill House**, E, dated 1825 in a perfectly dolls' house front. Back on Dale Street, buses return to the city centre.

Colwick Hall

100. Colwick Hall, south front, remodelled by John Carr of York, 1776

Colwick Hall can be reached by bus CL2 from Sneinton Market (Manvers Street).

Church and Hall once made a famous picture near the River Trent. Now the unroofed C14–C15 **church** hides among trees, a romantic spot. Single-bay chancel of 1684. However, the hall has been restored as a hotel. The medieval manor, acquired by the Byron family *c.* 1362, passed *c.* 1660 to the Musters. A wall of local stone survives between the library and entrance hall. As rebuilt *c.* 1690s, Colwick was a brick block of two storeys, with on the entrance (N) front, a five-bay recess two bays deep (cf. Melbourne Hall, Derbyshire, E front, remodelled 1706). The windows have simple stone surrounds and the angles quoins.

John Musters succeeded in 1770. He married an heiress in 1776, and through Whig connections turned to *John Carr* of York for alterations and additions. The rainwater heads are dated '1776 JWM' and a painting by Stubbs from 1777 shows the S front in its present form. Carr's builder was *Samuel Stretton*.

Exterior. Carr added only a balustrade and colonnade to the **entrance front**. A central 1690s cupola has gone. The **S front** was transformed – though the 1690s brickwork remains visible – with an attached Ionic portico. The original block was then flanked by Carr with two five-bay wings for a ballroom and dining room (altered), with Doric pilasters and guttae over the friezes.

The exquisite **interior** is in Carr's version of the Adam style. The low entrance hall, its plasterwork and doorcases, are clearly 1690s. The main stairs are set in a new hall, right; two flights returning from a half-landing. A second staircase survives against the old S front. Here, too, is the former library, with a columned screen at each end, a Chinese-style bookcase at the E, and an anthemion frieze. The ballroom leads off it, W, its apsed ends with screens of Corinthian columns, plaster cornices and a plain coved ceiling.

Walk 9.

The Meadows and Trent Bridge

This walk heads s from Midland Station through the Meadows, enclosed in 1845. It contrasts an area of workers' housing with mainly recreational buildings alongside the River Trent, in both Nottingham and West Bridgford, a suburb under county jurisdiction.

101. Walk 9

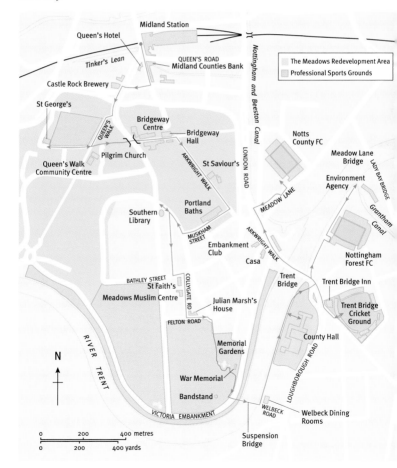

On the corner of Queen's Road and Arkwright Street the former **Midland Counties District Bank**, by *Lawrence Bright*, 1902, with Ionic columns. Opposite, the **Queen's Hotel**, *c.* 1865, rendered with first-floor pediments; ground-floor bays by *A.N. Bromley*, 1905. Down **Arkwright Street**, No. 3, the **Nottingham Royal Naval Association**, originally a doctor's house, by *William R. Gleave*, 1902–3, a judicious balance of gables and bays. One block w on the corner of Queen's Bridge Road and Traffic Street, a warehouse, its round-headed corner over an Ionic porch, by *Lawrence Bright*, 1905–6. Opposite is Castle Rock's **micro-brewery**, installed here 1997, its warehouse by *Sutton & Gregory*, 1913; the brewery tap, the **Vat and Fiddle** (formerly The Grove), Moderne, by *W.B. Starr & Hall*, 1938.

The rebuilt Meadows area of 1972–80, low-rise medium-density housing by the *City Architect's Department*, is best entered via **Queen's Walk**, a tree-lined promenade created 1855 from an old track, given over to cars in 1926 but restored in the 1970s. E, the **Pilgrim Church**, a former Congregational chapel rebuilt by *C. Nelson Holloway*, 1902. Rock-faced gabled front, brick behind. Next door, the **Queen's Walk Community Centre**, a tall Board School by *A.N. Bromley*, 1878–9, extended 1886. Kirkewhite Street West leads w to **St George's church** [102], the nave by *R.C. Sutton*, 1887–91. Rock-faced, Mansfield stone banding, with a bellcote and low aisles; plate tracery; chancel, organ chamber (N) and vestries added by *G.F. Bodley*, 1897, his appointment demanded by the anonymous lady donor. The high E window resembles Bodley's St Alban (p. 149). His intended Lady Chapel, s, was realized on a larger scale by *Cecil G. Hare*, 1914–15. Reticulated tracery windows to the s; blind E end – like his St Stephen. Another bellcote, and a Blessed Sacrament Chapel at the E end. Hare also planned a wider s aisle, shown by the weatherboarded and brick w wall. Inside, Sutton's artisanal brick

102. St George, Kirkewhite Street West, chancel, 1897, by G.F. Bodley; nave by R.C. Sutton, 1887–91

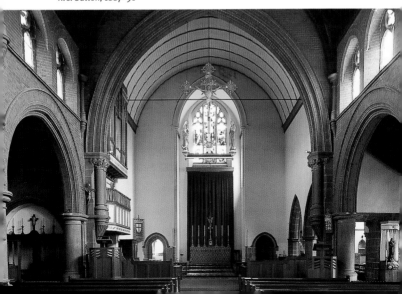

103. Bridgeway Hall Methodist Mission, Kirkewhite Street, by Terry Bestwick, 1963–7

arcade on Mansfield columns contrasts with Bodley's spare E end, and Hare's refined Lady Chapel, with a high arcade and arched altar recess below a late Dec triple niche (**figures** 1938). Chancel **fittings** by *Peter Currey*, 1934, **pulpit** 1938. **Organ case** by *Bodley*, 1905–6 in an otherwise unrealized chancel scheme, redecorated 1962. Hanging **rood**. Blessed Sacrament Chapel fitted *c.* 1920, decorated 1932; Resurrection (N) chapel: **altar** 1924; **mosaic** 1934. Square **font**, W end. **Stained glass**: E window, 1902, probably by *Burlison & Grylls*. The Blessed Sacrament Chapel has small windows of Our Lord in Glory, n.d., and St George, probably German. Lady Chapel windows by *Whitefriars*, 1948–9; N aisle, six windows 1924–34, mostly English saints, by *H.T. Hincks* of *Hinchcliffe, Hincks and Burnell*. Splendid W window contrasting SS George and Michael, 1927 by *Burlison & Grylls*, St Michael revised when realized in 1938. Outside, **Calvary**, 1921 by *Pask & Thorpe*.

E down Kirkewhite Street, an underpass leads to the **Bridgeway Centre**. Beyond is the **Bridgeway Hall Methodist Mission** [103], by *Terry Bestwick*, 1963–7, when its red brick evangelism shone amidst sooty streets; now lost under foliage, still honest and robust. The church itself faces SE, its corner prow with tall opaque windows facing Arkwright Walk, the spine of the Meadows redevelopment. Its centre is **St Saviour**, by *R.C. Sutton*, 1863–5. Rock-faced Dec, with star-traceried clerestory windows and low broach spire (rebuilt 1955). Arcades with lifelike heads; hammerbeam roof. E end remodelled by *Thomas Wright*, 1913. The sombre **vicarage** added by *Frederick Bakewell*, 1867. Schools behind by *R.C. Sutton*, 1865–6.

At the end, right into **Muskham Street**. **Portland Baths**, classical, by *Arthur Dale*, City Architect, dated 1914 in its broad gable with Diocletian window. Then right into **Wilford Crescent East**, where C19 housing begins. At the corner with Wilford Grove, the **Southern Library**, by *Arthur Dale*, 1923–5. V-planned, its prow with a domed porch on Roman Doric columns and a pretty cupola. Down **Mundella Road**, s, council semis by *T. Cecil Howitt*, Housing Architect, 1920–2 with catslide roofs. On the corner of Collygate Road, s, **St Faith** by *Sutton & Gregory*, 1913–15, now closed. Orientated s–n, with n bellcote, octagonal baptistery, five-bay nave and two-bay chancel. Dec tracery (flowing in the transepts), with a broad, five-light e window. Arcades, but only the n aisle built; narrow s aisle by *F.W.C. Gregory*, 1939–40, with the suburban-style vicarage. Down **Collygate Road**, s, is a jolly gabled **Board School**, by *Evans & Son*, 1898–9, now the Meadow Muslim Centre. On the corner with Felton Road, No. 20 is *Julian Marsh*'s own house, 2007–8, a s-facing courtyard shaded by solar panels. Contrasting black zinc to the upper, living, rooms, with rooftop greenhouses.

To the s, playing fields, gifted 1923–7 by Jesse Boot; an extension to **Victoria Embankment**, an embanked carriage drive made by Borough Engineer *Arthur Brown*, 1898–1901, in a loop of the river between Trent and Wilford bridges. The **War Memorial Gardens** lurk behind a belated war memorial, left, 1927. A **triumphal arch** by *T. Wallis Gordon*, City Engineer, flanking colonnades and wrought-iron gates. **Statue** of Queen Victoria by *Albert Toft*, 1905, moved from the Market Square, 1953; stunning reliefs around the plinth. Moderne **bandstand**, s, 1932. Opposite, the **Suspension Bridge** [104], 1906, by *Arthur Brown*, is also a conduit for water pipes serving Wilford Hill reservoir, and gas mains. Rock-faced arched base; columned, classical, piers support the steel suspension cables.

Across the river to **West Bridgford**. Ahead, the **Welbeck Dining Rooms**, on the corner of Welbeck Road, built as a Masonic lodge by *A.E. Lambert*, 1909. Fruity Baroque with a cupola. Banqueting rooms to the river, a clubroom facing a rear bowling green. Along **Trentside**, embankment steps, remodelled 1953 after flooding. *Marriott Ogle Tarbotton* was commissioned to rebuild **Trent Bridge** in 1867, constructed 1868–71. Ashlar abutments, piers with rock-faced cut-waters, Aberdeen granite columns and Venetian Gothic mouldings; the three cast-iron arches decorated with tracery designed by *Farmer & Brindley* and cast at Derby. Widened 1926 to the w, repeating Tarbotton's details. The first wooden bridge across the Trent (Hethbeth Bridge) was probably early C10, rebuilt in stone by Henry II *c.* 1156, and again in 1374. This survived until the C19, despite many deprivations and rebuildings, particularly in the C17. Two s arches, round with longitudinal ribs, are preserved in the traffic island, s.

104. Suspension Bridge, by Arthur Brown, City Engineer, 1906

105. County Hall, staff entrance, by E. Vincent Harris, 1935–60

County Hall dominates the riverside, overlooking the city yet (from 1951) in the county. Castigated by Pevsner in 1951 for classicism 'as dead as mutton', while still unfinished. *E. Vincent Harris*, a civic centre specialist, was commissioned in 1935. He conceived an **H**-shaped block and corner clock tower, revised in 1938 to a campanile with a Wrennish spire, intended as a seventeen-storey bookstack. The main entrance was in the N wing facing Trent Bridge, while a central open colonnade served the members. A council chamber and assembly hall were planned for the s wing. Work halted at attic level, 1941, but staff increases after 1945 meant the unplastered interiors – even of the council chamber and hall – became offices. Harris designed a T-shaped addition, but in 1955 the Government suspended grants for building council offices, and the Modernist *Donald Gibson*, appointed County Architect that year, sought an alternative.

Harris's block combines Worcestershire Blockley brick with Portland stone and a copper roof [105]. The N portico, typifying his late work, has a bell-cast roof. Baseless Tuscan colonnade, glazed 1958–60, making an entrance hall (altered 1989). Relief figures either side by *Robert Kiddey*, 1939, depict Notts industries (s) [106], Agriculture and Arts (N). Foundation stone 1939 by *Eric Gill*. Inside, the first-floor **council chamber** and **assembly hall** created only in 1964–8, lined in rosewood; appliqué hanging by *Gerald Holtom*, 1965–8.

Additions were made in CLASP (Consortium of Local Authorities Special Programme), Donald Gibson's light steel school-building system. The three-storey riverside meeting rooms and canteen, and four-storey offices, by Gibson's successor *Dan Lacey* (County Architect), 1962–3, were among its first non-school uses (pre-dating York University). Elegant, but bonding awkwardly with Harris's work.

106. County Hall, Miners, panel by Robert Kiddey, 1939

107. Trent Bridge Cricket Ground, Fox Road stand, by Maber Associates, 2001–2

Across the bridgehead, **Ladbrokes**, a former National Provincial Bank (initials in segmental gable and railings), by *Walter Holden, c.* 1926. The **Trent Bridge Inn**, s, Queen Anne, is by *W. Wright, c.* 1883, a corner tower and extensions to Radcliffe Road in harder brick by *Thomas Jenkins*, 1919; a large bar for match days. The **Trent Bridge Cricket Ground** [108] was developed by William Clarke from 1837. Rebuilt since 1985, save the Queen Anne pavilion by *H.M. Townsend*, 1886, s, unbalanced by the professionals' dressing room, 1890s, and press box 1956. Interior restored 1995. New work since 1992 by *Maber Associates* (*Hugh Evans*) began with the Radcliffe Road stand, 1997–8, N, details aping the pavilion on a massive scale. Theirs, too, the ingenious Fox Road stand [107], 2001–2, E, a raised steel frame exploiting air rights after car parking was leased to adjoining county offices, built 1973. The upswept canopy minimizes shadows, a feature repeated on *Maber Associates*' West and Parr stands, 2007–8, w.

Downstream is **Nottingham Forest F.C.**'s City Ground, 1898, noted for the first elliptical goalposts. It is now dominated by the E (Brian Clough) stand, by the Sheffield specialists *Husband & Co.*, 1979–80, a model for post-1990 all-seater stadia. The Trent End by the *Miller Partnership*, engineers *Thorburn*, 1994–5, is a suspended structure with a colonnade along the riverside.

Lady Bay Bridge was built in 1875–9 by the Midland Railway's engineer *John Crossley* for its Melton line. Three wrought-iron spans on cast-iron piers, with brick flood arches either side. Adapted for road traffic 1978–9. Next to it is the energy-efficient **Environment Agency**, by *Maber Associates*, 1997–8. Below it lies the entrance to the Grantham Canal, 1797 by *William Jessop* and *James Green*.

108. Aerial view showing Trent Bridge Cricket Ground (foreground), Nottingham Forest F.C., and (across the river) Notts County F.C.

109. Top Knot, Victoria Embankment, by Calvert & Gleave, 1904

Back across Trent Bridge, up **London Road**. On the left, **Casa** was the Town Arms, also rebuilt by *Tarbotton*, 1869–71. Grand gates serve **Victoria Embankment**, 1901. On the corner, **Top Knot** [109], shops and houses by *Calvert & Gleave*, 1904; stepped gables and a corner turret. At the junction of Turney Street, the **Embankment Club**, a Boots shop and tea rooms, by *A.N. Bromley*, 1905; timber oriels and corner spirelet. Right, Turney's leatherworks, now flats, 1911, Baroque. Probably by *Elliott & Brown*, whose other buildings were demolished for **Turney's Quay**, 1990s Neo-vernacular town houses by the *William Saunders Partnership*.

Off London Road, E, **Meadow Lane Bridge**, stone, 1792–3 by *Jessop* and *Green* for the Nottingham Canal Co. On **Meadow Lane**, left, the **Trent Navigation** pub, 1842, with deep bracketed eaves. **Notts County F.C.** moved here in 1910. The ground was rebuilt in 1991, rare success coinciding with legislation requiring all-seater stadia for the higher Divisions. Three stands erected in seventeen weeks, builders *Mowlem* and *John Reid & Sons*, engineer *R.J. James*, effective despite modest means. The Derek Pavis stand followed, 1994.

Buses return to the city centre, or it is a short walk along the canal.

The Railway and Canal Area

This is the area between the historic city and the canal and railway, which lie just s of the old line of the River Leen. This was the centre for Nottingham's most noxious industries, and of transportation. It expanded after the enclosure of the Westcroft in 1837–9 and Eastcroft in 1845, when land s of the old town was taken by the railway companies and by the Corporation as a waste depot and abattoir. Three companies built lines into Nottingham, linking the coalfields N and w and offering services to London: chronologically, the Midland, Great Northern and Great Central. Those of the Midland Railway survive, along with the Great Northern's line to Grantham, although the viaduct built by the Great Central through the city centre has been partly rebuilt to serve the tram system opened in 2004. This walk starts at Nottingham Station [110], then loops E, returning via the canal and heading w along Castle Boulevard. The canal makes a pleasant route back to the station from any point along the walk.

110. Midland Station, by A.E. Lambert, 1902–4, Carrington Street front

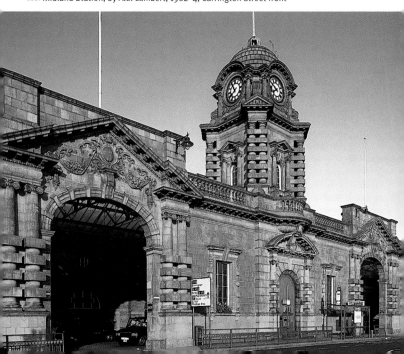

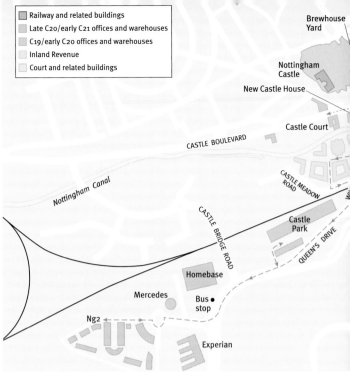

111. Walk 10

Circumnavigating the Station

Nottingham Station (Carrington Street and Station Street) was built for the Midland Railway in 1902–4 by *A.E. Lambert,* countering his ambitious Victoria Station for the Great Central and Great Northern. It is impressive for its terracotta frontage, rugged rather than grand, and for its completeness [110].

The plan of setting the booking hall on a road bridge above the platforms was pioneered at Crewe and Preston, but Nottingham owes much to the Midland Railway's architect Charles Trubshaw, designer of Sheffield and Leicester stations. Like Leicester it has a porte cochère across its frontage, 320 ft (98 metres), and a clock tower. Carriage entrances either side with paired blocked columns under pediments, and larger end entrances, the s one retaining wrought-iron gates with heart motifs. The tower has rusticated corner piers and a dome. Behind, three arches (the centre blocked) lead to a central booking hall, with higher carriage arches to either side now utilized for ticket office and bookshop. The hall has more terracotta, and green tiling at either end. The island platforms are canopied: wooden valances and riveted steel stanchions interrupted by red brick waiting rooms and offices – functional yet not undecorative. A lattice overbridge connects to the trams, their line presently ending here on the remains of the Great Central bridge that once spanned the station. On Station Street, N, the

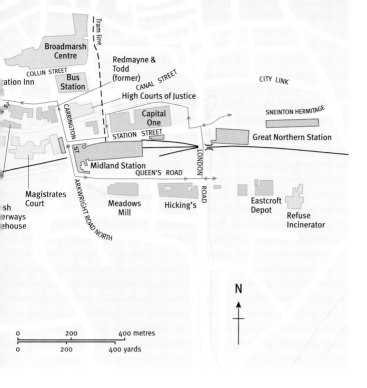

Broadmarsh
Centre

Tram line

Redmayne &
Todd
(former)

COLLIN STREET

Bus
Station

ation Inn

CANAL STREET

High Courts of Justice

CITY LINK

Capital
One

ST

CARRINGTON

STATION STREET

SNEINTON HERMITAGE

Great Northern Station

ST

Midland Station

QUEEN'S ROAD

LONDON

Magistrates
Court

sh
erways
ehouse

ARKWRIGHT ROAD NORTH

Meadows
Mill

Hicking's

ROAD

Eastcroft
Depot

Refuse
Incinerator

N

0   200   400 metres
0   200   400 yards

parcels office with its own timber canopy also from 1903–4, on the site
of the Midland's previous station (1848).

In **Carrington Street**, N, is a **bridge** over the Nottingham and
Beeston Canal (*see* topic box, p. 172). By *Moses Wood*, it was sponsored
by the Midland Counties Railway in 1842 (widened 1902). The site of
Nottingham's first station, 1839, W, is occupied by the grittily classical
railway **goods office**, 1873–4, now part of the Magistrates' Courts
complex, its shed rebuilt behind the N façade for car parking. The
Magistrates' Courts, 1992–5 by the *County Architect's Department* with
William Saunders Partnership and *Cullen, Carter & Hill*, has ambition in
its planning, including naturally lit courtrooms, not sustained through
the dreary façades around the Postmodern atrium entrance. (Back on
Carrington Street, the **Midland Counties Bank** and **Queen's Hotel**, S,
herald the Meadows walk, p. 155).

E, therefore, into **Queen's Road**. Here, the Midland Railway's
passenger offices (now Transport Police offices), domestic-scaled. Right
(S), behind low, later frontage buildings, the mighty **Meadows Mill** (for
cotton, later lace) by *T.C. Hine*. U-shaped, one wing *c.* 1865, raised 1874
and extended 1887; round-arched windows and stair-turrets. **Hicking's**
vast lace warehouses beyond are now flats (topshops remodelled as
penthouses); the nearest and reddest seven-bay finishing rooms by
A.N. Bromley, 1915–16. Flats behind by the *Weedon Partnership*, 2005–6.

112. Great Northern Station, off London Road, by T.C. Hine, 1857–8

To Queen's Road, a narrow carriageway block, by *Brewill & Baily*, 1908, was added to a thirty-four-bay range with a parallel block behind, all perhaps by *Truman & Pratt*, before 1881. The earliest building is now **Hoofers** bar, set back, dated 1873 on the clock and in the scrolly pediment facing London Road, E.

London Road has the canal running along its E side. Beyond was the small Eastcroft field, served by a bridge by *Frederick Jackson*, 1848. **Eastcroft Depot** is denoted by the turreted clock tower of its offices, dated 1878, still under *Tarbotton*'s imprimatur. Beyond is the gabled **hide, fat and skin warehouse**, 1878–9 by *S. Dutton Walker*, admired for its ease of cleaning and clad in his favoured Leicestershire terracotta. Dominating is the chamfered hulk and chimney of its municipal **incinerator**, by *John M. Gill*, City Engineer, 1970–3, which (via Boots' heat station on the corner of Station Street) warms several public buildings and housing schemes.

N of the railway bridge, E side, is the **Great Northern Station** [112], by *T.C. Hine*, 1857–8, for the Ambergate, Nottingham & Boston & Eastern Junction Railway, who – having failed to secure tracks to Ambergate or Boston – leased it to the Great Northern. Venetian windows, French gable and pavilion turret behind a deep porte cochère; long, shallow wings either side with Hine's distinctive white header cornice behind. The continuous platform canopy, with four higher, later and decoratively riveted bays, E, was restored by *Marsh Grochowski* and converted by *Colman Architects* into a health club 1998–2001. Beyond, rotting in gaunt isolation, are two massive derelict blocks, **James Alexander Warehouse**, E, thirteen bays, partly five storeys, 1905; **Great Northern Warehouse**, nearer and slightly lower, by *T.C. Hine*, 1857, roofless, with roundels, relieving arches and four large carriage arches. The office range, w, has a suspended floor structure similar to that at the Adams Building (p. 106).

To the w, Station Street and the canal towpath are linked by **Jury's Inn** and the timber-boarded **Stadium** apartments, both by *Corrigan & Soundy & Kilaiditi*, 2003–6. Then Boots' power station, 1950–3, now serving the city, and former printworks, by *Percy Bartlett*, 1951, with mushroom concrete columns behind a long Portland stone façade, still classical. Restored as **Trent House**, offices for Capital One by *DEGW*, 1998–2000. Its success led Capital One to build headquarters alongside, **Loxley House** [113], named for Nottingham's earlier financial operator. *ORMS* won a competition, 1999, with open-plan offices around a full-height atrium, opened 2002, a silvery louvred version of DEGW's addition at Boots (p. 217).

113. Loxley House, Station Street, by ORMS, 1999–2002

On the N side of the canal, highly glazed flats and offices by *Levitate*, 2007–8. **Trent Street** links the towpath with Canal and Station streets, and serves the tram bridge. On Canal Street, w, is the **High Court of Justice** and **Crown Court**, Canal Street, by the *Property Services Agency* (architects *P. Harvard*, *K. Bates* and *J. Mansell*); planned 1976, progressively opened 1981–7; its strip-glazed second-floor restaurant perched over stone-faced first-floor courts. s on Station Street, older buildings survive. First H. Hopkinson's brass factory, now the **Art Organisation**, a narrow part-stone frontage, before 1891, perhaps by *Truman & Pratt*, cast-iron columns inside. Next door, the **Granby Hotel**, Venetian classical, by *Truman & Pratt*, 1886, overshadowed by *Pratt*'s later offices, 1904, Baroque with a high rounded pediment. On a corner the **Bentinck Hotel**, by *Walter O. Hickson*, 1904–5; gable and corner oriel, another gable squashed into the busy elevation on **Carrington Street**. Next door here, **Fletchers'** offices began as the Nottingham and Nottinghamshire Bank by *Watson Fothergill*. Dated 1900 between first-floor oriels over a granite office front; above, arcading under a plain gable. The Temperance **Gresham Hotel** is by *W. Dymock Pratt*, 1898–9. First-floor pedimented windows and high ends. On the w side here, a long, jagged, gabled range ending in a prominent clock tower, for long the premises of Redmayne & Todd, sports outfitters, by *Gilbert S. Doughty*, 1896–7.

The s side of Canal Street retains late C19 warehousing for **Fellows, Morton & Clayton**, coal carriers. A narrow office block, dated 1895, by *W. Dymock Pratt* has, behind, former stables and smithy. Across Pratt's raised roadway is his double-gabled warehouse, 1895, one side arched over an arm of the canal, with steel girders to the floors above. In 1980 the City Council and a brewery jointly opened a museum here, closed 1998, and a pub restaurant, which thrived. E along Canal Street, another gabled warehouse, dated 1897, also by *Pratt*, now surrounded by *Franklin Ellis*'s **Castle Wharf**, 1996–9, red brick gables above balconies and tinted glass. A fully glazed corner turning into Wilford Street houses the *Evening Post*. The dominant building is the **British Waterways warehouse** [114] behind, *c.* 1919, six storeys over a concrete basement and twenty-one bays long, divided by pilasters and kinked like the canal. 'Trent Navigation' survives in tiles in the parapets under the present inscription; converted to offices and restaurants by *Franklin Ellis*, 1998, 2000.

Lenton Boulevard opened in 1884, its E–W section nearest the city renamed **Castle Boulevard**, 1906. It formed part of the Corporation's enterprising inner ring road w of the city, begun with Gregory Boulevard, 1883. N, a long red brick warehouse in three sections, the centre with a rusticated ground floor, 1903–7 by *William Woodsend*. Across Castle Road, the Waterworks offices and Brewhouse Yard, *see* Walk 1 (p. 65).

114. British Waterways warehouse, Canal Street, *c.* 1919, converted to offices and restaurants by Franklin Ellis, 1998, 2000

The Nottingham and Beeston Canal

115. Nottingham and Beeston Canal, showing Park Rock, Castle Boulevard, by Letts Wheeler, 2002–4

The Nottingham Canal, running from the Erewash at Langley Mill to Trent Bridge, was surveyed by the specialist engineer *William Jessop* in 1790 and developed by him and *James Green*. The first stage, from Trent Bridge to wharves by the town, opened in 1793, and the canal was completed in 1796. Meanwhile, the Trent Navigation Co. commissioned *Jessop* to build a canal from the river at Beeston to join the Nottingham Canal at Lenton, 1794–6, whence boats rejoined the river at Trent Bridge. The N arm of the Nottingham Canal (branching some hundred yards E of the A52 road bridge) closed in 1937. Part of its course was culverted for the River Leen (1952), and more survives NW of the city. E of Trent Bridge, the Grantham Canal opened in 1797, again by *Jessop* and *Green* (closed in 1936).

In 1975 Maurice Barley and Robert Cullen reported for the Nottingham Civic Society on the Nottingham and Beeston's sorry state. Their recommendations formed the basis of council plans for recreational use, centring on the easily accessible area between Carrington and Wilford streets, developed with bars and restaurants. W of Wilford Street is a lock, and a landscaped walk to the Castle Marina, 1982–3. Apartment blocks have sprung up here from the 1990s, the best Park Rock by *Letts Wheeler* [115], 2002–4, with landscaping by *Fiona Heron* that incorporates the medieval caves of St Mary de la Roche in the cliff behind. E of Carrington Street the canal runs to London Road, where ahead, the Poplar Arm (1797, extended 1835) has been infilled. The canal swings sharply right, then straight to the Trent at Meadow Lane Lock (no public access).

On the s side, **New Castle House** [116], by *Frank Broadhead*, 1931–3, for William Hollins & Co., manufacturers of Viyella fabric. Its concrete flat-slab construction is akin to Boots' D10 (p. 212), and shows how developed use of the system had become before it was finally permitted in London in late 1934. The mushroom columns still close-set here; one right behind the entrance. Continuous glazing, genuinely Modern. Converted to offices by *James McArtney*, 1987–91, retaining Broadhead's veneer-panelled boardroom; lumpy stair-towers to rear. Next door, **Castle Court** is almost symmetrical, a central carriage entrance between conical topped square towers. But a narrow attic and lively oriel dated 1894, right, denote *Watson Fothergill*'s hand.

116. New Castle House, Castle Boulevard, by Frank Broadhead, 1931–3

The Former Railway Lands, South-West

Back at the w corner of Wilford Street and Castle Boulevard is the **Labour Exchange** by *P.M. Stratton* of the *Office of Works*, 1935. Men and women signed on separately at the rear and side. Next door, **Woodward, Clark and Co.**, by *Heazell & Son*, gabled, 1897. The **Irish Centre** occupies stabling and warehousing to the four-square **Navigation Inn**, *William Stretton*'s building of 1787, all rebuilt in 1887 (no architect).

Across the canal, the large **Inland Revenue** development sparked the area's regeneration as an office centre. The Government's first 'design and build' proposals were so widely condemned that it held a competition in 1991, won by *Michael Hopkins & Partners*, built 1993–5. It was Hopkins's first Nottingham project, and combined his distinctive tented structures with the brick contextualism first seen in his additions to Lord's Cricket Ground, London, 1984–7. His use of brick was developed further with the remodelling of Bracken House, London, opened 1992, its proportions inspired by Guarini, and especially with his Glyndebourne Opera House, 1989–94. At Nottingham there are six office buildings, the two central ones full quadrangles, the others L-shaped, and a central sports and café building (a tented structure reminiscent of the Schlumberger factory near Cambridge that made Hopkins's name), with streets between them angled on the Castle behind. The expression of load-bearing brick as an honest, modern structure owes most to Louis Kahn. But red bricks reflect local traditions and C19 jack-arch construction, with concrete folded slabs set between masonry columns pre-formed off site. The projecting top storeys clad in lead. Natural light and ventilation, early energy

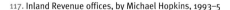

117. Inland Revenue offices, by Michael Hopkins, 1993–5

118. Landmark House, for Experian, by Sheppard Robson Corgan, 2003–4

conservation, were part of the brief, inspiring the narrow plans, heavy construction and façade design. The quirky glass-brick stair-towers at the corners act as solar chimneys [117]: as they heat up they draw air through the work spaces below, though heat gain remains problematic. Glass 'light shelves' provide shading and reflect daylight up on to the ceiling. Windows are triple-glazed, a Venetian blind in the outer cavity.

s across the railway line on **Queen's Drive** is **Castle Park**, factory units by *Nicholas Grimshaw & Partners*, 1979–80. One of his first independent works and rare speculative sleek sheds at a time when British High Tech was just becoming noticed, following the opening of Piano & Rogers's Pompidou Centre, Paris, in 1977. A long steel shed hard against the tracks, with green service towers of glass-reinforced polyester, battered but still sleeker than later neighbours.

Further sw, a new business park is emerging, **Ng2**, to a masterplan by *Maber Associates*, 2002, incorporating **Homebase**, by *Chetwood Associates*, 2001–3, and modified when **Experian** took the entrance site. Their **Landmark House** [118], by *Sheppard Robson Corgan*, 2003–4, is a partly transparent office building with an entrance atrium housing a café and shop. Behind are buildings by *Mabers* on a roundabout, a circular **Mercedes** garage, 2004–5, and curved **Arc** offices, 2004–5, extended w 2007–8. Behind is *Mabers'* **The Triangle**, neatly glazed small office units. Ng2 is on one of the proposed new tram routes; until then a bus must suffice to return to the centre.

Lenton and New Radford

Lenton was an important centre in the Middle Ages, with the most powerful monastic house in Notts – holding the Nottingham parish livings, and an annual fair larger than Nottingham's Goose Fair. The village retained a picturesque character through the C18 and early C19 thanks to the Gregory family. But as Nottingham strangled itself in the 1820s, a new settlement emerged between the village and future city, New Lenton. Here and in New Radford, immediately N, developed Nottingham's industrial base in textiles, and later in bicycles and cigarettes. This walk starts at the site of Lenton Priory on the corner of Abbey and Gregory Streets, and looks at old Lenton village. It then looks at New Lenton around Church Street, before heading up Lenton Boulevard, N into New Radford. The radial roads – Abbey Street, Castle Boulevard, Derby and Ilkeston roads – have frequent buses into the city.

Lenton

The Cluniac **priory** founded by William Peveril at Lenton in 1102–8 is known from excavations and slight remains E of **Priory Street**, the site of the nave. It was aggressively dissolved in 1538. Partial excavations in the C20 showed the C12 church had a three-bay choir with apse, ambulatory and E Lady Chapel, and a ten-bay nave. The first three piers w of the crossing were of a curious compound type, the main face consisting of a large three-quarter column attached to a rectangular core. Between N transept chapel and choir a recess was found, possibly for a stair, and between the second piers w of the crossing was a stone screen. At the corner with Old Church Street, 'The Stump' is an exposed NE ambulatory pier. Up to 7 ft (2.2 metres) of the N and w walls survive in those bounding the churchyard, s, with 9 ft (2.8 metres) of the w buttress. The conventual buildings and prior's lodging, s of the church towards the River Leen, survived into the C17; a gatehouse stood until the C19 at the junction of Gregory and Abbey streets.

William Stretton built himself **Lenton Priory** on the site of the prior's lodging, s, in 1802. A symmetrical crenellated box with label stops over conventional sashes, and a Gothic doorcase with slender shafts. Extensions for the Sisters of Nazareth, 1880 onwards, were replaced with housing 2007–8. In Priory Street, the **Boat Inn**, rebuilt by *W.B. Starr & Hall*, 1922–3, faience frontage.

After the priory's destruction the parish built a new church, to the N, incorporating as its chancel a **chapel**, *c.* 1170, probably that of the

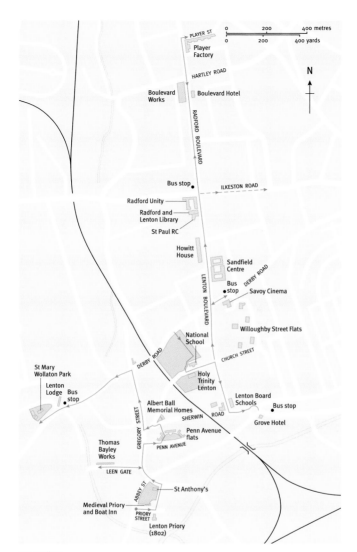

119. Walk 11

hospital and dedicated to St Anthony. Much reused stone was found when the nave was demolished in 1842 after a new church was built (*see* Holy Trinity, p. 180). The single-cell chancel was restored 1883–4 as a chapel of ease. One old lancet window, a piscina, and Norman carving on the altar step – arcading similar to that on Holy Trinity's font [123]. Nave, 1883–4, Dec, with only a little bell-spike; octagonal piers to its four-bay arcades. Over the chancel arch, the arms of Charles I. w window, 1949, to Sir Albert Ball, d.1946, developer, Mayor and father of Albert Ball, air ace; by *Harry Grylls*, Ball's favourite Dalmatian at the Nativity. Foundations of an attached building (the hospital hall?) were found

inside the present nave. Churchyard: stone **wall** and **gates**, 1811, chestnut trees 1812. – **Chest tomb** of William Stretton (1755–1828), SW corner.

Lenton village centred on Gregory Street, N, with vestiges of a picturesque Gothick character imparted by the Gregory family, early C19. On the NE corner, the **White Hart**'s 1804 frontage, with ground-floor cellarage, right, shields a C17 rear farmhouse range, which became the Lenton Coffee House in the C18. An outshut served as a debtors' prison until 1849. Inside, a sinuous stick baluster stair. Opposite, a gabled brick C17 cottage. Left, some way down **Leen Gate**, N side, **Thomas Bayley & Co**, a leather factory, 1860s, polychrome brick with prominent clock tower.

On **Penn Avenue**, E, three blocks of **maisonettes** [120] by *Arthur Eaton & Son*, 1924–6, replacing houses demolished for Abbey Bridge, part of Jesse Boot's University Boulevard scheme. In a semicircle round communal gardens, and early for stacked two-storey units; classical, the upper tier with balconies. W, the **Albert Ball Memorial Homes**, by *Brewill & Baily*, 1919–20. A central clock tower behind the First World War memorial recording Ball's V.C. On the junction, N, with Derby Road, is the **Three Wheatsheaves**, a farmhouse of *c.* 1690, first record-ed as a pub in 1810. L-shaped, with a turned-baluster dog-leg stair on the upper floors.

Continuing W, the **William Woodsend Memorial Homes**, right, six Jacobethan-style flats by *Woodsend*, 1912–13. Next door is the **Rose and Crown**, 1937 by *Eberlin & Darbyshire*, Tudor. W, beyond the line of the Nottingham Canal, the imposing **Lenton Lodge** [121], built for Wollaton Hall (*see* p. 196) but now separated from it by housing. By *Sir Jeffry Wyatville*, 1823–5. C16 in style but designed to defend Wollaton from the mob: no windows on the ground floor, stone floors, and massive gates reinforced with cast iron. Behind, **St Mary**, Wollaton Park, serves the Middleton lands developed as a garden suburb after 1924. By *T. Cecil Howitt*, 1937–9, where he worshipped. High and light. Wrennish chancel fittings and organ case (divided, at W end) of a piece. Stencilled ceilings. The square font inspired by Holy Trinity's (below). Howitt's **church hall** and **vicarage** cluster domestically round the W end.

121. Lenton Lodge, Derby Road, by Sir Jeffry Wyatville, 1823–5

122. Holy Trinity, Lenton, interior looking east, by H.I. Stevens, 1842

New Lenton

E along Derby Road over the railway bridge, and through the recreation ground (right, 1887, entrance by the lodge) appears the sooty w tower of **Holy Trinity**, Church Street. *H.I. Stevens* built a new Holy Trinity in expanding New Lenton, superseding that at the Priory. Tall, with lancet windows, solidly done. The interior high and light [122], on tall quatrefoil piers. A new w balcony and reordered chancel, 1892. **Reredos**, with tiled dado and inscription, by *Powell & Sons*, 1911, with *Frederick Ball*. Chancel **screen** by *J. Rigby Poyser*, 1931, incorporating an earlier dwarf wall. **Stained glass**. Unusual floral glass, E window, to Francis Wright, the church's founder, d.1873. N aisle: Boer War memorial 1901; stained glass to Lady Ball, d.1931, by *Heaton, Butler & Bayne*.

To the s is the **churchyard**, extended 1858, a rugged mêlée of tombs: slate slabs made in Lenton into the C20. **Lenton National School**, N, is dated 1841. To the E, **Castle Ward Conservative Club**, an 1840s house, behind *Frederick Ball*'s frontage, 1912–13. His, too, the **Lenton and**

The Lenton Font

Holy Trinity has one superlative feature: the mid-C12 font from Lenton Priory, one of the most interesting in the country and one of only five rectangular narrative fonts. It is almost square, of stone, 30 in. (75 cm.) high. All four sides are richly carved, framed by shafts with cushion capitals to the corners; the top decorated with trefoil leaves. Traces of

123. Holy Trinity, Lenton, C12 font, w side

original colour. The N side has a Maltese cross and Tree of Life, the others figure scenes of richness and beauty. E, two tiers of arcades, each filled by a row of cherubim with a row of seraphim beneath, except the centre of the lower tier, which shows the Baptism of Christ in an arch of double width. S, the Crucifixion (with the soul of the penitent thief emerging from his mouth and soaring upwards, that of the impenitent thief being consumed by a large dragon), contrasting with Life on the N side. W, four scenes divided by a foliated cross, at the top the story of Lazarus and below the Resurrection, with the Three Marys at the Sepulchre in contemporary fashion. The carving, in common with other Cluniac sculpture in England, has no French parallels. The closest Crucifixion iconography is in a manuscript of *c.* 1140 at Pembroke College, Cambridge, itself indebted to the St Albans Psalter and North German prototypes. (George Zarnecki, 'The Romanesque Font and Lenton', in *Southwell and Notts, Medieval Art, Archaeology and Industry*, British Archaeological Association, Conference Transactions 21, 1998.)

Nottingham Co-operative Society store, dated 1899 in high gables, adjoining **Lenton Boulevard**. As architect brother of Sir Albert, *Ball* laid out most of the housing here. S to **Lenton Schools**, left, the only work of the Lenton School Board, 1872–4; right, the boys' school for the Nottingham Board, by *A.N. Bromley*, 1887, extended 1889, 1897–8; girls' school, behind, by *Ernest R. Sutton*, 1897–9, pretty Jacobean gables and a central lantern. Across the roundabout, SE, the **Grove Hotel**, Renaissance style, 1887, on Castle Boulevard, whence it is a short walk or ride back to the city (Walk 10, especially pp. 171–2).

North from Lenton to Radford

An alternative walk heads N into C19–20 Nottingham's industrial heart, where lace gave way to bicycles and cigarettes, and the land of Alan Sillitoe's *Saturday Night and Sunday Morning* (1958). N of Church Street, more distinctive houses on the E side of **Lenton Boulevard**, those on the corners of Willoughby Avenue and Derby Road by *Frederick Ball & Lamb*, 1896, 1897, decorative gables; between them Nos. 104–106 by *Brewill & Baily*, Jacobethan, 1895–7. Behind, in contrast, pre-cast concrete, seventeen-storey **tower blocks** by *Miall Rhys-Davies & Partners* and *Bovis*, 1965–9; estate plan by *David Jenkin*, City Architect. In Derby Road, the **Savoy Cinema,** by *Reginald Cooper*, 1935, Nottingham's only 1930s cinema still in use; curved frontage remodelled 1970.

Opposite, and extending N along Lenton Boulevard, the **Sandfield Centre**, schools of 1931–2 by *T. Wallis Gordon*, City Engineer; low courtyard blocks espousing the domestic style championed by Henry Whipple, Director of Education 1924–33. A little further up Lenton Boulevard, left, **Howitt House**, formerly offices for Raleigh Cycles. By *T.C. Howitt*, 1931, original design prepared in the name of *Arthur Eaton & Son* of Derby, 1929–30, a giant order across the long façade either side of a rusticated three-bay centrepiece. Panels between the two main storeys depict cherubs latheing bicycle frames. An imposing double-height entrance hall serves panelled boardrooms, right, and the attic Marcus Garvey Ballroom. Then a line of public buildings, left. **St Paul** (**R.C.**), 1929–30 by *Joseph T. Lynch*, was hugely extended by *Reynolds & Scott*, 1966–7, with a new roof and open campanile. **Radford and Lenton Library**, 1925–6, by the *City Engineer's Dept*, Elizabethan. Next door, former **Sunday Schools** for All Souls' church, red brick Perp, by *Frederick Ball*, 1914. On the w corner with Ilkeston Road, **Radford Unity** is the former Radford Boulevard Board School, by *G.T. Hine*, 1885–6 (date on girls' entrance), extended 1893–4.

The largest building on **Radford Boulevard**, 500 yds N, is **Boulevard Works** [124], perhaps the finest surviving tenement lace factory, 1883. Thirty-nine bays long, polychrome brick and segment-headed windows. w addition by *Lawrence Bright*, dated 1896 on Hartley Road, over a sweeping porch on dumpy columns. Opposite, E, the grandiose **Boulevard Hotel**, still Gothic, by *Herbert Walker*, 1883. NW, the decapitated **clock tower** is all that remains of **John Player & Son's** mammoth No. 3 Factory, left, by the *Imperial Tobacco Co.'s Engineer's Office*, 1930. **Radford House**, Player's former offices (E side), by *McMorran & Whitby*, is weatherboarded, with neo-colonial C18 sashes and columned entrance, 1965–7 (condemned as 'superficial' by the City Architect David Jenkin). Behind in Player Street is **Player's** original factory, shared with lace manufacturing, with which his wife had connections. By *R.C. Sutton*, 1881–2. The lace standings quit in 1902. Four storeys, 387 ft (119 metres) long and 38 ft (12 metres) wide; internally, forty-six bays denoted by iron columns.

Head back E into town up Ilkeston or Alfreton roads (many buses).

124. Boulevard Works, Radford Boulevard, 1883

The University of Nottingham

Main campus between Lenton and Beeston, entered from Derby Road or University Boulevard; Jubilee Campus (to the N) from Wollaton and Triumph roads.

Nottingham University College opened in 1881 on Shakespeare Street (p. 132). But the C20 saw a preference for green-field campuses on the American model, exemplified by Birmingham, where Lord Calthorpe's munificence secured land and university status. Jesse Boot similarly

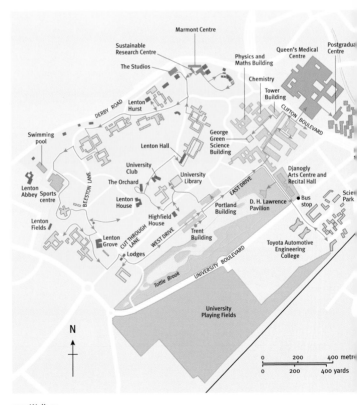

125. Walk 12

126. Nottingham University, Trent Building, by P. Morley Horder, 1922–8

wished Nottingham to become the University of the East Midlands. In 1919–20 he had purchased Highfields, Lenton House and Lenton Hall, major villas built on the Milward Estate following its sale in 1798. His first proposals were for a factory and model settlement, with Boot himself occupying Lenton House – but then he sold the business, while Mrs Boot refused to leave The Park. Instead, possessed of time and money, in 1921 he and his architect *Percy Morley Horder* developed a scheme of university buildings for the rising land, N of a public park, with sports grounds to the s, separated by a boulevard, *W.H. Radford*, engineer. Highfields Lake was enlarged E and w for drainage. Horder designed the University's administrative Trent Building, first residences and park buildings. Boot was created Lord Trent in 1928.

Nottingham belatedly achieved university status in 1948. *Sir Percy Thomas* then produced an 'American' campus plan, with administrative and arts faculty buildings aligned behind the Trent Building, leading to a library. On either side, informally disposed, he planned halls of residence amid the earlier villas, following Horder's division of men to the E, women w. He tucked the science area in the featureless SE corner, nearest the city. *Geoffrey Jellicoe*'s revisions, 1955, created the N entrance and rolling landscape around Cripps Hill. *Sir William Holford* succeeded as master planner, 1962, although outside the science area Modernism appeared only after 1970.

This tour makes an anti-clockwise circumnavigation from the Trent Building, ending at the s gate on University Boulevard, where buses serve the city. Free bus services connect the subsidiary Jubilee Campus, by *Michael Hopkins & Partners*, opened 1999, extended by *Make Architects* 2007–9.

Trent Building [126], 1922–8 by *P. Morley Horder*. The university's headquarters, set across the lake axially with the park entrance. Portico and tower are not quite in line. Nevertheless *Horder's* is a refined academic classicism in Portland stone, a giant Roman Doric order under a central pediment and a tall clock tower with aedicules and an Italianate roof, heralding their brief fashion among institutions. Two wings, the left housing the great hall without first-floor windows. Behind, a courtyard has arches giving long views E and W. The modest hall is lined in stone, with a trabeated ceiling; galleries over aisles supported on square acanthus columns. Right, the gawky **Portland Building**, by *T. Cecil Howitt*, 1949–56, respectful in style and materials, with a high portico. The *piano nobile* corresponds with the rear ground level. Its grand Neoclassical rooms epitomized the seriousness of 1950s students. Remodelling, 1994, retained the central double staircase with trabeated ceilings; *Lord Mottistone's* collegiate chapel was reordered. The glazed rear arcade added by *Michael Hopkins & Partners*, 2001–3.

N, the **University Library** [127] by *Faulkner-Brown, Hendy, Watkinson & Stonor*, 1971–3. An innovative deep plan, air-conditioned with open stacks, for maximum flexibility, inspired by the American theoreticians Ralph Elsworth and Keyes Metcalfe; the concrete

127. University Library, by Faulkner-Brown, Hendy, Watkinson & Stonor, 1971–3

128. Nottingham University, Lenton Hall, by William Stretton, 1804

cladding, pre-cast with granite aggregate, designed to avoid staining and still smart. The **Social Sciences and Education Building**, w, by *Donald McMorran*, 1960–1, lone legatee of Thomas's plan. Originally L-shaped, entered under a Scandinavian-style corner tower. Stone piers between the segmental-arched ground-floor windows suggest an arcade. Extended in matching style by *Dykes Naylor*, 2003–4: w, a courtyard, and NE, a lecture theatre. This adjoins *Diana Thomson*'s barefoot D.H. Lawrence **statue**, 1994, resited 2004.

To the s, behind a walled garden, **Highfields**, by *William Wilkins the Elder*, 1798, is U-shaped with low sashes; incised, unpainted render. More villas N of Social Sciences. **The Orchard**, by *W. Dymock Pratt*, 1904, with timber gables and octagonal bays, overlooks the **Millennium Garden**, conceived 1998 as a secret garden, a competition won by *Quartet Design*, Postmodern geometry and symbols. E, the **University Club**, another house by *Pratt*, 1906–7.

Up Lenton Hall Drive, E, to **Lenton Hall** [127]. By *William Stretton* for John Wright, 1804, with machicolations like Stretton's own Lenton Priory (p. 176), a Gothic porch but tall sash windows; remodelled 1905 by *Lawrence Bright*. It became **Hugh Stewart Hall**, the first men's hall, adapted by *Horder*, 1930–2. An austere open quadrangle in unmoulded stone added by *W.B. Starr & Hall*, 1935–8, with dining and common rooms set NW on two levels where the hill falls away.

129. Nottingham University, Cripps Hall, by Donald McMorran, 1957–9

Post-war halls followed to the N and W along **Beeston Lane**, as the university bought up C19 villas. For demonstrating the continued inventiveness of classical architecture after 1945 only Durham University compares. Earliest and most elegant is **Cripps Hall**, 1957–9, the gift of the Northants family who later endowed college buildings at Cambridge. One of *Donald McMorran*'s most confident works, fine materials and proportions combined in understated quadrangles, enhancing the virtuosity of the clock tower and open belfry over the dining hall. Details are indebted to 1920s Sweden, particularly Ivar Tengbom in the baseless Ionic columns framing the entrance [129].

Across Beeston Lane, buildings for the **School of the Built Environment** explore environmental, not architectural, issues. The **Sustainable Research Building,** by *David Short*, 2002–3, exposed steel amid tile cladding; rooftop solar panels. It forms a quadrangle with the **Marmont Centre for Renewable Technology**, by *Martin Noutch*, 1998–2000 – solar-heated water pipes, photo-voltaic cells, and vertical wind turbine. A low timber gallery by *Noutch*, 1997. Right, **Lenton Firs**, early C19, remodelled by *T.C. Hine*, 1862, by *Evans & Jolley*, 1888 and *Evans & Son*, 1903, Old English. A Gothic **lodge** by *Hine*, dated 1862. Staff **cottages**, E, by *T.C. Howitt, c.* 1956, lead to the **David Wilson Millennium Eco-House**, 1999–2000, with *Maber Associates*, a conventional spec house for testing renewable energy devices. Six 'creative energy homes', 2006–9, S, will demonstrate sustainable eco-technologies. Most of these by the School's *Guillermo Guzman* and *Mark Gillott*, but the **EON House** is by *Julian Marsh*, and **BASF House** by *Derek Trowell Architects*. Across Lenton Hall Drive is **Paton House**,

130. Nottingham University, Rutland Hall, by James Fletcher Watson & Partners, 1963–5

by *Evans & Jolley*, 1881, and **The Studios** (Environmental Education Centre), part photo-voltaic barn-like roofs and glazed gables, by *S & P Architects*, 2003–4.

McMorran & Whitby's **Lenton Hall**, 1963–5, w, exemplifies their late style, more Soane, less Scandinavia; based around an arched motif. 1820s-style railings bound its bastion setting; a timber lodge introduces a formal axis. Changes in level contained by retaining walls and steps, forming partially enclosed courtyards. It incorporates **Lenton Hurst**, by *Marshall & Turner* for W. G. Player, handsome Arts and Crafts, 1896. A panelled hall with an open screen, and a garden by *Gertrude Jekyll*.

Lincoln Hall is the strangest of the halls. By *Frederick Woolley*, previously Howitt's assistant, 1961–2. Soanic pilasters to the cupola-topped entrance; Wrennish dining hall and a Doric library: a cacophony of textbook details answering changes of level in one bid for glory. Upstaged by the calm sophistication of *Brian O'Rorke*'s **Derby Hall**, 1960–3. A courtyard entered at one end. The dining hall and common rooms at the other share a stark pyramidal roof – a tiny turret and niches under an arcade the only ornaments. Elsewhere, globe capitals and doorstep risers repeated from O'Rorke's observatory at Herstmonceux, Sussex, reference points heralding a Postmodern classicism.

More eclectic are the linked **Sherwood** and **Rutland halls**, w, by *James Fletcher Watson & Partners*, 1963–5. Both have weatherboarded libraries with pyramidal roofs, on stilts, inspired by Wymondham market hall in Watson's native Norfolk. Rutland Hall is the more intense for its cloistered courtyard [130], white concrete piers contrasting with deep brown brick. Grotesquely scaled coats of arms conflate the contorted path between traditionalism and Modernism. N across

131. Nottingham University, Chemistry Building, by Basil Spence & Partners, 1961, completed by Andrew Renton

playing fields is *FaulknerBrowns'* **swimming pool**, 1994–6, Postmodern, its gable indebted to Robert Venturi and clad in opaque glass; jewel-like next to *F.S. Eales*'s sports centre, a wartime hangar relocated 1970.*

Back on Beeston Lane, s, **Lenton House** is set within its own grounds, now Boots' company guest house. 1800, stuccoed, with full-height w bow and canted s bays, entered through a courtyard. Three-storey extension 1816. Stables dated 1890. **Lodge** for Captain John Boot, 1926, including the Gothick windows. Opposite are former **women's halls of residence**. A competition in 1950 was won by *Turley & Williamson* of Durham. Nevertheless the first to be built, **Nightingale Hall**, 1955–6, was by *T. Cecil Howitt*, four wings around a pyramidal core, gently Scandinavian next to Neo-Georgian tutors' semis. Next to **Lenton Fields**, *c.* 1837, a stuccoed box. W.A. Williamson built only in the 1960s, with **Cavendish** and **Ancaster halls**, a mirrored pair, by *Williamson, Faulkner-Brown & Partners*, classically proportioned with copper roofs. Three-storey additions with pale tile cladding, by *Cartwright Pickard*, 2002. *W.A Williamson*'s **Willoughby Hall**, w, is a six-storey slab with four-storey wing, 1962–5. It is set behind fellows' housing, the village green effect enhanced by **Lenton Grove**, stuccoed, *c.* 1800. The pre-war confines of the campus are denoted, s, by classical entrance **lodges**, 1932 by *Morley Horder*. The plans are annotated that Boot personally approved these before his death that

****Lenton Abbey,** w along Derby Road, is a lone section of the Milward Estate outside university ownership. 1798–1800 for the surveyor James Green, incorporating an earlier farmhouse, but now superficially 1850s. A large brick stable yard. The spurious name has been adopted by the surrounding area.

year. They lead to Morley Horder's **Florence Boot Hall**, 1927–8, the only coherent element its s-facing courtyard, but with a pleasantly domestic dining hall and library.

E of the Trent Building is **Science City**, its plan determined by Ministry of Works huts acquired with the site in 1949 and replaced piecemeal. *Basil Spence* was appointed architect in 1955, the job handled by his partner *Andrew Renton*, to whom it passed in 1961. Spence imposed a more urban character than that of the rest of the University, successful only in the w–e vista between library and tower. **Geology, Psychology and Cell Biology**, E of the Portland Building, begun 1950, when *David du R. Aberdeen*'s linear modern design was rejected for mundane quadrangles, blocking logical access. The **School of Pharmacy**, E, forms an equal barricade. By *Renton Howard Wood Associates*, 1967, brown brick piers intimating machicolations; lecture theatres of exposed concrete. A narrow entry and a left turn lead, N, to the raised **George Green Science Library**, the area's heart, by *Andrew Renton & Associates*, 1961–4. *In situ* concrete ribs of rough aggregate; extended 1969–70. The long **Coates Building** for engineering, a quintessential *Spence* teaching spine, with bands of windows and Derbyshire stone panels, shields landscaped quadrangles, N, from noisy laboratories in three s spurs. An elegant glazed stair hall links *Spence*'s **Pope Building**, N, dividing the quadrangles. These are faced, N, by **Physics and Mathematics**, 1961–3, and **Chemistry** [131], brick-clad with delicate slivers of stone to the columns, credited to *Basil Spence & Partners*, 1961, completed by *Renton*. Its entrance set in an internal courtyard reached through pilotis. The E vista is closed by *Renton*'s sixteen-storey **Tower Building**, more gnarled concrete ribs infilled with dark pre-cast panels and tightly planned above a sunken entrance, 1963–5. Facing Clifton Boulevard, E, the **Institute for Pharmaceutical Science** is a smartly glazed box with eye-like louvres, by *Pick Everard*, 1998–9. In between, the **Centre for Biomolecular Sciences** by *Benoy*, 2002–6, beige blocks with wing-like roofs, incorporates a bridge link across the boulevard to the Medical School.

The **Queen's Medical Centre** was the first regional hospital and medical school built under the National Health Service, planned from 1965, built 1971–5 by the *Building Design Partnership*. Four hollow five-storey blocks, three housing the wards and the fourth the medical school. The wards face the perimeter for natural light and outlook. The scale is vast. Stark and repetitive, bands of golden brick and dark tinted windows with a halo of white asbestos cladding on the top floor. Elegance is reserved for the double-height medical school entrance, where the university bridge connects. In the stairwell, stainless steel panels by *Gillian Wise*, 1974. A double stained-glass window by *Brian Clarke*, 1978, refreshingly abstract, in the chapel. The **residential village** for staff and students, by *Keith Ingham* of *BDP*, brick and white weatherboarding with monopitch roofs, quintessential 1970s housing, partly survives to the s.

132. D. H. Lawrence Pavilion, by Marsh Grochowski, 1998–2001; cafe to right, 2004

Highfields, Boots' public park, retains Victorian planting, with bowling and putting greens, 1924. At the Corporation's main entrance, axial to the Trent Building, Boot's **bust** by *Charles Doman*, 1934. *Morley Horder*'s Neoclassical lido and tea pavilion, E, were replaced, respectively, by the **Djanogly Arts Centre and Recital Hall**, and the **D. H. Lawrence Pavilion**. The Arts Centre, by *Graham Brown*, 1989–92, Postmodern classicism jumbled over a steel frame. Inside, Soanic reeding to the gallery and recital hall, the café Modern. The Pavilion is by *Marsh Grochowski*, 1998–2001. Awkward shapes mixing materials and stylistic motifs, inspired by Robert Venturi, dominated by the theatre's boat-like pre-patinated copper roof [132]. Equally contrasting spaces within, including the intimate Djanogly Theatre, and cool foyer café (added 2004). A lakeside amphitheatre incorporates balustrading and seats from *Horder*'s pavilion.

Highfields Science Park lies across University Boulevard, S, 1985. Offices laid out semi-formally E of a central axis. The best is the first, **Faraday House**, by *William Saunders & Partners*, 1984–5, yellow steel with cross-bracing. W of the axis the **Toyota Automotive Engineering College**, by *Hawkins\Brown* with *Studio Egret West*, 2006–8, loud yellow- and green-clad pavilions.

Jubilee Campus

Michael Hopkins & Partners won a competition, 1996, for a university extension one mile N up Western Boulevard. The **Jubilee Campus**, opened in 1999, lies on the site of the Nottingham Canal and Raleigh factory. Behind, John Player & Son's three bonded **warehouses** dominate, Mouchel system concrete, by *William Cowlin & Son*, Bristol builders, 1938–9, grouped as a T linked at ground level.

Following the earlier building line, Hopkins lined the teaching buildings along the E shore of a new lake. The faculty buildings are simple and economical, using standard forms in different combinations. Three-storey rectangular blocks, clad in sustainable Canadian Red cedar, are paired by glazed atria and fronted by a lakeside colonnade that coordinates the campus. Staircases in timber-clad towers are topped by oast-house-like cowls [134]; a system of passive solar and wind energy partly heats and cools the buildings. Insulation is from recycled newspaper and green roofs. The **Exchange**, in the centre, has a broader atrium, serving stacks of lecture theatres; the area between the Schools of Computer Science and Education, N, is glazed as a food court.

The campus's landmark is the polygonal **Learning Resource Centre**, on an island in the lake reached over a causeway [133]. The interior has a continuous spiral ramp past segmental book-lined alcoves, with a

133. Jubilee Campus, by Michael Hopkins & Partners, 1996–9, Learning Resource Centre

134. Jubilee Campus, by Michael Hopkins & Partners, 1996–9, teaching block

central helical stair and lifts; the continuous floor offers flexibility. **Newark** and **Sherwood halls**, E, are brick courtyards of undergraduate accommodation, while a crescent-shaped terrace of postgraduate residences overlooks the lake. S of the main buildings, a **Business School** added 2003–4, by *Hopkins* but losing finesse in execution by *Maber Associates* and the contractors. A N–S atrium makes it more introverted, with a rounded block of lecture theatres. At the lake's foot, S, the **National College for School Leadership**, 2001–2, three blocks linked by two atria, balconies overlooking landscaping by *Battle McCarthy*. It is stylistically between the main buildings and business school and superior in internal fittings.

Work began in 2007 on an extension by *Make Architects* (*Ken Shuttleworth*). The site is being expanded eastwards along a boulevard leading from the lake to the River Leen, angled on the Willoughby Street flats (p. 182). **International House** and the **Amenities Building**, clad in terracotta tiles and glass, contrast with the slinkily silver, dumb-bell **Gateway Building** for young businesses, all with green energy credentials. The formal boulevard and curvaceous landmark resemble Shuttleworth's work with Foster & Partners at More London, by Tower Bridge. It includes Shuttleworth's red and orange steel **sculpture**, Aspire, at 195 ft (60 metres) the UK's tallest public art in 2008, but dull.

Excursions

Wollaton Hall

Wollaton Park, between Derby Road and Wollaton Road

Wollaton Hall [135] is among the most important Elizabethan houses in England. It was built by *Robert Smythson* in 1580–8 for Sir Francis Willoughby, nephew of the Duke of Suffolk and connected with the Seymour and Dudley families, noted builders. Wollaton lay on coal, so Willoughby had the means to impress, and a Cambridge education informed his architectural enthusiasm. The house's cost (over £8,000), business failures and family disputes left him in debt, and convinced that his family and agents were out to swindle and perhaps murder him. The house reflects Willoughby's character, a supreme logic combined with extravagance and shades of lunacy; a passion for tradition perhaps determined its medievalizing aspects. Wollaton in turn was imitated by prosperous Victorians.

Robert Smythson (*c*. 1535–1614) first appears as a mason in Wiltshire, at Longleat in 1568, then at Wardour working for Sir Matthew Arundell, Willoughby's cousin and brother-in-law, *c*. 1576. He settled at Wollaton, and built several houses in the North Midlands, notably Hardwick Hall. His memorial in Wollaton church reads 'Architector and surveyor', a reflection of his rising status. But Wollaton's accounts still call him 'master mason'. Other masons included *Christopher Lovell*, *John* and *Christopher Rodes* (father and son, from Longleat) and *Thomas Accres*, who later worked at Hardwick. In 1588 *William Styles* succeeded Smythson as master mason, and Robert's son *John Smythson* worked as a mason.

Sir Francis's successors preferred their more comfortable Warwickshire estates, and Wollaton was neglected. The interior was damaged by fire in 1642, and restored only in 1687, when the house was occupied by Francis and Thomas Willoughby (1st Baron Middleton) and their sister Cassandra. She produced a valuable history of the house from estate papers subsequently lost. Downpipes dated 1746 and 1749 indicate repairs, while *John Johnson* worked here in the 1790s. The interior was transformed for the 6th Baron, mainly *c*. 1801–8, but projects continued into the 1830s, including the w service range by *Jeffry Wyatt* (later *Sir Jeffry Wyatville*). Still the house remained little used, and in 1924 it was sold to the City Corporation. It was restored in 2005–7 by *Purcell Miller Tritton*.

Wollaton is showy, set on a raised platform crowning a steep hill overlooking the site of the Willoughbys' old hall in the village. It is also

135. Wollaton Hall, s front by Robert Smythson, 1580–8

the most bookish Elizabethan house, its plan related to designs in du Cerceau's *de Architectura*, 1559, known to have been in Willoughby's library. A variant, in an unknown hand, is in the Middleton archive. Smythson adopts its symmetry, with a central hall instead of a court-yard, and a basement kitchen, while reflecting the Elizabethan fascination with devices in both geometrical and symbolic shapes. Wollaton is rectangular, though the N and s fronts step back behind terraces, with an almost free-standing tower at each corner. Mark Girouard suggests a source in Mount Edgcumbe, Cornwall, begun in 1546 by a distant relative. Elizabethan designers struggled to combine a symmetrical, central entrance with a great hall entered in the traditional manner via a screens passage at one end. Wollaton has an L-shaped lobby taking the visitor to the screens passage at the w so that the hall's bulk is central. Above rises a spectacular turreted 'prospect room', probably used solely for its panorama, since it had only two narrow newel staircases and no fireplace. Smythson adopted an interlinking structure of short joists for the hall roof from Serlio's *Architettura* (1566), known as the 'Chinese Lattice'. Staircases either side of the hall's dais end served first-floor suites and a long gallery; a service stair led additionally down to the vaulted kitchens. Basement kitchens were themselves novel in the late C16.

Wollaton's **elevations** are of Ancaster stone, but the foundations use salvaged stone from Lenton Priory (*see* p. 176). The storeys are almost equal in height, articulated by pilasters of the correct classical orders (divided by niches on the first floor), large square mullion-and-transom windows (larger on the first floor), and straight parapet. These are derived from Longleat, but Wollaton is not classical – here there is a more medieval silhouette: curved gables and groups of chimneys are brought together in a form reminiscent of medieval market crosses or

conduit heads, and reflecting Willoughby's taste for tradition. Linked chimneys in rendered brick were added to the corner towers by Wyatville [136]. The tracery windows of hall and prospect room recall those of the C15 Prior Overton's tower at Repton or the tower at Mackworth, both in Derbyshire. The classical column chimneys and busts of Plato, Aristotle, Diana, Virgil, Hercules and many others had appeared at Longleat, but other ornament is gaudily Netherlandish. It owes much to Vredeman de Vries's *Architectura*, 1577, although the scrolled tower gables, the main frieze with its metopes of circular paterae and bucrania, and the first-floor capitals come from the 1565 edition; a panel over the N door derives from Claude Paradin's *Héroïques*, 1557.

The N **front** is particularly magnificent. The central projecting bay, framed by single Doric columns and Ionic pilasters, has an elongated corbel keystone supporting an entablature; above, a panel of figures holds a cartouche. The steps with their square turned balusters by *Wyatville*, 1804. On the S **front** [135] the Saloon fenestration was remodelled by Wyatville. A plaque commemorates Willoughby's building and, in the raised balustrade above, Hercules and a monk appear from the family coat of arms. Double flights of steps, shown in a painting of *c*. 1790, incorporate a skittle alley. Wyatville filled the windows with casements and sashes, and introduced copper tracery into the hall clerestories. He also created the W **terrace**, when in 1823 he extended the service basement in Hollington sandstone. He may also have partly refaced the W front.

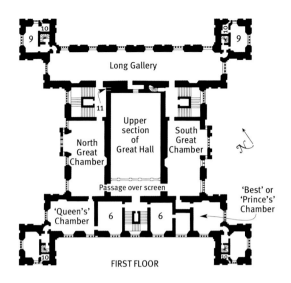

Long Gallery

9   10   10   9

11

North Great Chamber

Upper section of Great Hall

South Great Chamber

Passage over screen

'Queen's' Chamber

6   6

'Best' or 'Prince's' Chamber

10   10

FIRST FLOOR

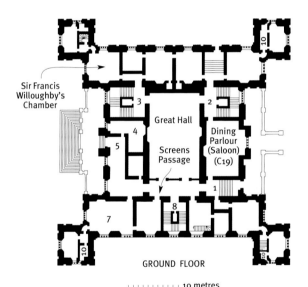

10

Sir Francis Willoughby's Chamber

3   2

Great Hall

Dining Parlour (Saloon) (C19)

4

5

Screens Passage

1

7

8

10   10

GROUND FLOOR

10 metres
30 feet

1	'Garden' Stairs	7	North-west Corner Chamber
2	South State Staircase		(Dining Room C19)
3	North State Staircase	8	Service Staircase
4	Porter's Lodge	9	Bedchamber
5	Entry	10	Garderobe
6	Withdrawing Chamber	11	Stairs to Leads and High Hall

137. Wollaton Hall, ground- and first-floor plans

138. Wollaton Hall, Great Hall, c16 screen with balustrade by Wyatville, 1831; c18 organ, Hammerbeam roof with additions of 1823

The **interior** is awkward [137], dominated by the tall hall. Wyatville opened up the central axis, and remodelled the entrance vestibule with segmental coffered alcoves, *c*. 1804. At the w end of the **Great Hall** [138] is the stone screen. The design, with spandrel figures like those in

Middle Temple Hall, comes originally from French choir screens, with metopes and strapwork panels from de Vries. An early c18 organ atop. Serlio's Book III provided the pattern for the Doric fireplace, perhaps originally one of a pair. The roof is a fake hammerbeam, as at Longleat, carved by *Lewis*, possibly the son of John Lewis, Longleat's head carpenter. *Wyatville* added the shields and tracery panels in 1823. He gave the screen its balustrade and renewed the panelling in 1831. He also opened up a door, s, to the **Saloon**, created in 1823 out of the former parlour and extended in 1832 to incorporate the garden stair; *Johnson*'s Coade stone fireplace was moved from the n **Great Chamber** in 1988. NW is the **Dining Room**, its buffet alcove elaborately decorated with floriate panels. On the E side Wyatville created a **library**, its frieze decorated with owls, a Willoughby emblem.

The N **and** S **state staircases** are reached through carved doorcases of the late 1690s and *c*. 1712, that to the N with fluted Corinthian pilasters and a segmental pediment. The stairs, probably remodelled then, were rebuilt by Wyatville *c*. 1804, in timber with lattice balustrades. The N stair hall has **wall paintings,** first recorded in 1699, depicting the life of Prometheus by *Sir James Thornhill*, Mercury and Argus in the overdoors. The ceiling, by *Laguerre*, *c*. 1699, was given additional figures by *Thornhill*. The s stair hall has a Thornhill ceiling, by 1712, depicting Pandora. Classical detail by *Johnson* in the N Great Chamber; the other rooms firmly Wyatville.

The back stair was extended to the **Prospect Room** *c*. 1690. Its ceiling is most likely *Johnson*'s, with a bucranian frieze; the shell niches in the window reveals 1690s. The painted wood pelisses over the windows are by *Wyatville*, who inserted a new floor, the original having sunk drastically. This was covered in turn by steel girders *c*. 1925–35 to stop the walls from spreading outwards, removed in 2005–7.

The basement **service rooms** are wrapped around the rock core under the Great Hall. The principal 1580s survivor is the vaulted **kitchen** on the N side, its stone vault supported on round columns and with a vaulted larder beyond, a saucery, and on the NE corner the wine cellar under Francis Willoughby's own chamber. In the 1690s a larger ale cellar was dug and the old cellar was converted into the servants' hall – demonstrating the growing separation of master and servant. Wyatville completed this separation, moving all the servants' accommodation to this level, some in new mezzanines. His service wing included a new servants' hall (the Education Room), reusing a c17 fireplace. Cellars lead to an underground well, the Admiral's Bath.

The Grounds

Between 1753 and 1790 the formal gardens were swept away and the park landscaped. *William Stretton* designed new N **gates**, 1790.

The **stable block**, w of the house, is dated 1743 (hopperheads), with a lower, second courtyard, added *c*. 1774. Engaged Ionic portico, its pediment with a carved tympanum and clock, over arched ground-

139. Camellia House, by Jones & Clark, 1822–3, probably designed by Sir Jeffry Wyatville

floor openings partly blocked by the 6th Lord. An industrial museum opened in the stables in 1971, with to w, Beam Engine House by *Terry Bestwick*, 1972–6, a glass and steel showcase for an 1858 engine from Haydn Road (Bagthorpe) Pumping Station, Basford.

sw of the house, the **Camellia House** [139] is perhaps the oldest surviving prefabricated metal building anywhere. It was ordered in 1822 from *Jones & Clark* of Birmingham, builders of iron conservatories since 1818. 100 ft (40 metres) long, the plan resembles a squashed octagon. The design may be *Wyatville*'s; he designed a screen for Jones & Clark in 1823. The n and w walls are brick, backing into the terrace, but the former entrance section, e, consists of iron sheets bolted together, and the s and w façades facing the ornamental garden are cast-iron panels with brass glazing bars bolted on to pairs of iron Doric columns. Iron columns with foliage capitals divide the interior into four top-lit flowerbeds; the walkways between have iron barrel vaults. Heating came through bronze floor grilles.

Lord Middleton feared a popular uprising, and rebuilt the boundary **wall** in 1823, with two new lodges. **Beeston Lodge**, s, has castellated towers and machicolations. For Lenton Lodge [121], *see* p. 178.

Newstead Abbey

10 M. N, on the Mansfield Road

140. Newstead Abbey, east front with south-east wing, C13–C19

Not an abbey. It was founded *c.* 1163–73 by Henry II as a priory of
Augustinian Canons. The scale was absurdly big for just fifteen to
twenty canons, but this was a royal foundation, superbly located for
hunting in Sherwood Forest. What survives today is largely of *c.* 1270,
partly recast with Perp windows *c.* 1450; the prior's lodgings and great
hall were remodelled in the early C16. In 1540 Henry VIII granted
Newstead to Sir John Byron of Colwick (p. 207). Though erasing most
of the church, Byron retained the w front complete – as a guilt-struck
token or for its picturesqueness? The s transept and cloister ranges
became his house. Sir John assumed the prior's lodgings and great hall
as his own, made a great chamber out of the refectory, and split the
dormitory over the chapter house into chambers.*

More alterations were made in the C17, particularly by the 1st Lord
Byron *c.* 1630–3, and by the 4th Lord before 1720, by which time the SE
family wing had taken shape. The 'wicked' 5th Lord spent prodigiously
on the grounds, but subsequent financial difficulties were compounded

---

*This account is indebted to new research by Dr Rosalys Coope and Colin Briden; see
pp. 218–19 for further reading. Haidee Jackson has also been extremely helpful.

by spite against his son. He stripped the estate in his final years, spent reclusively after a conviction for manslaughter. So when his great-nephew, the poet Byron, inherited in 1798 aged ten, Newstead was near ruinous.

That the mansion appears as it does is due to Col. Thomas Wildman, Byron's schoolfellow, who purchased it in 1817. *John Shaw* of London produced plans in 1818, not all realized, but Wildman was himself a competent designer who worked into the 1850s, having first made the SE wing comfortable. The building described by the poet as 'of rich and rare mix'd Gothic' thus today owes most to his successors. Tourists flocked to Newstead following the poet's death, 1826, and guide books survive from the 1850s.

After Wildman's death Newstead was bought, 1861, by W.F. Webb, explorer friend of Dr Livingstone, who made minor alterations, employing briefly *M.E. Hadfield* and then *Charles Alban Buckler*. Buckler worked more extensively after 1899 for Webb's daughters Geraldine (Lady Chernside) and Ethel. It was bought in 1931 by Sir Julien Cahn, who presented it to Nottingham Corporation. The Roe Byron Collection of manuscripts, books and pictures was bequeathed in 1937, and is exhibited with the Fraser Collection of Byron relics and the Gatty Collection of Byron and Webb family furniture.

Exterior. Shaw's **Sussex Tower** stands at the s end of the w front, balancing the intricate, paper-thin church façade on the N. His composition pivots around the Sussex Tower, a Norman piece; revivalism extended to Tudor details and a 'Glastonbury'-style kitchen. But the most striking feature remains the **w front** of the church [141], an exceptional late C13 work without the bittiness of many Early English Gothic façades. A few large, logically composed motifs, broadly laid out and lightly executed. Narrow buttresses divide the front into three. The ground floor has tall, blank arcading, cusped where the arches are broader. The capitals are partly still stiff-leaf, partly naturalistic. A mullion divides the central portal into two, slim and quatrefoil in section. A quatrefoil appears in the tympanum, not yet composed solely of tracery but still blank, with a seated figure of Christ. The first floor had a vast six-light window, as big as any of the Perp style, with Geometrical and, probably, intersecting tracery. To left and right, high blank four-light windows with sexfoil and cinquefoil circles in the tracery, exactly like the Salisbury chapter house of *c*. 1270, and stylistically earlier than Southwell's. The only feature not exactly in symmetry is the side portals. That into the N aisle exists, much simpler than the central one; the s side has a C19 window replacing a Byronic insertion. A portal would, however, never have led into a s aisle, for there never was one. There simply was the N end of the w range with, behind, the N walk of the cloisters. It is a remarkably early instance of an aesthetic sham. The façade is crowned by a gable with a niche, containing a seated figure of the Virgin. The window inserted below it is Perp, as is the openwork quatrefoil frieze over the aisles.

141. Newstead Abbey, west front, late C13

In the centre lie the **prior's lodgings** with, N, a canted bay lighting the prior's chambers, and next the three tall bay windows of the hall, carried on a low, largely pre-C18 arcade, extended S by Shaw *c.* 1820. Probably only the N, dais end, window predates the Byrons. The second window replaced the exterior chimney-breast *c.* 1726–30, and Shaw added the third. He moved a first-floor porch dated 1631 (*see* below),

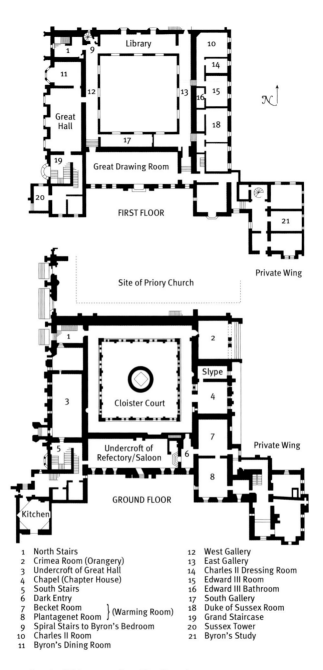

1	North Stairs
2	Crimea Room (Orangery)
3	Undercroft of Great Hall
4	Chapel (Chapter House)
5	South Stairs
6	Dark Entry
7	Becket Room
8	Plantagenet Room } (Warming Room)
9	Spiral Stairs to Byron's Bedroom
10	Charles II Room
11	Byron's Dining Room
12	West Gallery
13	East Gallery
14	Charles II Dressing Room
15	Edward III Room
16	Edward III Bathroom
17	South Gallery
18	Duke of Sussex Room
19	Grand Staircase
20	Sussex Tower
21	Byron's Study

142. Newstead Abbey, ground- and first-floor plans

reached by external steps (presumably an entrance at this level existed earlier), transferring the entrance to the ground floor, with a vaulted Gothick porch, modest for a large house. Between it and Shaw's tower a semicircular bay lights the main staircase.

The N **front** is almost plain save for minor C19 windows and a stair. The E **front**, overlooking the formal garden, has at the N end *Buckler*'s large bay window, *c.* 1905. Then, between buttresses, three lancets with C19 tracery light the chapter house. The projecting SE **wing**, first shown by Tillemans, *c.* 1728–30, incorporates medieval work (perhaps the infirmary) and (internally) a Tudor lancet on the line of the straight joint and buttress revealed on the s front; under the w lobby is a medieval drain. Shaw relocated the 1631 entrance porch here, part of the 1st Lord Byron's improvements: a low round arch under a keystone carved with the Byrons' mermaid emblem, incorporated into a tripartite centrepiece; downpipes dated 1818. Shaw's most radical alterations were to the s **front**, undistinguished in C18 watercolours. At the w end his kitchen is polygonal and almost free-standing, yet dominated by the Sussex Tower and his stark SW **wing** – whose upper floor was added by Buckler's assistants after 1900, with larger lancets and plate tracery.

Interior [142]. The small w porch leads into the much restored **undercroft** (all Shaw's as now seen). Webb filled it with shooting trophies, but it now holds three Byron **monuments** brought from Colwick in 1937: the first Sir John Byron, d.1567, an alabaster tomb-chest, its top incised with depictions of him and his two wives, above their kneeling children and grandchildren; his son Sir John, d.1604, a large wall monument with two recumbent effigies, obelisk and achievement on top; and the latter's son and grandson, both d.1625 (modern style) and their wives, a small monument with figures kneeling opposite each other, the older generation above, the younger below.

143. Newstead Abbey, library, by Wildman, early C19, incorporating C18 work

Head up the **Grand Staircase**, for which *Wildman* signed a drawing, 1830. He refitted the **Great Hall** in the early 1850s with decoration by *Willement*, originally with *trompe l'œil* ashlar above the panelling, a recurrent theme. A late C13 doorway right of the fireplace by *T.C. Hine*. The realistic figures are plaster, while the timber minstrel gallery is dated 1818.

In the Byrons' time there were two rooms in the prior's lodging w of the hall, but Wildman replaced one with a staircase. They are reached via a **corridor** over the medieval cloister, whose rich roll mouldings are concealed in the floor void. The monks had few common first-floor parts and built stairs as required, but Sir John Byron established a *piano nobile* served by galleries. The surviving **parlour** N of the Great Hall, Byron's dining hall, retains an overmantel, bearing the Byron crest and motto '*Crede* Byron', dated 1556, probably from Colwick, sold by the Byrons in 1649. There are four such overmantels (only this one is dated), first recorded by S.H. Grimm, 1770; all now set over Shaw fire-places. A spiral stair leads to Byron's **bedroom**, subdivided by Shaw; he blocked a C16 window made in the westworks. Wildman installed a **library** [143] above the N cloister, in the C17–C18 the 'great gallery', with handsome oak bookcases and painted Gothic wall decoration, incor-porating an C18 fireplace, one of two credited to *Thomas Carter*.

The E cloister runs alongside the s transept, and the first-floor gallery has, concealed, an arch of *c.* 1270 associated with the chapter house below. The guest rooms formed from the dormitory were presumably set *en filade*.* To the N are fragments of the night stairs and to the s more fragments leading to the refectory. The **Charles II Room** and dressing room were one until remodelled by the 4th Lord Byron, who installed the cornices and oval ceiling centrepiece; coats of arms in painted panels of grisaille grotesques date the work before his third marriage in 1720. The **Edward III** and **Duke of Sussex rooms** have more C16 overmantels, the latter recast by Shaw. The **Henry VII lodging** was redecorated *c.* 1900 after the Webb daughters visited Japan, with screen paintings and timber panels, those to the frieze and overdoors antique. They also heightened the attic storey for guests.

The s gallery leads to the Great Dining Room [144] (used by the poet for fencing and shuttlecock, and now the **Great Drawing Room**), formed from the monastic refectory and two superimposed chambers, E, by the 1st Lord Byron, 1631–3. His floor is 6 ft higher than that of the medieval refectory, from which a fragment of wall painting, *c.* 1200, was exposed following a fire in 1965. Sir John inserted a plaster ceiling, with timberwork of a piece – magnificent despite losing its carved corbels in early C20. Eight panels at the dais (E) end are decorated with antique heads based on Abraham Ortelius's engravings (Antwerp 1573); Juno is dated 1631. The other twenty-four panels vivaciously depict foliage,

---

*As suggested by Neil Burton and supported by Dr Coope.

144. Newstead Abbey, Great Drawing Room, 1631–3, c18 fireplace

animals and figures, one in the NW corner dated 1633 (and 1966 following restoration). Sir John commissioned a marble fireplace from *Nicholas Stone*, 1635; the present c18 one is identical to *Carter*'s at Uppark, Sussex.

From the 1720s the SE wing contained the **family apartments**, the first floor (entered first) remodelled for Wildman using imported panelling. The staircase was rebuilt for the Webbs. On the ground floor, the **Plantagenet Room** and **Becket Room** occupy the monastic warming room, divided by Wildman, the former remodelled with a new fireplace and W door by Buckler *c.* 1900–5, closely resembling his work at Arundel. Then follows, N, the c13 **Dark Entry**, a monastic passage to the cloisters, entered through a c12 doorway. The s cloister walk has the shafts of the blocked dormitory stairs and the stone staircase that replaced them. Beyond, the stone ledge of the lavatory. In the depth of the N wall of the cloister (i.e. the s wall of the church) are the shafts of the E and w nave doorways. The cloister garth contains a hexagonal **conduit**, with shell niches on the lowest stage, a quatrefoil frieze, a battlemented parapet and a topknot with lozenge decoration. Each stage is topped by six grotesque figures. The inscription reads 'WB 1724', but the topknot appears c16; the conduit was moved by the 4th Lord to the w front and returned by Wildman. At the end of the N walk, on the site of the transept, the **orangery**, an indoor–outdoor room or grotto. The alcove fountain or buffet survives, resembling the c18 one at Swangrove, Gloucestershire; 1760s descriptions suggest the room contained some real medieval work as well as c18 Gothick. But it was enclosed in 1905 and remodelled in c17 style, though the ceiling's central element is original c17 work.

145. Newstead
Abbey, former
Chapter House (left),
c. 1270

146. Newstead
Abbey, former
Chapter House,
detail of decoration
(right), 1860s

The **Chapter House** [145, 146] off the E cloister dates from *c.* 1270. Rectangular, with six ribbed vaults on two slender composite shafts and stiff-leaf capitals. It became the Byrons' chapel, used – it seems – without separation between family and servants' pews. It was restored by Wildman when a family gallery was created in the upper part of the adjoining **slype**, previously the poet's plunge bath. In the 1860s Buckler remodelled the chapel with polychromatic tiling, stencilling, and *Hardman* glass, that in the gallery commemorating Wildman.

The **grounds** today are of three main phases. First is that of the 4th Lord Byron, whose father-in-law was the 1st Earl of Portland, superintendent of the Royal Gardens and Ambassador to Paris. His early C18 works show this French influence. To the SE was a long canal, later made a serpentine **lake**. E, the garden rises in **terraces** from the square Eagle Pond, with two lead figures probably by *John Nost*. In 1808 Byron buried his dog Boatswain there; his neat classical **monument** was intended to stand sacrilegiously over the High Altar but is actually SE of it. Secondly, the 5th Lord reshaped an upper lake and built castellated Gothick forts round it in 1749, i.e. only shortly after Sanderson Miller's first Gothicisms. In the 1770s he transformed the stables on the NE side of the lake into another 'castle' or fort. He also kept a twenty-gun ship (he had served in the Navy) and staged mock battles. More remodelling was undertaken by Wildman and the Webbs. *Hadfield* built the rumbustious **stables** W of the house, 1862–3, before the more decorous *Buckler* was preferred for the E and W **lodges** *c.* 1864. Mrs Webb introduced a **fernery** E of the lower lake, 1864, using Pulhamite artificial stone and Derbyshire tufa, and a **Japanese garden** was created for Ethel Webb from 1899 onwards.

Boots

Thane Road, Nottingham, and Humber Road South, Beeston

Boots acquired its featureless site between the railway and canal, w of the city, in 1926. Here is some of the most important c20 work in Britain: two factory buildings by *Sir Owen Williams*, civil engineer turned architect; and offices by the esteemed American partnership *Skidmore, Owings & Merrill* (in association with *Yorke Rosenberg & Mardall*). They sit at either end of a loose grid of buildings.

Boots' '**Wets**' building, **D10** [18, 148], by *Williams*, 1930–2, was erected for manufacturing and packaging creams and medicines. In 1920 Boot had sold his interests to the American United Drugs Company. Their new factory was dedicated to production-line processes like a contemporary Detroit car works, its massive scale impossible before buses and bicycles made greenfield sites a serious option. It was the first building designed under Williams's sole command. The commission came via the chief mechanical engineer of the Dorchester Hotel, London, where Williams had been eased out in favour of an architect. Williams went on to combine architecture and engineering with

147. Boots

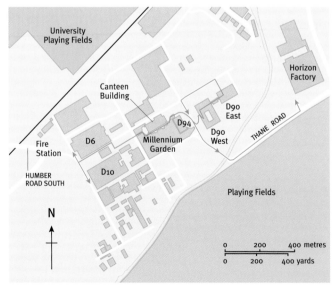

148. Boots, D10, 'Wets Building', by Sir Owen Williams, 1930–2, north-west corner, photograph of 1932

showmanship in a series of buildings that were functional, cheap, yet exciting. D10 was intended to be three times larger, for the manufacture of not only wet creams and toiletries, but also dry powders and cough sweets, later accommodated in a separate building (D6, below).

Williams advanced modern architecture in England to a different scale, with an enormous concrete structure whose form was truly determined by its function. D10 is the prime British example of flat-slab construction [18], where the concrete's reinforcement is spread across the floor structure, so beams are not required. The columns have bold mushroom-shaped tops where the reinforcement spreads out. Williams had witnessed the system emerge working for the American company Truscon in 1912–16. It was no longer novel by 1931, but Williams refined the columns to accommodate services; the sharp arrises on the columns are his signature. D10 also introduced a cantilevered section for the side delivery bay [148]. Most dramatic are the central atria; lecturing in 1927 Williams suggested that floors hampered manufacturing processes. He also believed that factory walls should not be structural, so that they could be fully glazed – important in so deep a plan. His first proposal was for a complete curtain wall; as built the glazing is set between the concrete floors, like Rotterdam's Van Nelle factory or London's Peter Jones, but as sophisticated as anything before 1945.

Unloading and manufacturing are concentrated on the ground floor, with the products stored on the three levels of galleries above until required for packing and dispatch. They are then gathered via cascading conveyor belts on the packing floor at the bottom of the main, 600-ft (185-metre)-long atrium, under a roof glazed by 150,000 glass prisms. The galleries are partly cantilevered, designed for further extension.

D10 was restored in 1992–4 by *AMEC Design & Management*, who gave the front façade new double-glazed Crittall units, improving working conditions at the price of the building's integrity and tactile qualities. Laboratories were adapted as offices and first-floor warehousing was converted to production facilities for dry goods.

The 'Drys' building, **D6** [149], was added by *Williams* in 1935–8, NW of D10. It is again a flat-slab construction, but manufacturing was on the middle floors, whence the raw materials were sent via lifts. They returned to the packing floor below with the aid (for powders) of spiral chutes in holes through the floor slabs. Offices were on the top floor, and unloading docks, sorting and preliminary production were in ambitious single-storey wings. These are roofed by 9-ft (2.75-metre)-deep, Z-section beams over columns at 30-ft (9-metre) to 60-ft (18-metre) centres, making unprecedented 30-ft (9-metre) cantilevers at the ends. To achieve a column-free space where the two structures met, Williams suspended the beam ends from concrete hangers, which were exposed on the elevations and themselves suspended from exposed beams at roof level. Ventilation shafts are also externally expressed. But despite its greater invention, D6 has none of D10's

149. Boots, D6, 'Drys Building', by Sir Owen Williams, 1935–8

150. Boots, D90 West, by Skidmore, Owings & Merrill and Yorke, Rosenberg & Mardall, 1967–9

grandeur. *AMEC* adapted the interior to offices, 1994–6. The ocean-liner exterior has a projecting prow over the entrance and the floor slabs expressed as horizontal sun shields to the windows between.

Williams also designed a **fire station** (**D34**, now offices) with a hanging roof mimicking D6 in miniature and a jaunty hose tower of reinforced concrete and glass bricks.

The Dutch-style brick **Canteen Building** (**D31**), E, was built in 1937–8 by *E.T. Dowling* and *W.H. Tanner* to feed 2,000 staff at a sitting. A **Millennium Garden**, S, by *James Knox* of Art for Work with the landscape designer *Mark Lutyens*, 1999–2000.

In the 1960s Boots turned directly to America for its **headquarters offices, D90** [150]. The director Ben Jefferies visited the US in 1962, when he was introduced to the Chicago office (then headed by *Bruce Graham*). The job was run by *Bill Hartmann* of SOM, with *Brian Henderson* of the British firm *Yorke, Rosenberg & Mardall* handling it on site and designing the furniture. Whereas SOM's New York office had pioneered sleek, steel-framed offices, the Chicago office was inspired by Mies van der Rohe's late, heavy steel aesthetic. Constructed in 1967–8, the two-storey bulk of what is now called D90 West – though not its vast 480-ft (148-metre) length – was masked by mounding earth from the central courtyard excavation round the lower storey to form a plinth for the colonnade of black steel that faces on to parkland. The roof cornice is heavier than in Mies's work, but the influence of his Mineral and Metals Research Building at Chicago's Illinois Institute of Technology is felt in the cut-away junction of the corner I-beam.

As remarkable as the purity of the welded exterior was the completeness with which the interior was designed. This survives in the precise symmetry of the inset ceiling lighting and the natural oak partitions with storey-height doors in the directors' wing (N side). The rest of the column-free upper storey has lost its work stations or carrels in favour of a clear open plan, but SOM/YRM's *café au lait* tones of carpet and tinted glass still dominate.

By the late 1990s D90 was considered too small and inflexible. *Stephen Greenberg* of the office specialists *DEGW* was commissioned to make alterations, and to add a subordinate building (**D90 East**), built in 1997–8, with *Roger Preston & Partners*, associate architects. Its core is an atrium, a tiny tribute to D10 with catering facilities, surrounded by open-plan 'neighbourhoods' with meeting rooms, break-out areas, and places for working quietly. Three atria facing N are light wells. The s façade, louvred against the sun, is more respectful of D90 West and the greensward on which the buildings float towards the Beeston Canal.

NE of Boots, across the canal but still on Thane Road, is the massive **Horizon Factory** [151] for John Player & Co. (part of Imperial Tobacco), by *Arup Associates*, 1968–71. A hefty British counterweight to D90 West's cool, its concrete frame and clip-on cladding of pre-cast concrete and fibreglass panels is nevertheless equally carefully considered. Horizon is an early integrated design where architects, engineers and contractors were involved from the first. It has a second-floor factory serviced from above and below, over ground-floor loading bays and plant.

151. John Player & Co., Horizon Factory, by Arup Associates, 1968–71

Further Reading

There is no **general introduction** to Nottingham architecture, though many articles on individual buildings and architects have appeared since Elizabeth Williamson's revision in 1979 of Nikolaus Pevsner's original *Nottinghamshire*, 1951. Dr Thoroton's 1677 *Antiquities of Nottinghamshire*, edited and enlarged by John Throsby, 1790–6, and reprinted with a new introduction by M.W. Barley and L.S.S. Train, 1972, remains the starting point. Charles Deering, *The History of Nottingham*, 1751, reprinted 1970, is the first history of the town, supplemented by Throsby's *History and Antiquities of the Town and County of Nottingham*, 1795.

The best historical introduction is *A Centenary History of Nottingham*, edited by John Beckett, 1997, reprinted 2006. More specialist information comes from the *Transactions of the Thoroton Society* (*TTS*), published annually since 1898, supplemented since the late 1970s by short articles and notices in the *Newsletters* of the Nottingham Civic Society. The Civic Society's invaluable series, 'Get to Know Nottingham', includes volumes on *Thomas Chambers Hine, Watson Fothergill, The Park, Shire Hall and Old County Gaol*, and *Mapperley Park*, all by Ken Brand. More lavish is *The Council House, Nottingham*, by John Beckett and Ken Brand, 2004. For recent architecture, Kenneth Powell's *Nottingham Transformed*, 2006, repays scrutiny.

Other books cover particular **building types**. Tony Waltham, *Sandstone Caves of Nottingham*, revised 2008, is excellent. On landscape, there is Robert Mellors, *The Gardens, Parks and Walks of Nottingham and District*, 1926. D.E. Varley, *A History of the Midland Counties Lace Manufacturers' Association, 1915–1958*, 1959, includes an account of the industry's earlier history. On railways, the best of an extensive literature is Michael A. Vanns, *Rail Centres: Nottingham*, 1992. On canals, see Charles Hadfield, *The Canals of the East Midlands*, 1966. David Wardle, *Education and Society in Nineteenth-century Nottingham*, 1971, is the best introduction to Board Schools and higher education.

Individual buildings have prompted more detailed study. Nottingham Castle has been covered by Trevor Foulds, e.g. ' "This Great House, so Lately Begun, and All of Freestone": William Cavendish's Italianate Palazzo called Nottingham Castle', in *TTS* 106,

2000, and '"The Warmest I Have": Henry, Second Duke of Newcastle and Nottingham Castle', in *Nottinghamshire Past: Essays in Honour of Adrian Henstock*, 2003. For the medieval castle, *see* Christopher Drage, *Nottingham Castle, A Place Full Royal*, 1999. For County House, *see* Adrian Henstock, 'County House, High Pavement, Nottingham: A Georgian and Regency Town House', *TTS* 80, 1976. The account of St Barnabas's Cathedral is based on that by Priscilla Metcalf with Andor Gomme and Rory O'Donnell, in N. Pevsner and P. Metcalf, *The Cathedrals of England*, 1985. Rosemary Hill's *God's Architect*, 2007, provided a valuable background. On the Convent of Mercy, *see* Timothy Brittain-Catlin, 'A.W.N. Pugin's English Convent Plans', in *Journal of the Society of Architectural Historians* 65/3, 2006.

Wollaton has an extended literature. The starting point is Mark Girouard, *Robert Smythson and the English Country House*, 1983. Alice T. Friedman, *House and Household in Elizabethan England*, 1989, controversial when published, is very useful, and informs Pamela Marshall, *Wollaton Hall and the Willoughby Family*, 1999. On decoration, *see* Anthony Wells-Cole, *Art and Decoration in Elizabethan and Jacobean England*, 1997, and Edward Croft-Murray, *Decorative Painting in England 1537–1837*, 1962, vol. 2. On the early C19 work, the most helpful article is Pete Smith, 'Comfort and Security', in Malcolm Airs (ed.), *The Regency Great House*, 1998.

Newstead Abbey has been exceptionally served by Rosalys Coope: on the C18 building works of the 4th and 5th Lords Byron, *TTS* 83, 1979; on the poet Lord Byron's Newstead, *TTS* 91, 1987; on the Wildman family, *TTS* 95, 1991 and *Architectural History* 44, 2001; a further article on the period 1540–1640 is forthcoming. For Colwick Hall, *see* Brian Wragg and Giles Worsley, *John Carr of York*, 2000. On Boots, the best survey remains David Cottam, *Sir Owen Williams, 1896–1969*, 1986. Two useful volumes on the University are Frank Barnes, *Priory Demesne to University Campus, a Topographical History of Nottingham University*, 1993; and A. Peter Fawcett and Neil Jackson, *Campus Critique, the Architecture of the University of Nottingham*, 1998, thorough if flawed.

Useful **websites** are those of the Lenton Local History Society, *www.lentontimes.co.uk*, and the diocesan church recording project, *http://southwellchurches.nottingham.ac.uk*.

The main source for **primary research** is the Nottinghamshire Archives, and particularly its CA/PL series of building plans beginning in 1875. The Park was excluded from Nottingham Corporation's Building Control regulations until 1939, but the Newcastle family papers at Nottingham University Archives (NPE series) include plans of individual buildings from *c*. 1900, and records of leases.

For a selection of buildings in suburbs not covered by this book, *see* Nikolaus Pevsner and Elizabeth Williamson, *The Buildings of England: Nottinghamshire* (1979).

Glossary

Acanthus: *see* [2D].

Aedicule: architectural surround

Ambulatory: aisle around the *sanctuary* of a church.

Angle buttress: one set at the angle or corner of a building.

Antae: simplified *pilasters*, usually applied to the ends of the enclosing walls of a *portico* (called *in antis*).

Anthemion: *see* [2D].

Apse: semicircular or polygonal end, especially in a church.

Arcade: series of arches supported by *piers* or columns (cf. *colonnade*).

Arch: for types *see* [4].

Architrave: *see* [2A], also moulded surround to a window or door.

Art Deco: a self-consciously up-to-date interwar style of bold simplified patterns, often derived from non-European art.

Ashlar: large rectangular masonry blocks wrought to even faces.

Atlantes: male figures supporting an *entablature*.

Atrium: a toplit covered court rising through several storeys.

Attic: small top storey within a roof. Also the storey above the main *entablature* of a classical façade.

Back-to-back houses: with a shared rear (spine) wall.

Baldacchino: solid canopy, usually free-standing and over an altar.

Balusters: vertical supports, often of outward-curved profile, for a handrail, etc.; the whole being called a balustrade.

Ballflower: globular flower of three petals enclosing a small ball.

Baroque: bold, free and emphatic European classical style of the C17–C18, revived in the late C19.

Barrel vault: one with a simple arched profile.

Basement: lowest, subordinate storey; hence the lowest part of a classical elevation, below the *piano nobile*.

Bay: division of an elevation by regular vertical features such as columns, windows, etc.

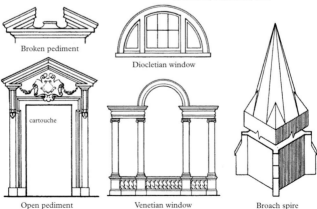

Broken pediment

Diocletian window

cartouche

Open pediment

Venetian window

Broach spire

1. Miscellaneous

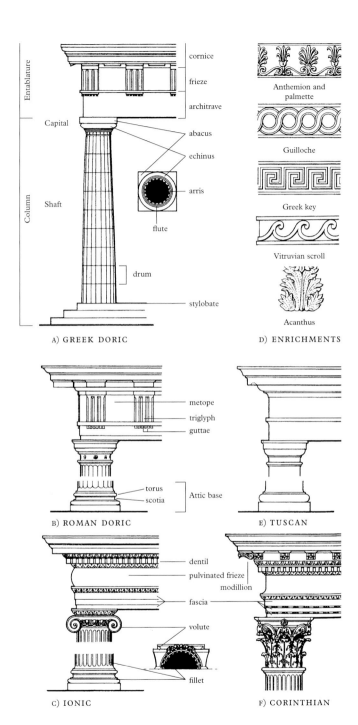

A) GREEK DORIC

Entablature
— cornice
— frieze
— architrave

Capital
— abacus
— echinus
— arris

Shaft
— flute

drum

stylobate

Column

D) ENRICHMENTS

Anthemion and palmette

Guilloche

Greek key

Vitruvian scroll

Acanthus

B) ROMAN DORIC

metope
triglyph
guttae

torus
scotia
Attic base

E) TUSCAN

C) IONIC

dentil
pulvinated frieze
modillion
fascia
volute
fillet

F) CORINTHIAN

2. Classical orders and enrichments

Bay window: one projecting from the face of a building. *Canted*: with a straight front and angled sides.

Beaux-Arts: a French-derived approach to classical design, at its peak in the later C19–early C20, marked by strong axial planning and the grandiose use of the *orders*.

Bellcote: small gabled or roofed housing for a bell or bells.

Bolection moulding: convex moulding covering the joint between two different planes.

Brise-soleil (French): a sunscreen of projecting fins or slats.

Broach spire: *see* [1].

Bucrania: ox skulls used decoratively in friezes on classical buildings.

Campanile (Italian): free-standing bell-tower.

Cantilever: horizontal projection supported at one end only.

Capital: head feature of a column or *pilaster*; for classical types *see* [2].

Cartouche: *see* [1].

Castellated: with battlements.

Catslide: a roof continuing down in one plane over a lower projection.

Chancel: the E part or end of a church, where the altar is placed.

Chapter house: place of assembly for the members of a monastery or cathedral.

Choir: the part of a great church where services are sung.

Clerestory: uppermost storey of an interior, pierced by windows.

Coade stone: ceramic artificial stone, made 1769–*c.* 1840 by Eleanor Coade and associates.

Coffering: decorative arrangement of sunken panels.

Colonnade: range of columns supporting a flat *lintel* or *entablature*

Corbel: projecting block supporting something above.

Composite: classical order with capitals combining Corinthian features (acanthus, *see* [2D]) with Ionic (volutes, *see* [2C]).

Corinthian; cornice: *see* [2F; 2A].

Cottage orné: artfully rustic small house.

Cove: a broad concave moulding.

Crenellated: with battlements.

Crocket: leafy hooks decorating the edges of Gothic features.

Crown-post: a vertical roof timber starting centrally on a tie-beam and supporting a collar *purlin*.

Crypt: underground or half-underground area, usually below the E end of a church.

Cupola: a small dome used as a crowning feature.

Dado: finishing of the lower part of an internal wall.

Decorated (Dec): English Gothic architecture, late C13 to late C14.

Dentil: *see* [2C].

Diaper: repetitive surface decoration of lozenges or squares flat or in relief. Achieved in brickwork with bricks of two colours.

Diocletian window: *see* [1].

Doric: *see* [2A, 2B].

Dormer: *see* [3].

Drum: circular or polygonal stage supporting a dome.

Dutch or Flemish gable: *see* [3].

Early English (E.E.): English Gothic architecture, late C12 to late C13.

Embattled: with battlements.

Entablature: *see* [2A].

Faience: moulded *terracotta* that is glazed white or coloured.

Fleurons: carved flower or leaf.

Flying buttress: one transmitting thrust by means of an arch or half-arch.

Freestone: stone that can be cut in any direction.

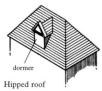

dormer

Hipped roof

Mansard roof

Flemish or Dutch gable

3. Roofs and gables

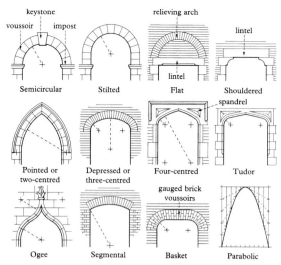

keystone

relieving arch

voussoir   impost   lintel

Semicircular   Stilted   Flat   Shouldered

spandrel

Pointed or   Depressed or   Four-centred   Tudor
two-centred   three-centred

gauged brick
voussoirs

Ogee   Segmental   Basket   Parabolic

4. Arches

Frieze: middle member of a classical *entablature*, see [2A, 2C]. Also a horizontal band of ornament.

Geometrical: of *tracery*, a mid-C13–C14 type formed of circles and part-circles; *see* [6].

Giant order: a classical *order* that is two or more storeys high.

Gibbs surround: C18 treatment of an opening with blocked architraves, seen particularly in the work of James Gibbs (1682–1754).

Gothic: the style of the later Middle Ages, characterized by the pointed arch and *rib-vault*.

Half-timbering: non-structural decorative timberwork.

Herm: head or bust on a pedestal.

Hipped roof: *see* [3].

Hoodmould: projecting moulding above an arch or *lintel* to throw off water.

Hyperbolic paraboloid: of a roof, built to a double-curved profile suitable for thin shell construction.

Impost: horizontal moulding at the springing of an arch.

In antis: (Latin) of columns, set in an opening (properly between simplified *pilasters* called *antae*).

Ionic: *see* [2C].

Italianate: a classical style derived from the palaces of Renaissance Italy.

Jack arches: shallow segmental vaults springing from iron or steel beams.

Jamb: one of the vertical sides of an opening.

Kingpost roof: one with vertical timbers set centrally on the *tie-beams*, supporting the ridge.

Lancet: slender, single-light pointed-arched window.

Lantern: a windowed turret crowning a roof, tower or dome.

Light: compartment of a window.

Lintel: horizontal beam or stone bridging an opening.

Loggia: open gallery with arches or columns.

Louvre: opening in a roof or wall to allow air to escape.

Lucarne: small gabled opening in a roof or spire.

Machicolation: openings between *corbels* that support a projecting *parapet*.

Metope: *see* [2B].

Mezzanine: low storey between two higher ones.

Moderne: of 1930s design, fashionably streamlined or simplified.

Modillion: *see* [2D].

Moulding: shaped ornamental strip of continuous section.

Mullion: vertical member between window *lights*.

Narthex: enclosed vestibule or porch at the main entrance to a church.

Newel: central or corner post of a staircase.

Nogging: brick infilling of a timber frame.

Norman: the C11–C12 English version of the *Romanesque* style.

Œil de bœuf: small oval window, set horizontally.

Ogee: of an arch, dome, etc., with double-curved pointed profile.

Orders (classical): for types *see* [2].

Oriel: window projecting above ground level.

Overthrow: decorative fixed arch above a gateway.

Parapet: wall for protection of a sudden drop, e.g. on a bridge, or to conceal a roof.

Pargeting: exterior plaster decoration, either moulded in relief or incised.

Patera: round or oval ornament in shallow relief.

Pavilion: ornamental building for occasional use; or a projecting subdivision of a larger building (hence *pavilion roof*).

Pediment: a formalized gable, derived from that of a classical temple; also used over doors, windows, etc. For types *see* [1].

Penthouse: a separately roofed structure on top of a multi-storey block of the C20 or later.

Perpendicular (Perp): English Gothic architecture from the late C14 to early C16.

Piano nobile (Italian): principal floor of a classical building, above a ground floor or basement and with a lesser storey overhead.

Pier: a large masonry or brick support, often for an arch.

Pilaster: flat representation of a classical column in shallow relief.

Pilotis: C20 French term for pillars or stilts that support a building above an open ground floor.

Plinth: projecting courses at the foot of a wall or column, generally chamfered or moulded at the top.

Polychromy: the use of contrasting coloured materials such as bricks as decoration, particularly associated with mid-C19 Gothic styles.

Porte cochère (French): porch large enough to admit wheeled vehicles.

Portico: porch with roof and (frequently) *pediment* supported by a row of columns.

Portland stone: a hard, durable white limestone from the Isle of Portland in Dorset.

Postmodern: idiom associated with the 1980s that references older styles, notably classicism, not always reverently.

Presbytery: a priest's residence.

Purlin: horizontal longitudinal timber in a roof structure.

Quatrefoil: opening with four lobes or foils.

Queen Anne: the later Victorian revival of the mid-C17 domestic classical manner, usually in red brick or terracotta.

Queenpost: paired upright timbers on a tie-beam of a roof, supporting purlins.

Quoins: dressed or otherwise emphasized stones at the angles of a building; *see* [5].

Rainwater head: container at a *parapet* into which rainwater runs from the gutters.

Reeded: decorated with small parallel convex mouldings.

Render: a uniform covering for walls for protection from the weather, usually of cement or *stucco*.

Reredos: painted and/or sculpted screen behind and above an altar.

Reveal: the inner face of a jamb or opening.

Rib-vault: masonry framework of intersecting arches (ribs) supporting vault cells.

Rock-faced: masonry cleft to produce a natural, rugged appearance.

string course

channelled with glacial quoins

V-jointed with vermiculated quoins

5. Rustication

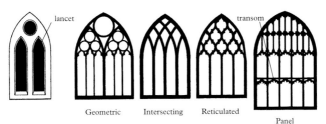

lancet · transom

Geometric · Intersecting · Reticulated · Panel

6. Tracery

Romanesque: round-arched style of the C11 and C12.

Rood: crucifix flanked by the Virgin and St John, carved or painted.

Rubble: of masonry, with stones wholly or partly rough and unsquared.

Rustication: exaggerated treatment of masonry to give the effect of strength; *see* [5].

Sacristy: room in a church used for sacred vessels and vestments.

Saddleback roof: a pitched roof used on a tower.

Sanctuary: in a church, the area around the main altar.

Sedilia: seats for the priests in the *chancel* wall of a church or chapel.

Sexfoil: a six-lobed opening.

Shaped gable: with curved sides, but no pediment (cf. Dutch gable, [3]).

Spandrel: space between an arch and its framing rectangle, or between adjacent arches.

Splayed: angled; (of an opening) wider on one side than the other.

Stanchion: upright structural member, of iron, steel or reinforced concrete.

Stiff-leaf: carved decoration in the form of thick uncurling foliage; originally late C12–early C13.

Strapwork: decoration like interlaced leather straps.

Stringcourse: horizontal course projecting from a wall surface.

Stripped classicism: buildings whose proportions conform to classical precedent but where the usual classical decoration is implied or removed altogether.

Stucco: durable lime plaster, shaped into ornamental features or used externally as a protective coating.

System building: system of manufactured units assembled on site.

Terracotta: moulded and fired clay ornament or cladding (cf. *faience*).

Tie-beam: main horizontal transverse timber in a roof structure.

Tile hanging: overlapping tiled covering on a wall.

Trabeated: having a post-and-beam structure, i.e. not arched.

Tracery: openwork pattern of masonry or timber in the upper part of an opening; *see* [6].

Transept: transverse portion of a church.

Transom: horizontal member between window lights; *see* [6].

Trefoil: with three lobes or foils.

Triforium: middle storey of a church interior treated as an arcaded wall passage or blind arcade.

Truss: braced framework, spanning between supports.

Tunnel vault: one with a simple elongated-arched profile.

Tuscan: *see* [2E].

Tympanum: the area enclosed by an arch or *pediment*.

Undercroft: room(s), usually *vaulted*, beneath the main space of a building.

Vault: arched stone roof, sometimes imitated in wood or plaster. See also Barrel vault.

Venetian window: *see* [1].

Vitruvian scroll: wave-like classical ornament.

Volutes: spiral scrolls, especially on Ionic columns (*see* [2C]).

Voussoir: wedge-shaped stones forming an arch.

Wagon roof: with the appearance of the inside of a wagon tilt.

Wainscot: timber lining of a room (cf. Panelling).

Index

of Artists, Architects and Other Persons Mentioned

The names of architects and artists working in Nottingham are given in *italic*, with entries for partnerships and group practices listed after entries for a single name. Page references in italic include relevant illustrations.

Index
of Localities, Streets and Buildings

Principal references are in **bold** type; page references including relevant illustrations are in *italic*. 'dem.' = 'demolished'

Illustration Acknowledgements

Every effort has been made to contact or trace all copyright holders. The publishers will be glad to make good any errors or omissions brought to our attention in future editions.

We are grateful to the following for permission to reproduce illustrative material:

Author: 2, 3, 4, 5, 6, 7, 9, 11, 14, 15, 16, 17, 18, 23, 24, 30, 31, 32, 33, 34, 35, 36, 37, 40, 41, 42, 44, 45, 46, 47, 50, 51, 52, 53, 54, 56, 57, 58, 60, 61, 62, 63, 65, 66, 67, 68, 69, 71, 72, 73, 75, 78, 79, 80, 82, 83, 84, 88, 89, 90, 91, 93, 95, 96, 97, 98, 99, 100, 102, 103, 104, 105, 106, 107, 109, 110, 112, 113, 114, 115, 116, 117, 118, 120, 121, 122, 123, 124, 126, 127, 128, 129, 130, 131, 132, 133, 134, 135, 136, 138, 139, 140, 141, 144, 149, 150, 151
Boots Archive: 148
Caruso St John Architects: 22
Crown Copyright (NMR): 70

English Heritage (Steve Cole): 8, 25, 26, 43, 55, 74, 87, 92, 143, 145, 146
English Heritage (Derek Kendall): 21, 38
English Heritage (NMR): 8, 12, 77, 108
English Heritage (Photo Library): 13
Alan Fagan: 29, 137, 142
Nottingham City Council (Picture the Past): 27, 28
Nottingham City Council (Picture the Past) and the Nottingham Evening Post: 20
Nottingham City Museums and Galleries: 49
Nottinghamshire Archives: 10, 19
Oxford Designers & Illustrators: 1, 39, 48, 59, 64, 76, 81, 86, 94, 101, 111, 119, 125, 147
Pete Smith: 85

A special debt of gratitude is owed to Steve Cole at English Heritage for photographing the most difficult interiors.